# Ancient Christian Texts

## Commentaries on Galatians–Philemon

## Ambrosiaster

TRANSLATED AND EDITED BY

Gerald L. Bray

SERIES EDITORS

Thomas C. Oden and Gerald L. Bray

IVP Academic

An imprint of InterVarsity Press
Downers Grove, Illinois

*InterVarsity Press*
*P.O. Box 1400, Downers Grove, IL 60515-1426*
*World Wide Web: www.ivpress.com*
*E-mail: email@ivpress.com*



*InterVarsity Press® is the book-publishing division of InterVarsity Christian Fellowship/USA®, a movement of students and faculty active on campus at hundreds of universities, colleges and schools of nursing in the United States of America, and a member movement of the International Fellowship of Evangelical Students. For information about local and regional activities, write Public Relations Dept., InterVarsity Christian Fellowship/USA, 6400 Schroeder Rd., P.O. Box 7895, Madison, WI 53707-7895, or visit the IVCF website at <www.intervarsity.org>.*



*Design: Cindy Kiple*

*Images: Saints Peter and Paul by Carlo Crivelli at Accademia, Venice/Art Resource, NY*

*ISBN 978-0-8308-2904-0*

*Printed in the United States of America ∞*

green press INITIATIVE *InterVarsity Press is committed to protecting the environment and to the responsible use of natural resources. As a member of Green Press Initiative we use recycled paper whenever possible. To learn more about the Green Press Initiative, visit <www.greenpressinitiative.org>.*

**Library of Congress Cataloging-in-Publication Data**

*Ambrosiaster.*
*[Commentarius in XIII Epistulas Paulinas. Pars 3. English]*
*Commentaries on Galatians-Philemon / translated and edited by Gerald L. Bray.*
*p. cm.—(Ancient Christian texts)*
*Includes bibliographical references.*
*ISBN 978-0-8308-2904-0 (cloth: alk. paper)*
*1. Bible. N.T. Epistles of Paul—Commentaries. I. Bray, Gerald Lewis. II. Title.*
*BR65.A323A43213 2009*
*227'.077—dc22*
2009021519

**P** 24 23 22 21 20 19 18 17 16 15 14 13 12 11 10 9 8 7 6 5 4 3 2 1
**Y** 30 29 28 27 26 25 24 23 22 21 20 19 18 17 16 15 14 13 12 11 10 09

# CONTENTS

General Introduction / page vii

Translator's Introduction / page xv

Commentary on Galatians / page 1

Commentary on Ephesians / page 35

Commentary on Philippians / page 64

Commentary on Colossians / page 81

Commentary on 1 Thessalonians / page 101

Commentary on 2 Thessalonians / page 113

Commentary on 1 Timothy / page 120

Commentary on 2 Timothy / page 142

Commentary on titus / page 155

Commentary on Philemon / page 161

Scripture Index / page 165

# GENERAL INTRODUCTION

The Ancient Christian Texts series (hereafter ACT) presents the full text of ancient Christian commentaries on Scripture that have remained so unnoticed that they have not yet been translated into English.

The patristic period (A.D. 95-750) is the time of the fathers of the church, when the exegesis of Scripture texts was in its primitive formation. This period spans from Clement of Rome to John of Damascus, embracing seven centuries of biblical interpretation, from the end of the New Testament to the mid-eighth century, including the Venerable Bede.

This series extends but does not reduplicate texts of the Ancient Christian Commentary on Scripture (ACCS). It presents full-length translations of texts that appear only as brief extracts in the ACCS. The ACCS began years ago authorizing full-length translations of key patristic texts on Scripture in order to provide fresh sources of valuable commentary that previously was not available in English. It is from these translations that the ACT Series has emerged.

A multiyear project such as this requires a well-defined objective. The task is straightforward: *to introduce full-length translations of key texts of early Christian teaching homilies and commentaries on a particular book of Scripture*. These are seminal documents that have decisively shaped the entire subsequent history of biblical exegesis, but in our time have been largely ignored.

To carry out this mission the Ancient Christian Texts series has four aspirations:

1. To show the approach of one of the early Christian writers in dealing with the problems of understanding, reading and conveying the meaning of a particular book of Scripture.

2. To make more fully available the whole argument of the ancient Christian interpreter of Scripture to all who wish to think with the early church about a particular canonical text.

3. To broaden the base of the biblical studies, Christian teaching and preaching to include classical Christian exegesis.

4. To stimulate Christian historical, biblical, theological, and pastoral scholarship toward deeper inquiry into early classic practitioners of scriptural interpretation.

**For Whom Is This Series Designed?**

We have selected and translated these texts primarily for general and nonprofessional use by an audience of persons who study the Bible regularly.

In varied cultural settings around the world, contemporary readers are asking how they might grasp the meaning of sacred texts under the instruction of the great minds of the ancient church. They often study books of the Bible, verse by verse, book by book, in groups and workshops, sometimes with a modern commentary in hand. But many who study the Bible intensively hunger to have available to them as well the thoughts of some reliable classic Christian commentator on this same text. This series will give the modern commentators a classical text for comparison and amplification. Readers will judge for themselves as to how valuable or complementary are their insights and guidance.

The classic texts we are translating were originally written for anyone (lay or clergy, believers and seekers) who would wish to reflect and meditate with the great minds of the early church. They sought to illuminate the plain sense, theological wisdom, and moral and spiritual meaning of an individual book of Scripture. They were not written for an academic audience, but for a community of faith shaped by the sacred text.

Yet in serving this general audience, the editors remain determined not to neglect the rigorous requirements and needs of academic readers who until recently have had few full translations available to them in the history of exegesis. So this series is designed also to serve public libraries, universities, academic classes, homiletic preparation and historical interests worldwide in Christian scholarship and interpretation.

Hence our expected audience is not limited to the highly technical and specialized scholarly field of patristic studies, with its strong bent toward detailed word studies and explorations of cultural contexts. Though all of our editors and translators are patristic and linguistic scholars, they also are scholars who search for the meanings and implications of the texts. The audience is not primarily the university scholar concentrating on the study of the history of the transmission of the text or those with highly focused interests in textual morphology or historical critical issues. If we succeed in serving our wider readers practically and well, we hope to serve as well college and seminary courses in Bible, church history, historical theology, hermeneutics and homiletics. These texts have not until now been available to these classes.

**Readiness for Classic Spiritual Formation**

Today global Christians are being steadily drawn toward these biblical and patristic sources for daily meditation and spiritual formation. They are on the outlook for primary classic sources of spiritual formation and biblical interpretation, presented in accessible form and grounded in reliable scholarship.

These crucial texts have had an extended epoch of sustained influence on Scripture interpretation, but virtually no influence in the modern period. They also deserve a hearing among modern readers and scholars. There is a growing awareness of the speculative excesses and spiritual and homiletic limitations of much post-Enlightenment criticism. Meanwhile the motifs, methods and approaches of ancient exegetes have remained unfamiliar not only to historians but to otherwise highly literate biblical scholars, trained exhaustively in the methods of historical and scientific criticism.

It is ironic that our times, which claim to be so fully furnished with historical insight and research methods, have neglected these texts more than scholars in previous centuries who could read them in their original languages.

This series provides indisputable evidence of the modern neglect of classic Christian exegesis: it remains a fact that extensive and once authoritative classic commentaries on Scripture still remain untranslated into any modern language. Even in China such a high level of neglect has not befallen classic Buddhist, Taoist and Confucian commentaries.

**Ecumenical Scholarship**

This series, like its two companion series, the ACCS and Ancient Christian Doctrine (ACD), are expressions of unceasing ecumenical efforts that have enjoyed the wide cooperation of distinguished scholars of many differing academic communities. Under this classic textual umbrella, it has brought together in common spirit Christians who have long distanced themselves from each other by competing church memories. But all of these traditions have an equal right to appeal to the early history of Christian exegesis. All of these traditions can, without a sacrifice of principle or intellect, come together to study texts common to them all. This is its ecumenical significance.

This series of translations is respectful of a distinctively theological reading of Scripture that cannot be reduced to historical, philosophical, scientific or sociological insights or methods alone. It takes seriously the venerable tradition of ecumenical reflection concerning the premises of revelation, providence, apostolicity, canon and consensuality. A high respect is here granted, despite modern assumptions, to uniquely Christian theological forms of reasoning, such as classical consensual christological and triune reasoning, as distinguishing premises of classic Christian textual interpretation. These cannot be acquired by empirical methods alone. This approach does not pit theology against critical theory; instead, it incorporates critical historical methods and brings them into coordinate accountability within its larger purpose of listening to Scripture.

The internationally diverse character of our editors and translators corresponds with the global range of our audience, which bridges many major communions of Christianity. We have sought to bring together a distinguished international network of Protestant, Catholic and Orthodox scholars, editors, translators of the highest quality and reputation to accomplish this design.

But why just now at this historical moment is this need for patristic wisdom felt particularly by so many readers of Scripture? Part of the reason is that these readers have been longer deprived of significant contact with many of these vital sources of classic Christian exegesis.

**The Ancient Commentary Tradition**

This series focuses on texts that comment on Scripture and teach its meaning. We define a commentary in its plain sense definition as a series of illustrative or explanatory notes on any work of enduring significance. The word "commentary" is an Anglicized form of the Latin *commentarius* (or "annotation" or "memoranda" on a subject or text or series of events). In its theological meaning it is a work that explains, analyzes or expounds a biblical book or portion of Scripture. Tertullian, Origen, John Chrysostom, Jerome, Augustine and Clement of Alexandria all revealed their familiarity with both the secular and religious commentators available to them as they unpacked the meanings of the sacred text at hand.

The commentary in ancient times typically began with a general introduction covering such questions as authorship, date, purpose and audience. It commented as needed on grammatical or lexical problems in the text and provided explanations of difficulties in the text. It typically moved verse by verse through a Scripture text, seeking to make its meaning clear and its import understood.

The general western literary genre of commentary has been definitively shaped by the history of early Christian commentaries on Scripture. It is from Origen, Hilary, the *Opus imperfectum in Matthaeum*, John Chrysostom and Cyril of Alexandria that we learn what a commentary is—far more so than in the case of classic medical or philosophical or poetic commentaries. It leaves too much unsaid simply to assume that the Christian biblical commentary took a previously extant literary genre and reshaped it for Christian texts. Rather it is more accurate to say that *the Western literary genre of the commentary (and especially the biblical commentary) has patristic commentaries as its decisive pattern and prototype.*

It is only in the last two centuries, since the development of modern historicist methods of criticism, that modern writers have sought more strictly to delimit the definition of a commentary so as to include only certain limited interests focusing largely on historical critical method, philological and grammatical observations, literary analysis, and sociopolitical or economic circumstances impinging on the text. While respecting all these approaches, the ACT editors do not hesitate to use the classic word *commentary* to define more broadly the genre of this series. These are commentaries in their classic sense.

The ACT editors freely take the assumption that the Christian canon is to be respected as the church's sacred text. The reading and preaching of Scripture are vital to religious life. The central hope of this endeavor is that it might contribute in some small way to the revitalization of religious faith and community through a renewed discovery of the earliest readings of the church's Scriptures.

**An Appeal to Allow the Text to Speak for Itself**

This prompts two appeals:

1. For those who begin by assuming as normative for a commentary only the norms considered typical for modern expressions of what a commentary is, we ask: Please allow the ancient commentators to define *commentarius* according to their own lights. Those who assume the preemptive authority and truthfulness of modern critical methods alone will always tend to view the classic Christian exegetes as dated, quaint, premodern, hence inadequate, and in some instances comic or even mean-spirited, prejudiced, unjust and oppressive. So in the interest of hermeneutical fairness, it is recommended that the modern reader not impose upon ancient Christian exegetes modern assumptions about valid readings of Scripture. The ancient Christian writers constantly challenge these unspoken, hidden and indeed often camouflaged assumptions that have become commonplace in our time.

We leave it to others to discuss the merits of ancient versus modern methods of exegesis. But even this cannot be done honestly without a serious examination of the texts of ancient exegesis. Ancient commentaries may disqualify as commentaries by modern standards. But they remain commentaries by the standards of those who anteceded and formed the basis of the modern commentary.

The attempt to read a Scripture text while ruling out all theological and moral assumptions—as well as ecclesial, sacramental and dogmatic assumptions that have prevailed generally in the community of faith out of which it emerged—is a very thin enterprise indeed. Those who tendentiously may read a single page of patristic exegesis, gasp and toss it away because it does not conform adequately to the canons of modern exegesis and historicist commentary, are surely not exhibiting a valid model for critical inquiry today.

2. In ancient Christian exegesis, chains of biblical references were often very important in thinking about the text in relation to the whole testimony of sacred Scripture, by the analogy of faith, comparing text with text, on the premise that *scripturam ex scriptura explicandam esse*. When ancient exegesis weaves many Scriptures together, it does not limit its focus to a single text as much modern exegesis prefers, but constantly relates it to other texts, by analogy, intensively using typological reasoning, as did the rabbinic tradition.

Since the principle prevails in ancient Christian exegesis that each text is illumined by other texts and by the whole narrative of the history of revelation, we find in patristic comments on a given text many other subtexts interwoven in order to illumine that text. In these ways the models of exegesis often do not correspond with modern commentary assumptions, which tend to resist or rule out chains of scriptural reference. We implore the reader not to force the assumptions of twentieth-century hermeneutics upon the ancient Christian writers, who themselves knew nothing of what we now call hermeneutics.

**The Complementarity of Research Methods in this Series**

The Ancient Christian Texts series will employ several interrelated methods of research, which the editors and translators seek to bring together in a working integration. Principal among these methods are the following:

1. The editors, translators and annotators will bring to bear the best resources *of textual criticism* in preparation for their volumes. This series is not intended to produce a new critical edition of the original language text. The best Urtext in the original language will be used. Significant variants in the earliest manuscript sources of the text may be commented upon as needed in the annotations. But it will be assumed that the editors and translators will be familiar with the textual ambiguities of a particular text, and be able to state their conclusions about significant differences among scholars. Since we are working with ancient texts that have, in some cases, problematic or ambiguous passages, we are obliged to employ all methods of historical, philological and textual inquiry appropriate to the study of ancient texts. To that end, we will appeal to the most reliable text-critical scholarship of both biblical and patristic studies. We will assume that our editors and translators have reviewed the international literature of textual critics regarding their text so as to provide the reader with a translation of the most authoritative and reliable form of the ancient text. We will leave it to the volume editors and translators, under the supervision of the general editors, to make these assessments. This will include the challenge of considering which variants within the biblical text itself might impinge upon the patristic text itself, and which forms or stemma of the biblical text the patristic writer was employing. The annotator will supply explanatory footnotes where these textual challenges may raise potential confusions for the reader.

2. Our editors and translators will seek to understand the *historical context* (including social-economic, political and psychological aspects as needed) of the text. These understandings are often vital to right discernment of the writer's intention. Yet we do not see our primary mission as that of discussing in detail these contexts. They are to be factored into the translation and commented on as needed in the annotations, but are not to become the primary focus of this series. Our central interest is less in the social location of the text or the philological history of particular words than in authorial intent and accurate translation. Assuming a proper social-historical contextualization of the text, the main focus of this series will be upon a dispassionate and fair translation and analysis of the text itself.

3. The main task is to set forth the meaning of the biblical text itself as understood by the patristic writer. The intention of our volume editors and translators is to help the

reader see clearly into the meanings which patristic commentators have discovered in the biblical text. *Exegesis* in its classic sense implies an effort to explain, interpret and comment upon a text, its meaning, its sources and its connections with other texts. It implies a close reading of the text, utilizing whatever linguistic, historical, literary or theological resources are available to explain the text. It is contrasted with *eisegesis* which implies that interpreters have imposed their own personal opinions or assumptions upon the text. The patristic writers actively practiced intratextual exegesis, which seeks to define and identify the exact wording of the text, its grammatical structure and the interconnectedness of its parts. They also practiced extratextual exegesis, seeking to discern the geographical, historical or cultural context in which the text was written. Our editors and annotators will also be attentive as needed to the ways in which the ancient Christian writer described his own interpreting process or hermeneutic assumptions.

4. The underlying philosophy of translation that we employ in this series is, like the Ancient Christian Commentary on Scripture, termed *dynamic equivalency.* We wish to avoid the pitfalls of either too loose a paraphrase or too rigid a literal translation. We seek language that is literary but not purely literal. Whenever possible we have opted for the metaphors and terms that are normally in use in everyday English-speaking culture. Our purpose is to allow the ancient Christian writers to speak for themselves to ordinary readers in the present generation. We want to make it easier for the Bible reader to gain ready access to the deepest reflection of the ancient Christian community of faith on a particular book of Scripture. We seek a thought-for-thought translation rather than a formal equivalence or word-for-word style. This requires the words to be first translated accurately and then rendered in understandable idiom. We seek to present the same thoughts, feelings, connotations and effects of the original text in everyday English language. We have used vocabulary and language structures commonly used by the average person. We do not leave the quality of translation only to the primary translator, but pass it through several levels of editorial review before confirming it.

## The Function of the ACT Introductions, Annotations and Translations

In writing the introduction for a particular volume of the ACT series, the translator or volume editor will discuss, where possible, the opinion of the writer regarding authorship of the text, the importance of the biblical book for other patristic interpreters, the availability or paucity of patristic comment, any salient points of debate between the Fathers, and any special challenges involved in translating and editing the particular volume. The introduction affords the opportunity to frame the entire commentary in a manner that will help the general reader understand the nature and significance of patristic comment on the biblical texts under consideration and to help readers find their critical bearings so as to read and use the commentary in an informed way.

The footnotes will assist the reader with obscurities and potential confusions. In the annotations the volume editors have identified Scripture allusions and historical references embedded within the texts. Their purpose is to help the reader move easily from passage to passage without losing a sense of the whole.

The ACT general editors seek to be circumspect and meticulous in commissioning volume editors and translators. We strive for a high level of consistency and literary quality throughout the course of this series. We have sought out as volume editors and translators those patristic and biblical scholars who are thoroughly familiar with their original language sources, who are informed historically, and who are sympathetic to the needs of ordinary nonprofessional readers who may not have professional language skills.

Thomas C. Oden and Gerald L. Bray, Series Editors

# TRANSLATOR'S INTRODUCTION

The identity of Ambrosiaster and the history of the transmission of his great commentary on the Pauline Epistles are two of the great questions of patristic scholarship, neither of which is likely to be resolved in the foreseeable future. In her very thorough examination of the evidence, Sophie Lunn-Rockliffe has concluded that a search for his true identity is futile and that all we can say about the three different recensions of his commentary is that they are likely to have come from the author himself.[1] His motives for producing different versions remain obscure, however, as does the order in which they were produced. The texts are with us in over seventy different manuscripts, but beyond that inescapable fact all is speculation and uncertainty.

## The Identity of the Author

The name Ambrosiaster seems to have been given to the author of the Pauline commentary by its Benedictine editors (1686-1690). Before that time it had been attributed to Ambrose of Milan (d. 397) for more than a thousand years, despite the fact that it differs remarkably in style and approach from the genuine writings of the great Milanese bishop. Augustine of Hippo, who knew the commentary, attributed it to a certain "Hilary" perhaps because he thought it came from the pen of Hilary of Poitiers, though this is most unlikely. A more plausible candidate is Decimus Hilarianus Hilarius, a prominent Roman layman of the late fourth century, but this too is no more than speculation. Other suggestions, which range from Isaac the Jew to Evagrius of Pontus, are equally uncertain and open to serious objections, as Lunn-Rockliffe has shown. The tone of the commentary suggests that the author was a clergyman, and if his comments on Philemon are anything to go by, it seems that he regarded lay involvement in church affairs as anomalous. Most likely he was a presbyter of the Roman church who wanted to instruct younger clergy on how to preach and teach the Pauline Epistles. He does not appear to have had any special expertise for this task, though it is clear that he was a follower of Nicene orthodoxy and that he had an eye for pastoral questions. Many of his comments end with moral maxims which summarize principles that look very much like the message of a sermon, and it is probable that he exercised a regular preaching and teaching ministry at Rome. It may be that he deliberately chose to remain anonymous, perhaps in order to avoid the unwelcome controversy that his writings were likely to generate.

---

[1]Sophi Lunn-Rockliffe, *Ambrosiaster's Political Theology* (Oxford: Oxford University Press, 2007), pp. 11-32.

Ambrosiaster had a strong interest in Jewish laws and customs, though the suggestion that he was a Jew himself probably goes too far, since at many points in his commentary he identifies himself with the Gentile world. His knowledge of Greek was rudimentary, and perhaps it is just as well that he made virtually no attempt to correct false or inadequate renderings in the Latin version he was using by reference to the original language.

We know from internal evidence that Ambrosiaster was writing during the pontificate of Damasus I (366–384), who commissioned Jerome to produce a definitive Latin translation of the Bible. He did not use the Latin Vulgate, which was the result of Jerome's labors, nor did he comment on it where his own version differed from that of Jerome, so we may assume that his work was complete before the Vulgate translation became known. There is also no mention of the decree making Christianity the official state religion (February 27, 380) or of the first council of Constantinople, held in 381. The impression we get is that Nicene orthodoxy was still fighting its various enemies—pagan, Jewish and heretical—and that the final outcome was sufficiently in doubt that congregations were in constant need of warning about the dangers posed by each of these. It probably took several years for the commentary to be written, so that we can make a good guess that the task was underway during the 370s. The surviving recensions shed no further light on this question, which suggests that they were produced fairly soon after the initial composition. If they were the work of literary executors, it is possible that Ambrosiaster died sometime before 380, but this is pure conjecture and the evidence of his other work, the *Quaestiones* which deal with disputed points in the Bible, suggests that he was still alive in 384. What is certain is that by the end of the fourth century Ambrosiaster's commentary had become a standard work of Latin biblical study and that it retained its influence even after the publication of Jerome's new Vulgate translation.

**The Text and Its Translation**

Ambrosiaster's commentary can be broken down into two, or possibly three, principal recensions. Untangling these can be a delicate task, because in later centuries there was a good deal of cross-pollination, as monastic copyists incorporated elements from different recensions into their own text. It is possible that Ambrosiaster left his work in a semipolished state, which was then touched up for publication by literary executors who smoothed out some of its rough edges and filled in material that was either missing from the manuscript(s) they had or that was felt to be needed in order to make sense of what Ambrosiaster wrote. But it is also possible that Ambrosiaster produced the different versions himself, perhaps with a variety of audiences in mind. The style of the shortest recension is lapidary to the point of obscurity, and in some ways is more like a series of lecture notes than a finished commentary. It is often difficult or impossible to know what Ambrosiaster meant, and the second and third recensions were probably trying to explain the obscurities of the shortest text. Sometimes they are genuinely helpful and illuminate the commentary, but there are places when later hands digressed from Ambrosiaster's thought pattern and added material that is either irrelevant or contradictory. There is no reason to believe that anyone wanted to falsify Ambrosiaster's thought, though it is possible that the third recension contains comments that were felt to be more appropriate or helpful than the text of the primary and secondary ones. If they come from the pen of Ambrosiaster himself, then it would seem that he revised his work in the light of feedback received from readers of the earlier editions.

Given this situation, the task of a translator becomes extremely difficult. Reproducing the "original" Ambrosiaster is not a realistic goal, since even if this were possible, the result would be unreadable. Incorporating at least some of the later material is essential if we are to make sense of what Ambrosiaster was saying, and here we can only be guided by the weight of probability. Sometimes it appears as if whole phrases have gone missing or been transposed to other parts of the manuscript, but we cannot be certain of this. For this translation, editorial additions that round out the text and are uncontested by rival alternatives are included without further comment. Where a second possibility exists, it is put in a footnote. As a general rule the shorter version has been preferred for the main text and the longer one has been consigned to a footnote, on the assumption that the shorter text is more likely to be the older one. Interpolations that bear no relation to the rest of the text or that clearly contradict it have been omitted, though it should be said that there are very few of these. Possible transpositions have been ignored, though apparent lacunae have been filled in with conjectures that have been put in square brackets. The words and phrases thus supplied have been chosen in line with the general sense of the text, which makes them plausible, even if their accuracy cannot be guaranteed.

Ambrosiaster knew nothing of chapter or verse divisions in the Bible, and so the passages that he isolated for comment do not always coincide with what we are familiar with today. Modern readers cannot be expected to find their place in the text without chapter and verse, so these have been added to the translation of the commentary. His quotations from other parts of Scripture are more problematic. Those taken from the Old Testament follow Latin versions of the Greek Septuagint rather than the Hebrew text, which is sometimes quite different, and not every quotation is full or exact. Often he omits parts of a verse or paraphrases it slightly, which makes it hard to know whether he was using a different translation or merely adapting the text in front of him to his own literary style. In the Psalms, he used the Greek numbering, which usually differs by one from the Hebrew but is relatively unfamiliar to English-speaking readers. The Greek numbering has been preserved in the text, with a note signaling the numbering in the Hebrew (and English) system; footnotes regularly supply references to modern verse numbering. For this translation, the text of the Revised Standard Version (RSV) has been followed, mainly because it was the one chosen for the Ancient Christian Commentary on Scripture, but quotations have been given in the form Ambrosiaster used, regardless of what the RSV says. When the commentary is based on a reading that is not in the RSV or is contradictory to it, this is pointed out in a footnote. Once again, the frequency of this should not be exaggerated, and at least ninety percent of the text is identical (or nearly so) in both Ambrosiaster and the RSV. Nevertheless, it is only fair to point out discrepancies where these occur and leave judgment on the underlying textual questions to the experts. Most of the time, it will be found that Ambrosiaster was using a text closer to that of the so-called *Textus Receptus* (which is essentially the one underlying the Authorized or King James Version of 1611), rather than the text(s) behind the RSV or other modern English translations, but this is not an invariable rule and each verse must be considered on its own merits.

What Latin version Ambrosiaster was using is unknown. It was probably the one known to Lucifer of Cagliari, who was writing about the same time. It contained some egregious errors that a knowledge of Greek would have corrected, but beyond that it is impossible to go. Whatever text he was using, it was no doubt the translation that was most familiar to him. This may have been the *Itala,* referred to by Augustine as the best of the Latin versions circulating in his time, but if so, we can only say that it provides clear evidence of the need for a fresh translation, which Jerome was even then being commissioned to provide. He seldom quotes from the deuterocanonical books of the Old Testament, although when he does he treats them as Scripture, but he did not regard the epistle to the Hebrews as Pauline. We have to admit that Ambrosiaster's interpretive skills are conditioned and sometimes constricted by a faulty text, leading him to conclusions that cannot be justified, but the extent of this problem should not be exaggerated. On the whole, he made sensible judgments and was careful to present alternative possibilities when the meaning of Paul's words was unclear to him.

Ambrosiaster must be regarded as one of the greatest of the ancient biblical commentators, whose work can often stand alongside that of modern scholars. He was firmly wedded to the literal sense of interpretation and avoided allegory, though he was not averse to mentioning the spiritual dimension of the text when he thought that its grammatical or stylistic peculiarities required an explanation beyond the purely literal one. He was particularly sensitive to the rhetorical devices that the apostle Paul used, and sometimes we find interesting explanations of words taken from political, military or legal contexts that would have been well known to him but that might easily escape a modern reader less familiar with the Roman imperial context. One instance of this is his discussion of Paul's Roman citizenship, which he believed derived from a general enrollment of the people of Tarsus as Romans and not from a particular grant made to one of Paul's ancestors. Ambrosiaster clearly thought that grants of Roman citizenship were made collectively and not individually, but even if he was wrong in this case, his general sense of the way ancient societies functioned may give us a more faithful picture of the apostle Paul and his world than we usually get from modern commentaries.

### The Social and Theological Context

The importance of Ambrosiaster's feel for the cultural context of the Pauline Epistles is most noticeable when we consider the way that he brings out the close connection between the church of his day and that of the first century. For example, the fourth-century church was full of newly converted pagans whose behavior, particularly in matters related to idol worship, was fairly lax from the standpoint of more rigorously orthodox Christians. He felt he had to stress the importance of distancing himself from such pagan practices, even if they were theologically matters of indifference. Ambrosiaster understood that perception is often as important as the reality, and so he counseled his readers to avoid even the appearance of wrongdoing, whatever their consciences might tell them. Behind the dumb idols, he claimed, there lurked active and malevolent demons who would do all in their power to lead Christians astray, and it was they, not the wood and stone figures, who had to be feared. The apostle Paul did not make that connection, as far as we know, but Ambrosiaster reminds us that Paul also inhabited a world in which pagan religious practices were often regarded as essentially demonic and that he would not have been surprised by Ambrosiaster's conclusion, even if he would not necessarily have shared it.

Ambrosiaster's greatest worry was the prevalence of false teachers in the church, and here he felt a particular kinship with the apostle Paul, who also frequently warned against the influence of false apostles, who tried to subvert the congregations he had founded. In the fourth century, the enemies were different but the principle was the same, and Ambrosiaster did everything he could to prove that the great heresies of his own time were often merely rehashes of what the apostle warned against. In the course of his many discussions of this subject, we learn that the greatest danger came from the Manichaeans, whose dualism was foreshadowed by some of the proto-Gnostics attacked by Paul. Somewhat surprisingly, Ambrosiaster says very little about Arius, although he defends the Nicene faith in ways which were clearly anti-Arian in their substance. The reason for that may well have been political, since until the defeat of Valens at Adrianople in 378, the imperial family was Arian or semi-Arian, and Ambrosiaster may have been reluctant to express his views in a way that might have led to a charge of political disloyalty. On the other hand, his deep concern for sound doctrine was never in doubt, and by that he meant the Athanasian interpretation of the decisions taken at Nicaea in 325.

As befits his Roman background, Ambrosiaster had a keen eye for moral issues. He came down heavily against sexual immorality of all kinds, but he also highlighted Paul's condemnation of slanderous gossip, greed and selfishness. He particularly appreciated the link Paul had made between false teaching and greed, which he regarded as one of the most prevalent evils of the church both in his own day and in the first century. We have no way of knowing how widespread this problem was in Ambrosiaster's time, but the influx of wealthy people into the church must have raised the problem of financial corruption, and Ambrosiaster's reaction to this is understandable.

Despite his close identification with Paul and the Pauline legacy, Ambrosiaster had a clear understanding of the developments that had taken place in the church since the first century. For example, he knew that the apostles had performed signs and wonders that were no longer current in his own day. He was not a "cessationist" in the modern sense, but put this down to the fact (as he saw it) that signs and wonders were intended to impress unbelievers; Christians had no need of them. To reinforce this view, he made a particular point of saying that some of the apostle's companions, like Epaphroditus, had bouts of serious illness which the apostle had to pray about, because he could not automatically cure them.

Ambrosiaster was also aware that the structures of the church had evolved significantly over time, and he pointed this out when he could, especially in his commentaries on the Pastoral Epistles (1-2 Timothy and Titus). For example, he was prepared to say that in Paul's time there had been no distinction between the presbyterate and the episcopate, the difference having subsequently arisen because the qualifications of the former were not always high enough to allow them to exercise the ministry of the latter. Oddly, he seems to have been unaware that presbyters were the same as elders (*seniores* in Latin) and mentioned that the eldership, which the church had inherited from the synagogue, had died out over time for reasons unknown to him. Ambrosiaster did not use the term *sacrament* in the modern sense (to him it was just a translation of the Greek word *mystery*, which he also used), but he had what we would now call a highly sacramental view of the church's ministry. He did not hesitate to call the clergy *sacerdotes*, a usage unknown to the New Testament, and on several occasions he referred to them as men who stood "in the place of Christ" when leading public worship.

In other instances, Ambrosiaster recognized that there had been a continuity of traditions over the centuries, but that these traditions had sometimes been abused. He was particularly hard on the order of church widows, which still existed in his time but which had expanded to include women whom Ambrosiaster thought should have been kept out, in line with Paul's teaching that only those who had been wives of one husband and who had decided to dedicate their declining years to the service of God should receive any stipend out of church funds. By the late fourth century there were apparently many who had no such intention, but who were receiving charitable gifts from the church because they had somehow managed to get their names on the lists, whereas others (who were more deserving) were being overlooked.

### His Legacy

Ambrosiaster clearly belongs to the Latin theological tradition and was only minimally influenced by Greek, Jewish or other sources. He knew writers like Tertullian and Cyprian well enough to be able to quote them in support of his own views, and he was also familiar with the Roman schismatic Novatian. He never mentioned anyone from the

Eastern church, apart from an occasional reference to Arius. He could have known Origen's biblical commentaries but apparently did not, presumably because Rufinus had not yet translated them into Latin. He could also have met Athanasius during one of his periodic exiles in the West, but if he did so, he said nothing about it. It is hard to believe that he was an original thinker, and many of his ideas presumably came from elsewhere. But since his is the oldest Latin commentary on the Pauline Epistles to survive from ancient times, it is not clear what his sources were. He never mentioned any, but reticence in such matters was characteristic of most writers before the modern era and tells us nothing one way or the other.

We know that he was read by Augustine with profit and that certain theological themes generally associated with the great bishop of Hippo can be traced back to him. The links with Augustine are particularly noticeable when we compare him with his great contemporaries, Ambrose and Jerome. One might think that Ambrosiaster had some connection with Ambrose that would have justified the inclusion of his work with that of the bishop of Milan, but there is nothing that points clearly in that direction. Perhaps Ambrosiaster's work was edited by people close to Ambrose, but that is speculation and is not supported by any textual similarity between them. Nor is it clear to what extent Ambrosiaster knew Jerome or was known by him, although both men were probably in Rome in the early years of Pope Damasus I. Jerome was an accomplished linguist and therefore a better biblical scholar than Ambrosiaster could ever hope to be, and it would not be at all surprising if he had disliked Ambrosiaster's work and dismissed it as inferior to his own. Perhaps he did, but if so there is nothing in Jerome's works to tell us one way or another.

By the time Ambrosiaster's commentary was circulating widely, it had been subsumed under the name of Ambrose, and for more than a thousand years no one was aware of his separate identity. As the work of Ambrose, it was widely admired and imitated throughout the Middle Ages, when it did much to preserve both Pauline studies and a sense of the importance of the literal interpretation of Scripture. It was just as Ambrosiaster's distinct identity was being recognized that these two tendencies coalesced in a new outburst of scholarly energy that we associate with the Renaissance and the Reformation. But although Ambrosiaster was appreciated by humanists and reformers alike, his work was quickly surpassed, both in breadth of scholarship and in depth of theological insight, so that it never established itself as a standard reference for later biblical studies. His anonymity also worked against him at a time when there was an increasing focus on the accomplishments of particular individuals in the early church period. By showing that he was not Ambrose, his Benedictine editors effectively decanonized him, a disadvantage which persists to the present day and helps to explain why there has never before been a complete translation of his work, despite its obvious interest and importance.

Until very recently, Ambrosiaster was essentially unknown and disregarded by theologians, including those with a particular interest in the patristic tradition. He was better known to biblical scholars, but mainly because he regularly appears in the critical apparatus of the Greek New Testament as a witness to particular variant readings of the text. His skill as a commentator in his own right went unacknowledged, and it is only now that patristic biblical interpretation is coming into its own once more that his qualities are beginning to be more widely appreciated. It must be hoped that the publication of his commentaries on the Pauline Epistles will make it possible for a wider audience to hear and appreciate his message, and give him (at long last) the honored place in the history of biblical, and especially Pauline, studies, that he so richly deserves.

**For Further Reading**

The text of Ambrosiaster's commentary used for this translation is the one published in the series Corpus Scriptorum Ecclesiasticorum Latinorum (CSEL), *Ambrosiastri qui dicitur Commentarius in Epistulas Paulinas*, edited under the name of H. J. Vogels (3 vols., Vienna: Hoelder-Pichler-Tempsky, 1966–1969), though much of the actual work was done by others. A new translation under the direction of Professor David Hunter of the University of Kentucky is due to appear in 2010, which will include a full critical apparatus and introduction to the text.

The most important study of his identity remains the work of Alexander Souter, *A Study of Ambrosiaster* (Cambridge: The University Press, 1905), though this must be supplemented by further details found in the introduction to the Vogels edition. The only substantial examination of his theology available in English is the recent study by Sophie Lunn-Rockliffe, to which reference has already been made.

# AMBROSIASTER
## *Commentary on Galatians*

### Preface

Anyone who believes in Christ but still observes the law of works does not understand Christ correctly. An example of this would be the Symmachians, who trace their origin to the Pharisees.[1] They keep the whole law but call themselves Christians, although like Photinus,[2] they do not believe that Christ is both God and man, but say that he was only a man. If they understood that Christ was also God, they would have no faith in the law of works, that is, in new moons, the sabbath, circumcision and the food laws, since whoever worships the God and Lord of the law is above the law and cannot be judged by it, because he is in tune with the lawgiver himself.

Furthermore, the law was not given for the benefit of those who already worshiped God, but for those who believed and acted wrongly and who were contemptuous of the Creator. This is why Paul said to Timothy: *The law is not laid down for the just, but for the ungodly and sinners*[3] and Moses said: *You shall make the children of Israel to fear.*[4] The Galatians, or those who had undermined their faith, still had hearts shrouded in a cloud of error, and did not discern what the prophet Isaiah meant when he said elsewhere: *The Lord will execute his sentence upon the earth with rigor and dispatch.*[5]

If they had understood these sayings they would have turned away from the law, having learned from the preaching of John the Baptist that the law had come to an end and that once it was cut back, faith alone was necessary for salvation. What is made clear in the preaching about God the Father, Christ his Son and the Holy Spirit, was predestined in time by being contained in the law. If the children of Israel were circumcised as a sign that they were thereby children of Abraham according to the flesh, circumcision must naturally come to an end, because those who believe [in Christ] have the sign that death has been overcome. By this they are recognized as children of Abraham, but as his children by faith. Abraham was promised that the one who would come would overcome death.

Finally, Abraham was waiting for the one whose birth he rejoiced at in his spirit, knowing that he would soon be taken up into heaven. This is why the Lord said to the Jews: *Abraham wanted to see my day; he saw it and rejoiced.*[6] At the time when the children of Israel were still together in the desert, before they had Gentile neighbors, they were not circumcised. But when they began to mix with the Gentiles, Joshua had them circumcised by using a rock, and that rock stands for Christ. Paul said that the rock was Christ,[7] because it indicated that the future circumcision of the heart would come through Christ, as Moses and the prophet Jeremiah had both said: *Circumcise yourselves to God,*[8] and: *Circumcise the foreskin of your heart.*[9] Once the darkness had been removed by accepting the forgiveness

[1]Symmachus lived in the late second century A.D. and was a leader of the Ebionites, a Jewish Christian sect active at that time. He is best known today as a translator of the Old Testament into Greek. [2]Condemned in A.D. 351, he lived in Pannonia (now Western Hungary) and died in 376. [3]1 Tim 1:9. [4]Cf. Ex 20:20; Lev 19:3; 25:7. [5]Rom 9:28. Cf. Is 10:22-23. [6]Jn 8:56. [7]1 Cor 10:4. [8]Jer 4:4. [9]Deut 10:16.

of sins, they would become worthy of seeing the glory of God, which they could not see when they were still under the law, because of their sin. Therefore, in order to state that he meant that Christ was God and that he had not learned what he was teaching from other people, Paul begins as follows.

## Galatians 1

***1Paul an apostle—not from men nor through man, but through Jesus Christ and God the Father, who raised him from the dead—***

The apostle bears witness to the fact that unlike some, he had not been chosen and sent to preach by men who had been selected by the apostles and sent to churches in order to strengthen them, nor was he like others who had been sent by the Jews in order to upset the churches, whom he calls false apostles. Rather, he says that he was sent by the Son of God (whom, in this case, he almost seems to deny was a man, because he gave his commandments as God and not as a man, and chose whom he chose by divine judgment.) By this means he indicated that he was a good, solid preacher, because a person whom God chose was much better than one chosen by another man.

Paul says that he was not sent from men, because those who had forced the Galatians to be circumcised thought that Christ was only a man. He was sent by Jesus Christ, that is to say, by the one who is both God and man. This is clear from what follows, namely, *and God the Father, who raised him from the dead.* In saying this he condemned two heresies, that of Mani[10] and that of Photinus. Mani denied that Jesus was a man but did not deny that he was crucified. Photinus on the other hand did not accept that Christ was God and yet did not dare deny that he had come back to life from the dead. It seems stupid for Mani to deny that Christ was a man when he did not deny that he had been crucified, and likewise for Photinus to deny (by some ungodliness of his) that he was God, yet say that he had risen from the dead. He had read that the Lord had said: *Destroy this temple and I will raise it up in three days. He said this about the temple of his body.*[11] Therefore when he indicated that he would raise himself from the dead he meant his body. Yet at the same time Paul also said that Christ was raised by his Father, because all the Son's power comes from the Father, and the deeds of the Son are the deeds of the Father, from whom all things come.

***2and all the brethren who are with me,***
***To the churches of Galatia:***

After justifying his own authority, Paul backs up his point by claiming that all the others who had been with him were equally stirred up against the false apostles. His own authority would have sufficed and could not have been rejected, but in order to emphasize the seriousness of what they had done in abandoning their original faith, he pointed out that there were many with him who were equally incensed and determined to argue against their error. It would be easier for them to appreciate that error if they realized that they were being criticized for it by many others.

***3Grace to you and peace from God the Father and our Lord Jesus Christ,***

Paul claims that the human race has been blessed by both the Father and the Son. He indicates that the Son is not inferior [to the Father] when he calls him *our Lord,* and that the Father is not greater [than the Son], when

[10]A Persian who lived in the mid-third century and preached a dualistic doctrine which claimed that good and evil were equal forces battling one another for supremacy. [11]Jn 2:19, 21.

he calls him our God, because the Father will not truly be the Father unless he is also Lord, and the Son will not truly be Lord unless he is also God. Therefore, says Paul, if the grace of the Father and that of the Son which has been shown to us is one and the same, how is it that the Gentiles have thought less of Christ and equated him with the law, so as to serve Christ on the one hand and the law on the other? Had they not read how the Lord had said: *For the Son of Man is Lord also of the sabbath?*[12] In this way, Paul wanted them to realize how greatly they had offended God by comparing him with a servant.

***[4]who gave himself for our sins to deliver us from the present evil age, according to the will of our God and Father; [5]to whom be the glory for ever and ever. Amen.***

Paul shows quite clearly that the law is of no use when he says that Christ offered himself up to suffer on our behalf, in order to justify us (whom the law regarded as guilty), so that we should be delivered from the law by faith in Christ and be no longer sinners, but reckoned as justified by the second birth [given by] the Son of God. When the human race was still captive to the devil, the Savior offered himself up to him. and the devil was willing to take him. Christ's purpose was to deceive him by the strength of his power. The devil was willing to take him but unable to hold him, and in that way Christ was able to remove from him what he wrongfully held captive. Having looted hell, he brought his treasure of souls up to the Father, from whom all things come—something which the law could not do. Although the law had been given to be of use to us, in reality it turned us into sinners and thus became hostile to us, killing us instead of bringing us back to life.

But Christ forgave our sins and in so doing not only brought us back to life but also united us to himself, so that we might be called sons of God, made that way by faith. What a grave error it was therefore to return to the law after receiving grace, that is to say, to want to be a slave after having been set free. It was as if a gladiator had been discharged and then, ignoring his blessing, went and sold himself back to the gladiator-master![13] Such a person would in effect be turning on his liberator by abandoning him and going back to his first master.

*To deliver us from the present evil age.* Paul says this because the Lord surrendered himself to death in order to set us free from the error of this world, that is to say, from the wisdom of this world, so that as this present age hastens to its inglorious end, we have become strangers to it. Instead we now share in the mind of the one God in a future age which knows no end. The evil of the present world is that it does not give the appropriate reverence to God the Creator and to Christ the Liberator, either because human error concocts many gods for itself or because believers do not worship Christ with the honor due to him.

In order to confirm and validate what he says about Christ delivering us, Paul adds that he did this according to the will of God the Father.

***[6]I am astonished that you are so quickly deserting him who called you in the grace of Christ and turning to a different gospel—[7]not that there is another gospel, but there are some who trouble you and want to pervert the gospel of Christ.***

The gospel is good news, and for this reason the law is also the old gospel, apart from the law of works. The reason for this is that what it promised has been fulfilled and sinners have been summoned to get their reprieve. For that reason Paul says that he is astonished that the Gala-

[12]Lk 6:5. [13]Gladiators were mainly slaves who were forced to fight.

tians have turned away from so great a blessing and bound themselves to the law of works. As a result, they have lost what they had gained and have fallen right back into the slavery from which they had just been set free. Typically, a person moves over from bad to good behavior in stages, but these people had quickly been taken away from the good and been transported to the most serious works of the flesh.

It rarely happens that a person runs away from happiness to destruction, and for this reason Paul is astonished at the stupidity of people who had deserted their place of safety and subjected themselves to pointless travail. It is as if a crazy sailor who was anchored in port during a storm had decided to set sail and be tossed about by gusts on all sides. The Galatians were like this, because in their foolishness they had cut themselves off and subjected themselves to the pains of their shame and the yoke of the law, with no hope of relief in sight. They had been called away to another gospel, because although what the people who had turned them away preached was essentially no different from what the apostles had proclaimed, the false apostles claimed that it was because they were jealous of the apostle who had taught them. In order to deceive the Galatians by this lie, they had to say that the apostle preached another gospel than the one which the mind of the Savior had taught, and this was quite true because what they preached was in line with the old law. These were the same people who questioned Paul and Barnabas about this matter, as is contained in the Acts of the Apostles.[14] They taught that Gentile believers could not be saved unless they were circumcised according to the law of Moses and became Jews. It is clear that they were doing this in order to pervert the gospel of Christ by changing what had been taught and under cover of the name of Christ turning the Galatians into Jews.

***8But even if we, or an angel from heaven, should preach to you a gospel contrary to that which we preached to you, let him be accursed.***
***9As we have said before, so now I say again, If any one is preaching to you a gospel contrary to that which you received, let him be accursed.***

Nobody should be surprised that the apostle, who was known for taming wild behavior, should have been so worked up about this, because it was for the sake of the Galatians' salvation that he was so angry with the enemies of Christian discipline. This very anger shows that it was a serious sin to turn back to the law after having received the faith. He asserted that the gospel which he had preached to them was so firm and true that even if they themselves, that is the apostles, should change their minds and preach something different, they should not be listened to, even if their reputation as apostles had reached the ends of the earth. Even if the devil should pretend to be an angel of God, in order to get himself a better hearing, and appear from heaven, teaching things that went against what they had received, they ought to recognize as much and reject it as an abomination. So if the apostle Paul taught that even if apostles of Christ, who had acquired such a high reputation thanks to the signs and wonders which they had performed, or an angel from heaven, who might come with a spiritual recommendation, should be anathematized if they preached something other than what they had been taught by himself, how much more would this apply to those who had no persuasive testimony to commend them! For this reason he repeats his objection, so as to confirm them in their previous teaching, because repeating the rules makes those who ignore them more uncomfortable.

***10Am I now seeking the favor of men, or of God? Or am I trying to please men? If I were***

[14]Acts 15:1-29.

***still pleasing men, I should not be a servant of Christ.***

Paul says: "Am I trying to persuade you to return to the grace of Christ in order to please other people, or in order to please God?" It is obviously not to please other people, but to please God, so that by doing what he wanted they might return to the God whom they had rejected. After this he goes right on to add: *Am I trying to please men? If I were still pleasing men, I should not be a servant of Christ.* He means by this that those who had turned the Galatians away were not trying to please God by doing this, but other people, in precisely the same way that he himself had done in the days when he persecuted the church in an attempt to uphold his ancestral traditions. They were saying that the law had to be kept as they desired so that they would receive praise from the Jews, because if they had preached the true gospel of Christ, they would have fallen out with them instead. Here we see that the apostle Paul, who taught that we ought to please God with all devotion, was not afraid to offend other people as long as he was promoting the glory of God. Laying aside everything here and now, he devoted himself to the hope of future reward, like a faithful servant of Christ. Servants cannot be faithful if they look after their own interests while claiming to be working for the Lord.

But someone might object that those who were preaching the law, which God is supposed to have given, were really only servants of men. How can the law be said to be perfect if preaching it is compromised by human desires? Before the coming of the Lord, it was God's will that the law should be preached, for there was a time assigned to it during which it had to be kept. But when the Lord who had been promised in the law came, it was time for the law to cease, as the prophets had predicted. This is why the Lord said: *The law and the prophets are until John.*[15] It was not right for the authority of the law to be preserved once the Lord had come. Therefore, if anyone thinks he ought to go on keeping the law, he is not now obeying God's will but rejecting it and satisfying only other people like himself.

***[11]For I would have you know, brethren, that the gospel which was preached by me is not man's gospel. [12]For I did not receive it from man, nor was I taught it, but it came through a revelation of Jesus Christ.***

Here Paul explains the underlying principles of his epistle. He wants to make it clear that he had not learned what he was teaching from other people, in case some people doubted what he was teaching them. Nor had his preaching been adapted to suit human inclinations, which would make it appear unworthy of having divine authority. Rather, he says that he had learned it from the Son of God by way of revelation, since after the resurrection he was already in heaven, as I mentioned above, and the things which Paul learned fit well with the will and majesty of the one from whom he said he had learned them. They were spiritual commands, which stored up merit with God if they were kept. As for the carnal commandments [of the law], if they were kept beyond the time appointed for them, they earned neither merit nor demerit with God, but if they were not kept they would be a problem. This was because whoever did not keep the law was under a curse, but whoever kept it was not thereby justified before God, because *the just shall live by faith.*[16] Keeping the commandments of the law is therefore a burden, not a blessing.

***[13]For you have heard of my former life in Judaism, how I persecuted the church of God violently and tried to destroy it; [14]and I advanced***

[15]Lk 16:16. [16]Hab 2:4; Gal 3:11.

***in Judaism beyond many of my own age among my people, so extremely zealous was I for the traditions of my fathers.***

Paul mentions briefly how he had once lived according to the flesh and rejected the church, but that when he became a follower of Christ he gave all that up. He states that he was more dedicated than any of them in his attempts to defend the law, which he did not do in order to gain the favor of other people but because he thought it was what God wanted. It was through ignorance that he was pleasing men, because he thought he was serving God and had a clear conscience. He did not know that the time for keeping the law was over, and he was following the teaching of his declared ancestors either by mistake or out of malice. He was doing this with all his energy and devotion in order to look as if he stood head and shoulders above his peers in his zeal for the law. He was so incensed at the doctrine of Christ that he would not spare anyone who followed the covenant of faith. But when he had learned by God's revelation that all this work was futile and contrary to what God wanted, he gave it all up and submitted himself to the grace of faith, so that he might excel in it before God. Therefore if this man, who was an Israelite and held the rank of a teacher among the Jews, having studied with Gamaliel, a most learned man and who claimed a place beside the most accomplished men, abandoned the law, how much more should those who were outside the law not have to subject themselves to it! And if this man rejoiced at having got out from under the yoke of slavery, why should they bind their freedom by the chains of the law?

***15But when he who had set me apart before I was born, and had called me through his grace, 16was pleased to reveal his Son to me, in order that I might preach him among the Gentiles, I did not confer with flesh and blood,***

When Paul was putting his trust in the law he was unaware that the time for keeping it had come to an end, he struggled with all his might, thinking that he was doing this because God wanted him to, and combated the gospel of Christ. God saw that his zeal was good but that he lacked knowledge, and so it pleased him to call Paul to his grace, knowing that he would be just the right person to preach the gospel of his Son to the Gentiles. If Paul was as quick and as loyal in doing such a small thing because his conscience told him to and not because he was after the approval of other people, how much better would he be in preaching the gift of God with the hope of the promised reward.

By the foreknowledge of God, Paul had been set apart in his mother's womb, that is to say, before he was born, and from birth God knew what good he would do, as he says to Jeremiah: *Before I formed you in the womb I knew you, et cetera.*[17] In the same way, God knew what the apostle Paul would do in the future and so prepared him for his calling and conversion before they happened, because God needed him. Finally, as soon as he received the dispensation of God's gift he laid aside all worldly cares, and without seeking advice or referring his plans to anyone else, he went straight out and preached that Christ was the Son of God. Just as it often happens that good people turn out bad later on, so there are also occasions when bad people turn out to be good.

***17nor did I go up to Jerusalem to those who were apostles before me, but I went away into Arabia; and again I returned to Damascus.***

Paul says that since he was chosen by God, there was no need for him to go to see those who had been apostles before him in order

[17]Jer 1:5.

to learn something from them, because God had revealed to him by his Son how he should teach. He says this in order to show that no one should hold anything other than what he was teaching, nor should other people be believed, but only God, from whom he says he has learned it. For this reason he says that those who had led the Galatians away into the law were false teachers, because what they were teaching had not been given to them by God. From Damascus, Paul went off to preach in Arabia, where there were no apostles, in order to found churches and prevent false apostles from surreptitiously sowing the seeds of Judaism. After that he returned to Damascus to visit some simple people to whom he had preached the gospel of the grace of God.

***18Then after three years I went up to Jerusalem to visit Cephas, and remained with him fifteen days.***

It was right for Paul to want to see Peter, because he was the chief of the apostles to whom the Savior had delegated the care of the churches. It was not in order to learn something from him, because he had already learned everything from the author himself, just as Peter had, but because of his love for the apostles. He also wanted Peter to know that the same commission which had been given to him had been given to Paul also. Paul therefore went to Peter and was well received by him. He stayed there for fifteen days, and the two men were of the same mind as apostles. Paul tells us this in order to show that he was in complete agreement with the other apostles and did not disagree with them in anything, as the false apostles were whispering about him in an attempt to discredit him with the Gentile churches and introduce their own wickedness, claiming that it agreed with the teaching of the more important apostles.

***19But I saw none of the other apostles except James the Lord's brother.***

Paul also saw James at Jerusalem, because he had been appointed the city's bishop by the apostles. He too had been an unbeliever at first, as the Evangelist says: *Even his brothers did not believe in him.*[18] This James was the son of Joseph, which is why he is called the brother of the Lord. Joseph was his father and is also called the father of the Lord. This is what Mary says to Jesus in Luke's Gospel: *What have you done to us, son? Look, your father and I have been searching for you anxious and worried.*[19] And in John's Gospel, Philip says to Nathanael: *We have found him of whom Moses in the law and also the prophets wrote, Jesus of Nazareth, the son of Joseph.*[20] It is in this way that Jesus is said to be the brother of James and the others, for he too was called the son of Joseph. There are some people mad enough to make the ungodly claim that these men were the Lord's brothers because they were born of Mary, because they say that Joseph was not his true father. But if they were really his brothers, then Joseph was their real father, because whoever said that Joseph was his father also said that James and the others were his brothers.

***20(In what I am writing to you, before God, I do not lie!)***

Concerning his own recommendation, Paul says that God will be his witness so that the Galatians will take what he has to say and not think that he had made it all up, since it was not like him to do such things. In recommending himself Paul wants to help them, for his self-recommendation will help them know that what he has taught them is perfectly true.

***21Then I went into the regions of Syria and Cilicia. 22And I was still not known by sight***

[18]Jn 7:5. [19]Lk 2:48. [20]Jn 1:45.

***to the churches of Christ in Judea; [23]they only heard it said: "He who once persecuted us is now preaching the faith he once tried to destroy." [24]And they glorified God because of me.***

Paul says this because when he was defending Judaism in opposition to the faith, just as these Galatians had been seduced by some other people, he was chosen and taught to reject Judaism and preach the new law. Thus Jewish believers rejoiced at him who had previously persecuted them and gave thanks to God for having turned their persecutor into their defender. The Galatians would also come to realize that they had been led astray to the point where, claiming to be Christians, they actually professed Judaism. They were circumcising the flesh of their foreskins, although the law of Christ taught something quite different from Judaism. Its circumcision was of the flesh, whereas Christ's is of the heart. The Jews were tied to the elements and worshiped new moons and the sabbath, but Christians worshiped God alone in spirit, because they believed in their hearts. The Jews were in a situation which caused them to sin, but Christians enjoyed the freedom which comes from the forgiveness of sins. There is therefore a huge difference between Judaism and Christianity.

## Galatians 2

***[1]Then after fourteen years I went up again to Jerusalem with Barnabas, taking Titus along with me. [2]I went up by revelation; and I laid before them (but privately before those who were of repute) the gospel which I preach among the Gentiles, lest somehow I should be running or had run in vain.***

For a long time Paul's reputation was growing among the Jews although they never saw him because he was traveling about founding and strengthening churches, with his usual thoroughness, among the Gentiles. The Jews, however, were getting a bad impression of him because of the law and thought that he disagreed with the preaching of the other apostles. Many of them were worried and thought that the Gentiles might have to be put right, so as not to be led into something different from what the apostles who had been with the Lord were teaching. On this occasion the Galatians had been led astray by Jews who were saying that Paul was teaching something different from Peter. Thus it came about that Paul was told by a revelation from the Lord to go up to Jerusalem with witnesses of his preaching, that is, Barnabas and Titus, the one a Jew and the other a Gentile, so that if the Jews had some problem with him it could be resolved by their testimony, which would explain to them what the nature of his preaching was.

Paul had a private meeting with the apostles so that they would realize that he was not going away from the norm of the gospel, that is to say, that they would not think that he was running or had run into error,[21] as quite a few of the Jewish believers imagined. Paul had nothing to learn from them because he had been taught directly by God, but for the sake of harmony and peace God brought this about. This was so that any hesitation or suspicion on the part of his brothers or fellow apostles might be taken away and that Gentile believers might be reassured that Paul's gospel was the same as that of the other apostles, especially after they had decreed that Gentile believers would not be disturbed as long as they kept the law by refraining from blood, from fornication and from idolatry.

Now some clever Greeks, who boast of their natural talent for subtle arguments, might ask what exactly the Gentiles were told to do. What were they unaware of and what did they know? How can someone learn

[21]The Latin has *vacuum* here, meaning "emptiness" or "futility."

what he knows already? Therefore it must have been that they were told that certain things which they had previously thought were all right were in fact unlawful. For example, when they were told to abstain from blood, they were not being forbidden to commit murder. Rather, they were learning what Noah had also learned from God, that they should not eat raw meat.[22] After all, how could it have been that people who were steeped in Roman law and fully committed to keeping its commandments would have been unaware that killing others was wrong, especially since Roman law punishes adulterers, murderers, false witnesses, thieves, wrongdoers and people who commit other crimes? The only answer is that these three commands which were given to them by the apostles and elders are not found in Roman law, that is, that they should keep themselves from idolatry, from blood in Noah's sense and from fornication. But some clever Greeks who knew about the prohibition on blood but did not understand what it meant twisted Scripture by adding a fourth commandment, to the effect that they should not eat the meat of an animal which had been strangled. I think that God let them discover this, since what they added here had already been said above.

***3*But even Titus, who was with me, was not compelled to be circumcised, though he was a Greek.**

Titus was with Paul at Jerusalem. Paul says that even though they were in the company of the apostles and Jewish believers, nobody forced Titus to be circumcised. The subtext here is: "So why do you get circumcised when Titus was not forced to be but was accepted by the apostles, who after all counted for something, as an uncircumcised believer?"

***4*But because of false brethren secretly brought in, who slipped in to spy out our freedom which we have in Christ Jesus, that they might bring us into bondage—*5*to them we did not yield submission even for a moment, that the truth of the gospel might be preserved for you.**[23]

Paul says that Titus was not circumcised because he was a Greek, just like the Galatians. In saying this he was criticizing those Greeks who allowed themselves to be circumcised. But in order to avoid the objection that he himself had circumcised Timothy, he goes on to explain why he had done what he says ought not to be done. This is what these verses mean.

The Greeks retort: *We did yield for a moment,* and say that this supports their case, because whoever outlawed something should not then say that he has done it himself, because then he would be appearing to approve of it. But the apostle, being a holy man, knew that this objection might be made, and to prevent attackers of this kind, brought the matter up himself and gave the reasons why he was forced to act in a way that he did not want to.

Paul said that he acted *because of false brethren secretly brought in.* He puts it this way because they had entered by stealth, pretending to be brothers when in fact they were enemies. They entered with a great show of humility, pretending to be friends. To *spy out* is to enter in a way which says one thing but does another with the aim of attacking the *freedom which we have in Christ Jesus.* This freedom in Christ Jesus means that we are not subject to the law. *That they might bring us into bondage.* This means that they came in by stealth and with guile, with the intention of reducing our freedom to slavery by forcing us to submit to the law of circumcision. Paul is saying: "For a moment we submitted to slavery, humbling ourselves before the law so that by circumcis-

[22]Gen 9:4. [23]Ambrosiaster read v. 5 differently. In his version there was no "not," which meant that he had to explain why Paul had yielded for a moment (in the case of Timothy), although he thought it was wrong to do so in principle.

ing Timothy the Jews would have no reason to feel tricked or scandalized." It appears in fact that they were ready to stir up riot and rebellion against Paul, and indeed there was some reason why they had an excuse to attack him. Timothy had a Jewish mother and a Greek father, who was a convert. He had not been circumcised as a child, because his mother was already a believer, and the apostle wanted to take him on board and ordain him a bishop, which he did, since everyone had a good opinion of him, but at that point he suffered attacks from the Jews.[24] They were trying to discover whether Paul would accept the uncircumcised son of a Jewish mother, and were ready to rebel, because if he retorted that Greeks were not to be circumcised (as the letter on this subject had already been put out by the apostles), he did not forbid the sons of Israel from being circumcised, since the apostles had said nothing about that in their letter.

Thus, when he took Timothy on board he circumcised him for the sake of the Jews who lived in those places. They did not complain about Gentiles, which is why Titus was not obliged to be circumcised. He gave in, therefore, but only for a moment, so that the truth of the gospel might be preserved among the Gentiles who do not submit themselves to circumcision. This question did not arise among the Jews, who went on circumcising their sons even after becoming believers, *for in Christ Jesus neither circumcision nor uncircumcision is of any avail, but faith working through love.*[25]

In fact both the history and the epistle tell us that he gave in.[26] Paul has just said that Titus was not forced to be circumcised because he was a Greek, to which he added that it was because of the false brethren who had secretly been brought in. What does this sound like, other than that he gave in for a moment because of the false brethren who had been brought in secretly? Otherwise, what sense would the sentence make?

It is clear that Paul says that Titus did not have to be circumcised. What else does it sound like, except that he gave in? If he did not give in because of the false brethren, he did not give in of his own free will. If that is the case, he indicated that he would give in, but he did not give in because of the false brethren. But if there was no reason to give in, why does he call them false brethren, when he did not do anything for their benefit which did not have to be done? If that were the case, they would have done the apostle a favor, because he did not give what he had to give because of them. Why then are they called spies, if they did not want him to do what he was going to do, but did not do for their sake? If he was not going to do it, it was undoubtedly because of them that he did it. There is no other possibility.

The epistle indicates that he gave in, and the history proclaims the fact. Why would he deny that he had given in for a moment, when it is known that he had circumcised Timothy because of the Jews, and had gone up to the temple after purifying himself according to the law?[27] He could only have said that he had not given in even for a moment if it could be shown that he had never done so. Either he was prepared to give in and did not do so because of the false brethren, or he was not prepared to give in but did so because of them, and if he did not give in because of the false brethren, why would he have given in for the sake of true ones? So choose one option or the other. The false brethren were those who believed in Christ but continued to make people Jews.

***6And from those who were reputed to be something (what they were makes no difference to me; God shows no partiality)—those, I say, who were of repute added nothing to me;***

This means that the apostles were originally

[24]Cf. Acts 16:1-3. [25]Gal 5:6. [26]The "history" is the Acts of the Apostles. [27]Acts 21:26.

simple people with no education and no distinction in the law, but that this did not matter. Who would accuse someone if God excused him? The question is not what a person was, but what he is now. The past neither condemns nor affirms him. Paul wants people to understand that he was an expert in the law and of blameless life, and for that reason he turned into an outstanding minister of the gospel dispensation.

Paul says that he got nothing from the apostles; it all came from God. He says: "The one who imparted the meaning of Christian doctrine to the unlearned is also the one who was pleased to impart it to me as well, since I was learned in the law." Therefore how could Paul have learned anything from the apostles, when he was already learned and became even more so by the grace of Christ?

***[7]but on the contrary, when they saw that I had been entrusted with the gospel to the uncircumcised, just as Peter had been entrusted with the gospel to the circumcised [8](for he who worked through Peter for the mission to the circumcised worked through me also for the Gentiles),***

Paul mentions only Peter and compares himself to him, because he received the primacy and founded the church. Paul was also chosen in a similar way and given the primacy in founding Gentile churches, although of course Peter also preached to the Gentiles when the occasion arose, and Paul preached to Jews. Both men are recorded as having done both things. Nevertheless, Peter was recognized as having full authority to preach among the Jews just as Paul had the same full authority among the Gentiles. This is why he calls himself the teacher of the Gentiles *in faith and in truth.*[28] Each man received the gift according to his abilities. It is more difficult to attract those who are far away from God and persuade them than it is to attract and persuade those who are near to him.

***[9]and when they perceived the grace that was given to me, James and Cephas and John, who were reputed to be pillars, gave to me and Barnabas the right hand of fellowship, that we should go to the Gentiles and they to the circumcised; [10]only they would have us remember the poor, which very thing I was eager to do.***

Paul says that his gift, which he had received from God, was certified by the apostles who knew more than others did (which is why Paul calls them "pillars" on account of their firmness), who had always been with the Lord in his private moments, and who had been worthy to behold his glory on the mountain. This made him worthy to receive the primacy in preaching to the Gentiles, just as Peter had it in preaching to the Jews. And just as God gave Peter colleagues who were outstanding men among the apostles, so Paul associated Barnabas with himself because he had also been joined to him by a divine decision.

Nevertheless, Paul also claims that the grace of primacy had been given only to him, just as it had been given only to Peter among the apostles, so that the apostles of the circumcision might shake hands with the apostles of the Gentiles in order to demonstrate their agreement in fellowship, since they both knew that they had received from the Lord the Spirit of perfection in the dispensation of the gospel and could show that they were lacking in nothing. There was only one thing about which they had to agree among themselves because it had not been expressly taught them by a commandment or gift of the Lord, although it was easy to find it in the law. This was that they were to command those to whom they preached to remember the poor in order to foster the mercy by which they had been

[28]1 Tim 2:7.

redeemed by God. It was for this reason that Paul explains what had been agreed between him and the apostles, so that the Galatians would know that what they had received from him was true and agreed upon.

***11But when Cephas came to Antioch I opposed him to his face, because he stood condemned.***

After agreeing in fellowship and on the honor of primacy, which they accorded one another by the grace of God, something happened which caused the apostles to fall out with each another, either by negligence or because of some mistake they made. This had nothing to do with themselves, but concerned the care of the church. Paul says that he opposed Peter to his face. What can this mean except that he contradicted him to his face? To which he added the reason: *Because he stood condemned.* He was condemned by the truth of the gospel, which he had done something against. Which of them would have dared to oppose Peter, the chief of the apostles, to whom the Lord had given the keys of the kingdom, except someone on his own level who could rely on his election to know that he was not inferior and could continually rebuke him for having done something without thinking properly about it?

***12For before certain men came from James, he ate with the Gentiles; but when they came he drew back and separated himself, fearing the circumcision party. 13And with him the rest of the Jews acted insincerely, so that even Barnabas was carried away by their insincerity.***

All these Jews who consented to the policy of Peter and Barnabas were men of good faith, but because of the way in which those who came from James were scandalized—for they were zealous for the law and venerated both Christ and the law on an equal footing, which goes against the teaching of the faith—they did not eat with Gentiles when they were present because they were afraid of the reaction which would come from those who were zealous for the law. If that had been all there was to it, it would not have been so reprehensible, but Paul shows in what follows what the real error was. He himself had given in to the animosity and impudence of the Jews because he was afraid that otherwise he could easily have provoked a scandal which would have been difficult to put to rest. Examples of this are when he was forced to purify himself according to the law and when he unwillingly circumcised Timothy.

***14But when I saw that they were not straightforward about the truth of the gospel, I said to Cephas before them all: "If you, though a Jew, live like a Gentile and not like a Jew, how can you compel the Gentiles to live like Jews?"***

Paul lashed out only at Peter, because the others would get the message from the one who was their chief.

Here he reveals the cause of Peter's condemnation. There would have been nothing wrong if Peter had withdrawn from the Gentiles when Jews were present for fear of causing a scandal. The reason for the condemnation lay entirely in the fact that when the Jews came from James, not only did Peter cut himself off from the Gentiles with whom he had lived like a Gentile, but he went further and ordered those Gentiles to Judaize themselves because he was so afraid of them, with the result that the Gentiles had no idea what the truth was. They knew that Peter had associated with them as if he were not a Jew, and when they later heard from him that they were expected to follow Jewish customs, they started to wonder what the truth was. If it was true that they should adopt Jewish ways, then they thought that Peter must be a hypocrite because he had lived like a Gentile himself. But if it was better and right for them to live simply, then the Gentiles had been betrayed by Peter's cowardice, because the good which they had had been taken away from them, and in its place they had been given something burdensome and ineffective. When the apostle Paul had given in he had not gone that far, but maintained that he had done something unnecessary and foolish because of the anger of the Jews. He would not have surrendered on the point if there had not been a good reason, which was that the impudence of the Jews was too strong for him to resist. Timothy was the son of a Jewish woman, after all, although his father was a Greek convert, which meant that he should have been circumcised according to the law. The Judaizers therefore wormed their way in to find out whether Paul would take a Jewish assistant who was not circumcised. They thought that it was unlawful for a Jew to do this, and were looking for an example of Paul's breaking the law. It was for this reason that Paul momentarily gave in to their madness.

***15We ourselves, who are Jews by birth and not Gentile sinners, 16yet who know that a man is not justified by works of the law but through faith in Jesus Christ, even we have believed in Christ Jesus, in order to be justified by faith in Christ, and not by works of the law, because by works of the law shall no one be justified.***

Paul shows by clear reasoning that the Galatians have been deceived into keeping the law, by which no one is justified before God, when even those who are born Jews abandon the law and take refuge in Christ if they want to be justified. Paul says that no one is justified by the works of the law. Whoever is justified has been justified by faith, just like Abraham, Isaac, Jacob and the other saints.

***17But if, in our endeavor to be justified in Christ, we ourselves were found to be sinners, is Christ then an agent of sin? Certainly not!***

How can Christ who forgives sin be an agent of sin? Paul says that this is nonsense. If we want to be justified by faith in Christ and yet still keep the law, we are admitting that we are under sin, because faith delivers a person from the law so that he can be justified. Therefore if we give ourselves a law we end up as sinners, because those who are under the law are under a curse.

***18But if I build up again those things which I tore down, then I prove myself a transgressor.***

It is essential that whoever comes to Christ must give up the law, because the slave has been set free. Therefore if he goes back to the law, he will be his own accuser, because he is condemning what he is doing.

***19For I through the law died to the law, that I might live to God.***

Paul says that by the law of faith he has died to the law of Moses. The person who dies is set free from it and lives for God, whose slave he becomes, having been bought by Christ.

***20I have been crucified with Christ; it is no longer I who live, but Christ who lives in me; and the life I now live in the flesh I live by faith in the Son of God, who loved me and gave himself for me.***

Paul is nailed to the cross of Christ because by walking in his footsteps he is not bound by any desire of the world. By living to God he appears to be dead to the world, for whoever does not do worldly things is dead to the world. There is nothing unclear in saying that Christ lives in the person who has been delivered from death by faith. By granting pardon for sin to someone who is worthy of death, Christ dwells in him, for it is by his help that such a person has been rescued from death.

***[21]I do not nullify the grace of God; for if justification were through the law, then Christ died to no purpose.***

Because a future life is promised to Christians, the person who lives in this life armed with the help of God lives in the hope of the promised life [to come]. Such a person meditates on his image, which he has as a token of the future life, which through God's grace has been granted to us by Christ's love. Therefore the person who perseveres in the faith of Christ shows that he is not ungrateful to him for this, because he knows that he will get no benefit from anyone other than from him, and that he will only insult Christ if he compares him to someone else who can do nothing to help him.

There is nothing clearer than this—if a person could have been justified by the law, Christ would not have had to die. But because the law could not grant forgiveness of sins nor prevent the second death from robbing its captives, whom it held because of sin, Christ died to achieve what the law could not do, and for this reason he did not die in vain. His death is the justification of sinners.

## Galatians 3

***[1]O foolish Galatians! Who has bewitched you, before whose eyes Jesus Christ was publicly portrayed as crucified?***

These are the words of a man who is angry at the marvel that the Galatians were so depraved that they did not even realize that they had been led astray. He used the form of an introductory exhortation, for everyone who is bewitched moves from the good to the bad, just as these people had moved from freedom and security to slavery and anxiety.

It is clear that it was only in the eyes of stupid people that Christ appeared to be proscribed,[29] that is to say, degraded and condemned. To the eyes and senses of the wise not only was he not condemned, but he appears as the one who himself condemned death on his cross. The passion of the Lord is our life and the destruction of death, but since these people had begun to think in a way that was unworthy because they had gone over to the law, in their minds it looked as though Christ had been condemned. Paul therefore adds the words: *In you he has been crucified.*[30] This means: "In your minds he has been crucified as a man. The full hope [of salvation] is not to be found in him because he is only a man." Therefore the Galatians did not believe that the fullness of salvation was to be found in Christ, and so they put the law on the same level with him. Christ dwells in those who understand him correctly, but he was crucified in Photinus, since a man in whom Christ is said to have been crucified is really dead. This statement stands in place of an accusation [against such people].

***[2]Let me ask you only this: Did you receive the Spirit by works of the law, or by hearing with faith? [3]Are you so foolish? Having begun with the Spirit, are you now ending with the flesh?***

Paul's gut reaction to the Galatians continues here. He is extremely upset at their error, because he saw that the work which he had built up in them through the gospel had been destroyed. He was not moved to this degree by the Corinthians, because although he calls them carnal, they had not been so completely deceived as to allow themselves to be circumcised. The Galatians are called foolish and mindless, because they could not even take the

[29]Ambrosiaster interprets this word differently from the English translation "publicly portrayed." [30]This phrase is not in the English version.

pain of their own flesh into account. A person normally only goes this far if he likes something, or is indifferent to pain. The questions here are rhetorical and the answer to them is obvious from the way they are expressed. Paul wants them to tell him what they are proud of and could not deny, because they had received the Holy Spirit by faith and not through the law. By repenting they recognized that they had not received the gift of God, which they were so proud of, by the works of the law but by believing in Christ. They ought to have been so thankful to him that they would have abandoned the law, which contained nothing of any benefit to them.

Paul states this because at that time it was not possible to deny that the Spirit of God dwelt in believers. This gift of God had been manifested to people in order to back up the basic doctrines of the faith. The same thing had happened back at the beginning to the apostles and the other disciples, including those twelve whom the apostle Paul ordered should be baptized in the name of the Trinity because in the corrupt form of baptism which went under the name of John they had not been properly washed but only dressed in rags.[31] When hands were laid on them the Holy Spirit came down upon them and blessed them with the gift of other tongues along with the interpretation of them, so that no one would dare deny that the Holy Spirit was present in them. This is why Paul says that the Galatians are foolish, because although they were fully aware and conscious of all this, they lowered themselves and submitted to the concerns of the flesh.

*Having begun with the Spirit, are you now ending with the flesh?* Paul says this because the normal procedure is to rise from the lower to the higher, but these people had gone the other way and fallen from the heights to the depths. They had become spiritual by their faith, but by going over to the law they had lost the grace of the Spirit which they had received. The ending here refers to perdition, which really is the end.

***4Did you experience so many things in vain?—if it really is in vain.***

Paul points out that the Galatians had suffered a lot for their faith. At that time those who believed were hated by others, both at home and abroad, and were cursed as if they were criminals. The Galatians had also suffered a lot but the only result was that they came out madder than ever, because they had lost the merit of their suffering by putting themselves under the law. By adding the clause *if it really is in vain,* Paul is showing that he hopes it may still be possible to reform them.

***5Does he who supplies the Spirit to you and works miracles among you do so by works of the law, or by hearing with faith?***

The meaning here is the same, to which Paul adds the signs of power which provide a witness of their faith that their hope is reliable and reasonable. There is no power accompanying the law which would persuade anyone to place their hope in it, because things which are seen are not hoped for. They are merely temporal, like the law of works, which we expounded above.

***6Thus Abraham "believed God, and it was reckoned to him as righteousness."***

By using the example of Abraham, who is the father of faith, Paul shows that righteousness is not imputed by the works of the law, but by faith. The person who believes is the one who is justified. But in spite of this, the Galatians had stupidly and unwisely subjected

[31] Acts 19:1-7.

themselves to the law, which was not given for justification.

***[7]So you see that it is men of faith who are the sons of Abraham.***

It is true that believers are children of Abraham, because if Abraham was the first person to have been justified by faith, all those who have believed since then are his children, whether they are Jews or Gentiles.

***[8]And the scripture, foreseeing that God would justify the Gentiles by faith, preached the gospel beforehand to Abraham, saying, "In you shall all the nations be blessed."***

Paul says this because Abraham stands for all believers, so those who believe have been blessed in him. By following his faith they have become partakers of his blessing as well.

***[9]So then, those who are men of faith are blessed with Abraham who had faith.***

***[10]For all who rely on works of the law are under a curse; for it is written, "Cursed be every one who does not abide by all things written in the book of the law, and do them."***[32]

It is clear that those who believe will be blessed together with the one who [first] believed, just as those who do not believe will be punished along with other unbelievers. Those who live under the law are under a curse, because they have transgressed the law.

The quotation is from Deuteronomy, which says that if anyone goes against the law he will be regarded as cursed. The commandments are so great that it is impossible to keep them. This is why the apostle Peter says in the Acts of the Apostles: *Why do you put a yoke on the brothers which neither our fathers nor we have been able to bear?*[33] These things were given to a negligent and proud people so that they would have a law to guide them in every aspect of their lives.

***[11]Now it is evident that no man is justified before God by the law; for "He who through faith is righteous shall live";***[34]

By saying this, Paul is teaching the Galatians that they should turn away from the law so as not to lose the justification they have by faith.

***[12]but the law does not rest on faith, for "He who does them shall live by them."***[35]

The law is not based on faith, because it does not command us to believe anything. Everything in it is perfectly clear and says that the person who keeps it will live. Otherwise he must be punished, because he has done something which he knew should be avoided. It is possible to approach the matter from a different angle and say: "If no one is justified by the law, why should someone who breaks it be cursed?" It is quite true that no one is justified by the law, but this refers to justification before God. The person who keeps the law is justified before the world, and lives safely in this present life. But if he wants to be justified before God and obtain merit in his eyes on the day of judgment, he must come to faith in God. Otherwise the man who dwells in safety here below will be considered guilty in the future. The law is beneficial, but this refers to the ten commandments, because all the rest have been given as a burden to bear, as I have already said.

***[13]Christ redeemed us from the curse of the law, having become a curse for us—for it is written, "Cursed be every one who hangs on a tree"***[36]***—***

Since no one could fully keep the law, everyone

[32]Cf. Deut 27:26. [33]Acts 15:10. [34]Hab 2:4. [35]Lev 18:5. [36]Deut 21:23.

was subject to its curse, which ruled over them. Christ was born as a man, having been offered for us by the Father, and he redeemed us from the devil. By offering him up to a voluntary death, God made him a curse for the sake of those who were bound to the curse of the law, in the same way as under the law sacrifices offered for sins took the place of sin. The one who was offered for the accursed became the curse himself. Christ became a curse for the Jews because he was put to death as a sinner. This is why Paul does not say that Christ became accursed, but rather that he became a curse. The person who was offered up to death because of his own sin became accursed because he deserved to die. But if you consider this more closely, you will see that Christ became the curse of those by whom he was put to death, because the cross of the Savior was the sin and curse of the Jews.

In Deuteronomy Moses says of those condemned to death that it would be enough for those who were hung on a tree to stay there until the evening, when they should be taken down and placed in a tomb.[37] It was enough for a man condemned to death to be hung on the tree until he died but not longer, so that his death would not get more condemnation that it deserved and become a stain on his family's reputation if it were to be overpublicized. Moreover, the innocent Savior hung on the tree is not himself accursed, but is the curse of those by whom he was hung. This applies primarily to the Jews who made Christ a curse by offering him to Pilate as if he were a sinner who had to be put to death. They intended that he should be killed as a guilty man even though he was innocent, because someone who is worthy of death is accursed according to the law. When they saw how many people were being attracted to his teaching they got jealous and said: *Look, the whole world has gone after him.*[38] Thus Christ is said to have been put to death for our sake, and this in two ways. The Jews thought that he ought to be put to death in order to prevent him from teaching, but they did not succeed in this, because his teaching spread further and he destroyed the power of death by his passion. Descending into hell he set the dead free. It was for this reason that he allowed himself to be killed, because he knew that he was on our side against the devil.

***[14]that in Christ Jesus the blessing of Abraham might come upon the Gentiles, that we might receive the promise of the Spirit through faith.***

Paul says this because the Jews had been condemned and cursed. They flattered themselves into thinking that they possessed the righteousness of the law, but when they put the Savior to death because he was supposedly guilty of breaking the sabbath, the blessing of Abraham's promise went over to the Gentiles who inherited it by their faith in Christ Jesus. This is why the Lord said to the Jews: *The kingdom will be taken away from you and given to a nation producing the fruits of it.*[39]

***[15]To give a human example, brethren: no one annuls even a man's will, or adds to it, once it has been ratified.***

Paul says this because he wants to explain the sense of the divine promise by using a human example. It is true that the will of a deceased person cannot be legally annulled.

***[16]Now the promises were made to Abraham and to his offspring. It does not say, "And to offsprings," referring to many; but, referring to one, "And to your offspring," which is Christ.***

This is what Genesis says about Abraham.[40] It has been fulfilled in Christ, in whose name all

[37]Cf. Deut 21:23. [38]Jn 12:19. [39]Mt 21:43. [40]Cf. Gen 12:7; 13:15; 17:8; 24:7.

the nations are blessed by faith. The promise has not been fulfilled in many different people but only in one, who is Christ. By arguing in this way, Paul says that those who believe in Christ but still hope to get something from the law are like those who are guilty of falsifying a will, because salvation has been promised not only in Christ but in the law also. Therefore he proves that the promise of blessing has been fulfilled in Christ alone.

**[17]*This is what I mean: the law, which came four hundred and thirty years afterward, does not annul a covenant previously ratified by God, so as to make the promise void.***

Paul teaches that the blessing of the promise is fulfilled only in Christ by showing that the law did not come until four hundred and thirty years later. The promise was given first and the law was given afterwards. The law cannot weaken the force of the promise, but only say that it still lies in the future and indicate when it might come.

**[18]*For if the inheritance is by the law, it is no longer by promise; but God gave it to Abraham by a promise.***

The Jews defend two things which contradict one another. There was no way and no argument by which it was possible to persuade the Jews that the promise made to Abraham had been annulled by the law, and rightly so. But the other thing which they claimed because of their somewhat thoughtless presumption, and which went against the previous statement, was that they thought it was impossible to obtain justification without doing the works of the law, even though they knew that Abraham, who was the archetype of the whole thing, had been justified by faith alone, without the works of the law.

The Jews were blinded by their jealousy and therefore did not understand or consider that if justification comes through the law, the promise is cut out altogether, and if the promise is cut out, the faith of Abraham is undoubtedly voided. But the Jews would not hear of that, because they knew that the promise had been made to Abraham because of his faith. That promise justifies by faith, not by the law, just as Abraham was justified by his faith. Therefore the true heirs of the promise made to Abraham are those who follow him by taking on the faith by which Abraham was blessed and justified. The witness of the promise made to Abraham is called a testament, so that after his death they might be the heirs to the promise, having become his children by faith.

This state of affairs lasted until the coming of the Christ who had been promised to Abraham, so that after the death of Christ believers might become heirs to the faith of Abraham through the testament of Christ's blood. The gift which was promised to Abraham was given to his children in Christ, even though Abraham also received it in the place where he then was.

**[19]*Why then the law? It was added because of transgressions, till the offspring should come to whom the promise had been made; and it was ordained by angels through an intermediary.***

The law of works, that is to say, the law of Moses, was placed in the middle between the beginning of the promise and the seed to whom the promise was made, that is to say, between Abraham and the Savior. The law was given long after the promise had been made, so that by this distinction it would be clear that the law and the promise were different things. The intention was to segregate the people of God from the Gentiles so that they might learn in the fear of God and be made worthy to receive the promise, which was Christ. It is called the law of works because it teaches that what God commanded concerning sacrifices, the firstborn, tithes and things like that should be performed physically.

Paul calls the messengers of God, that is to say, Moses, Joshua the son of Nun and the other prophets up to John the Baptist, angels, about whom God said: *Behold, I am sending my angel before your face.*[41] By them the law and the prophecies were established and appointed by God in the hand, that is to say, in the power of the Savior. He is the mediator or reconciler between God and human beings, who saves those of them who had received the law by way of the above-mentioned angels whom he wants to save. He himself said: *Just as the Father raises the dead and gives them life, so the Son gives life to whom he will.*[42]

***[20]Now an intermediary implies more than one; but God is one.***

There can be no doubt that a mediator, that is to say, an arbitrator, acts for both parties and not just for one of them. When the two peoples (i.e., Jews and Gentiles) fell out with one another and disagreed to the point of becoming hostile because of their different doctrines, their Savior came as an arbitrator and took away from each people the cause of their disagreement so that they might live together in peace. Thus he took away from the Gentiles the number of their gods and their worship of the elements, which was a scandal to the Hebrews, and he took away from the Jews the works of the law, that is, new moons, circumcision, sabbath observance, the food laws and other things which the Gentiles detested. In this way, those who had previously been enemies could live together in peace.

If this was indeed the case, how could it be that the Galatians were so stupid as to ruin this act of mediation by converting to Judaism? They were reducing the Savior's judgment to nothing, because after peace had been made they were behaving as if they regretted it and instead were submitting themselves to all the things which had been hindrances to peace earlier on. As far as the Galatians were concerned, Christ was not the mediator, because by being grafted into the law they had reduced the two peoples to one, and no one can be a mediator for a single people only. Paul follows the same argument when he writes to the Ephesians: *For he is our peace, who has made us both one and has broken down the dividing wall of hostility, by abolishing in his flesh the law of commandments and ordinances, that he might create in himself one new man in place of the two, so making peace.*[43] If Christ has made peace in one new man, he has taken away from each of them the things which caused disagreement between them and established this for them by his own law, which gave them peace with one another. The Galatians had broken this peace by converting to Judaism.

*God is one.* Paul says this so that when he preaches that Christ is God, whom he calls the mediator, no one will think that he is somehow calling into question the existence of a single God, which would be against the law and the prophets. Paul teaches that Christ is the mediator because he has taken on human flesh, as he says to Timothy: *The mediator between God and men is the man Christ Jesus.*[44] Insofar as he is God he cannot be separated from the Father, but rather is one with the Father. Whether we are speaking of the Father or of the Son, there is only one God. "God" is the name given to his nature and power, and the logic inherent in the names Father and Son teaches that this nature is present in each of them.

***[21]Is the law then against the promises of God? Certainly not; for if a law had been given which could make alive, then righteousness would indeed be by the law.***

The law cannot go against the promises of God, because the law is not the enemy of the

[41]Ex 23:20; 32:34; Mal 3:1. [42]Jn 5:21. [43]Eph 2:14-15. [44]1 Tim 2:5.

promises, but the means by which they are confirmed. Moses was the first to say: *God will raise up a prophet for you out of the midst of your brothers.*[45] The apostle Peter shows in the Acts of the Apostles that this was said of Christ.[46]

Paul says that this righteousness, which is reckoned before God as righteousness, is the righteousness of faith. The law also had its own righteousness, but that was for this present age only, and did not count in the presence of God. The law could not forgive sins or make sinners righteous, but was given to frighten people into living a good life by punishing those who did not respect it. For that reason the law was given not because it could justify, but because it condemned.

***22But the scripture consigned all things to sin, that what was promised to faith in Jesus Christ might be given to those who believe.***

Paul says the same thing to the Romans: *God has concluded everything under sin so that he might have mercy on everyone.*[47] He says what I mentioned above, that the law was given in order to make sinners realize that they were guilty in the eyes of God. Once their sins have been made clear they are trapped and cannot make any excuses but only ask for mercy. The one who had been promised to Abraham would come and demand nothing from them except the faith which Abraham had, by which they would earn both forgiveness of their sins and justification. God had already made this clear through the prophet Isaiah, saying: *There will come from Zion one who will remove and turn away ungodliness from Jacob, and this will be a covenant from me with them, when I shall take away their sins.*[48]

***23Now before faith came, we were confined under the law, kept under restraint until faith should be revealed.***

What Paul is saying is that before Christ came we lived under the guardianship of the law, so that we would not sin and would be worthy of the promise when it eventually came. The law therefore kept us in this hope in order to present us (that is, the Jews) to Christ when he came.

***24So that the law was our custodian until Christ came, that we might be justified by faith.***

The meaning is the same as saying that we were under the care of the law until Christ came to justify us as believers.

***25But now that faith has come, we are no longer under a custodian; 26for in Christ Jesus you are all sons of God, through faith.***

The person who is under a guardian cannot act for himself. He is too young and is placed in the care of a guardian because of his propensity to sin. However, when Christ came he turned minors into adults, so to speak. We were set free from the power of our guardian, and by the washing away of sins we became children of God, although we had previously been slaves to sin.

***27For as many of you as were baptized into Christ have put on Christ.***

Paul says this because believers put on Christ when they are converted, at which point they are called what they believe.

***28There is neither Jew nor Greek, there is neither slave nor free, there is neither male nor female; for you are all one in Christ Jesus.***

[45]Deut 18:15. [46]Cf. Acts 3:22. [47]Rom 11:32. [48]Is 59:20-21; cf. Rom 11:26-27.

Paul says that there is no barrier among believers, and that nobody is judged according to what he was before his conversion. The same gift is given to everyone. With God there is no distinction of persons except in the realm of morals and lifestyle, with the result that people who share a common faith are distinguished by their merits and not by who they are.

***29And if you are Christ's, then you are Abraham's offspring, heirs according to promise.***

All believers are the seed of Abraham, because Abraham is the father of everyone who believes. If they are children they must also be heirs of his promise. We receive by faith what was promised to Abraham, so that we may become partakers of his justification in the kingdom of heaven.

## Galatians 4

***1I mean that the heir, as long as he is a child, is no better than a slave, though he is the owner of all the estate; 2but he is under guardians and trustees until the date set by the father.***

It is true that our ancestors made a law and set the age at which a minor would be declared an adult, so that as long as he was still a child he could not exercise his liberty nor control his property as an heir, but remained more like a slave in the care of guardians and agents. By using this example, Paul shows that those who were still under the law were like children and did not enjoy their liberty because they were subject to the law on account of their sin.

***3So with us; when we were children, we were slaves to the elemental spirits of the universe.***

*The elemental spirits of the universe* means new moons and the sabbath. New moons are days in the lunar calendar which the Jews observe, and the sabbath is the day of rest. Before the promise came, which is the gift of God's grace, to purify and justify us believers, we were immature and like children, subject to the law of God which kept us as if we had guardians. Freedom was foreign to us because of sin. On the other hand, the Jews did not believe in the elements in the way that pagans do, but worshiped God the Creator in his creation.

***4But when the time had fully come, God sent forth his Son, born of woman, born under the law, 5to redeem those who were under the law, so that we might receive adoption as sons.***

The fullness of time is the end of time which was predetermined by God the Father as the time when he would send his Son to be born of a virgin as a man. The Son would submit to the law until the time of baptism in order to establish a pattern by which sinners would be cleansed, delivered from the yoke of the law and adopted with the dignity of being sons of God, as God had promised to those who were redeemed by the blood of his Son. It was necessary for the Savior to be under the law and like a son of Abraham according to the flesh. That way the one promised to Abraham, who had come to justify the Gentiles by faith, would appear circumcised, bearing the sign given to Abraham, to whom he had been promised. For that reason, no one should be circumcised any more, because the sign was valid only up to the time when the one who had been promised came to restore the faith by which Abraham had been justified when he was still uncircumcised. Believers therefore have no need of circumcision. Abraham, however, was circumcised because he believed that he would have a son in whom all the nations would be blessed. Thus the sign continued in existence until the one who had been promised actually came. Otherwise, if someone believed that circumcision served no purpose because of Abraham's faith, would it not be objected that because Abraham believed and was circumcised, believers [in Christ] ought to be circumcised too?

***[6]And because you are sons, God has sent the Spirit of his Son into our hearts, crying, "Abba! Father!"***

Paul starts off writing to the Gentiles as "you" and then adds the Jews when he says "our." If Paul said that the Gentiles were children of God because they believed in Christ, although they had previously been enemies, there was no doubt that Jewish believers were also children of God, since it is clear they had already been called for a long time. In ancient times they had taken this designation as a metaphor, but afterwards it was confirmed by Christ, since it could not really be true without the Spirit. This is what Paul said to the Romans: *The Spirit bears witness with our spirit that we are children of God.*[49] In order to prove that we have been adopted by God as his children, God has given his Spirit to us, who reveals the sign of the Father in the children, so that we dare to say what we never would have said in our own weakness and inadequacy, which is *Abba*, meaning "Father." The Jews had never been allowed to say this.

***[7]So through God you are no longer a slave but a son, and if a son then an heir.***

The person who has been taken out of the power of the law and made a partaker of the blessing of God's own Son is not a slave. There is no doubt that anyone who adopts a son makes him his heir. But inheritance depends on someone's death. How is it then that mortals are said to be the heirs of the one who lives for ever? Here Scripture is speaking in human terms so that we can understand it. It shows that the Father will give his children what he has to give them out of his own possessions, and calls this gift our inheritance.

***[8]Formerly, when you did not know God, you were in bondage to beings that by nature are no gods;***

Those who worshiped idols in the past did so out of ignorance, Paul shows that this came naturally to them, just as in Genesis Abimelech says to God: *Lord, will you slay an ignorant people?*[50]

***[9]but now that you have come to know God, or rather to be known by God, how can you turn back again to the weak and beggarly elemental spirits, whose slaves you want to be once more?***

Paul notes their serious admission, that after coming to know God, they had begun to follow pagan things. He goes on to add that it was not so much that they knew God as that they were known by God. When they were not seeking him, he called them to his grace, and they were so ungrateful for this that they started to turn back to what they had worshiped before, when they did not know God, venerating weak and beggarly elements and not adoring Christ, in whom the whole Godhead dwells, with their whole mind. He says that the elements are weak and beggarly because they are imperfect and lack what is needed to rule the world. Perfect salvation is found in Christ.

***[10]You observe days, and months, and seasons, and years!***

Now Paul explains what he means by the elements. The sun makes the day, the cycle of the moon the months, and the seasons are spring, summer, autumn and winter. Taken together, these four make up the year. People who observe days are those who say things

[49]Rom 8:16. [50]Gen 20:4.

like: "We must not travel tomorrow," "Nothing should be started the day after tomorrow." In this way they are all the more deceived. The people who observe months are those who examine the course of the moon, saying things like: "It is wrong to buy a slave and take him home," which only makes it more likely that they will suffer adverse consequences. People who observe seasons are those who say: "Today is the first day of spring; let us celebrate!"; "The day after tomorrow is the feast of Vulcan" and other things like that. In the end, they hardly dare leave the house! Those who observe years say: "The new year starts on the first of January," as if every day were not the start of a new year. What they are doing is recalling the two-faced head of Janus, falling into a superstition which ought to be the last thing on the minds of God's servants. If we love God with all our heart we ought to worship him without the slightest sign or hint of such things. It is quite good enough simply to stick to the things which fall into the category of devotion to God.

**[11]*I am afraid I have labored over you in vain.***

The Galatians had been led astray in two ways. After receiving God's grace, not only had they been converted to the law, but they had also gone back to their previous ways. Whether they had been initiated into the law or had simply returned to it, they easily fell away into observing days and months, because the observance of the sabbath and new moons had attracted them to such things. This is why Paul said: *I am afraid I have labored over you in vain.* Watching them fall into such bad habits, he thought they might well turn away from Christ completely.

**[12]*Brethren, I beseech you, become as I am, for I also have become as you are. You did me no wrong;***

Paul says this so that the Galatians will make an effort to correct themselves. It was not impossible for them to become like him because he was a man just as they were, and when he was in error he persecuted the church until he was seized and converted.

Here Paul treads more softly with them and starts to recount their good points. His intention was that after such great criticisms, they would be encouraged by hearing of their good works and make an effort to reform themselves. He did not want them to be angered by being further pressured by even stronger rebukes. He says that they have not harmed him in any way; it was their own wrongdoing which stood in the way. The apostle was merely fulfilling the duty contained in the dispensation assigned to him, which was to preach to them with all diligence, as the Lord said to the prophet Ezekiel: *You preach. If they hear you, you will have benefited them, but if not, you will save your own soul.*[51]

**[13]*you know it was because of a bodily ailment that I preached the gospel to you at first;* [14]*and though my condition was a trial to you, you did not scorn or despise me, but received me as an angel of God, as Christ Jesus.***

Paul reminds them of the time when he first preached the gospel of God to them, since it was at that time that the apostle was afflicted with injuries and wounded by blows. A person appears to be wounded when he is humble and does not offer resistance on behalf of the gospel of God. In this matter Paul praises the loyalty of those who have not gone away from the faith. The apostle's wounds were a test for the Galatians, and they had come out of it strong, not doubting their faith. Those who had stumbled might have said, "Where is the power or hope in this faith, if the one who preaches it is humiliated?" But

[51]Ezek 3:19, 21.

because they had already filled their minds with future hopes, present sufferings for the name of Christ did not bother them. They knew that our faith has its glory not on earth but in heaven and that great rewards will be given for these tribulations. Paul makes them blush, because after all these praiseworthy accomplishments they had been deceived and made to appear despicable.

Paul praises the Galatians even more because when he was put under pressure, he did not lose his reputation among them but was praised more highly, because they knew that he was suffering these afflictions for the sake of those who believe. They therefore received the apostle as if he were an angel of God, believing that what he preached was the gift of God and deferring to him as they would to the Creator, the Lord Jesus Christ himself.

***15What has become of the satisfaction you felt? For I bear you witness that, if possible, you would have plucked out your eyes and given them to me.***

Paul says that the Galatians were blessed in the eyes of the other churches because they had not been broken by his sufferings but had grown in their faith. He shows that their dedication to religion was so great that not only had he been well received by them, but they had been found to be firm in their faith, and what was even more to their credit, they had given almost everything they had to him to do with as he pleased. Thus it was all the more painful that such great love had been undermined by false doctrine.

***16Have I then become your enemy by telling you the truth?***

Paul says this because what he means is this: "It is not possible for me to be your enemy when I have felt such support from you. But because nobody likes to be reproached when doing something wrong, I have become your enemy because I have rebuked you as you deserve."

***17They make much of you, but for no good purpose; they want to shut you out, that you may make much of them.***

Paul means that they have been led astray by the envy of the Jews. When they saw what great progress they were making in the gospel and how much love they had for the apostle, the Jews did all they could to deceive them. They were the apostle's enemies because of the law. They had kept the name of the Savior but made themselves Jews, who rejoiced in having perverted them, because they were not prepared to accept that the grace promised to them should be given to uncircumcised Gentiles. That is why the Jews wanted the Gentiles to follow their practices and be circumcised as they were.

***18For a good purpose it is always good to be made much of, and not only when I am present with you.***[52]

The better gifts are spiritual ones, and those who seek to imitate them will make an impression on God. Paul wants the Galatians to imitate these good and spiritual things all the time, and not just on occasion or when he is with them. After his departure they had turned away to other things, but he wanted them to go on persevering in what is good.

***19My little children, with whom I am again in travail until Christ be formed in you!***

Paul had originally given birth to them by faith in baptism, but because they had

[52]Ambrosiaster read this verse differently: "Seek to imitate the better gifts. Always try to imitate what is good, and not just when I am present with you."

been aborted and turned out to be weak and deformed, he now tries to reform them with the travail of his counsel. By conceiving faith but paying no attention to its meaning, the Galatians effectively denied that Christ had been formed in their minds. If they had understood the grace of God in Christ, they would not have been led astray into Judaism after believing.

***20 I could wish to be present with you now and to change my tone, for I am perplexed about you.***

Paul wants to go to them and rebuke them. He wants to change his voice from praise to criticism of them, so that they might be embarrassed for two reasons—partly because of their own error and partly because of the apostle's shame, which he suffered among those to whom he had preferred them.

***21 Tell me, you who desire to be under law, do you not hear the law? 22 For it is written that Abraham had two sons, one by a slave and one by a free woman.***

This comes from Genesis. Sarah could not have children because she was infertile, and so she offered her maid Hagar to her husband Abraham as a concubine, so that he might adopt whatever she gave birth to. Thus it happened that Ishmael was born of Hagar. Afterwards, by God's grace, a son was promised to Abraham from his wife Sarah, who was infertile. She bore Abraham [a son] Isaac. As a result, Abraham ended up with two sons, one from the maid and one from the free woman.

***23 But the son of the slave was born according to the flesh, the son of the free woman through promise. 24 Now this is an allegory: these women are two covenants. One is from Mount Sinai, bearing children for slavery; she is Hagar.***

Ishmael, who was the child of the maid Hagar, was born according to the flesh, because he was born in the normal way. Isaac however, was not born in the normal manner, but providentially by the power of God, since Sarah was both old and infertile. Isaac was born as a type of Christ. Thus Paul says that these things were said as an allegory, and that the persons of Ishmael and Isaac stood for other things. Ishmael represents the birth of the Jews and of those who are slaves to sin, whereas Isaac represents the birth of Christians who are born into freedom. Whoever receives the forgiveness of sins becomes a free person.

Moses placed the blood of a calf in a bowl and sprinkled the people with it, saying: *This is the blood of the covenant which God has made with you.*[53] The law was given on Mount Sinai. Moses appealed to it when he read the book of the covenant to the people and then he sprinkled them with the blood, as I said. This law considered sinners guilty and so they became slaves of sin, turned into children of Hagar the maid.

***25 Now Hagar is Mount Sinai in Arabia; she corresponds to the present Jerusalem, for she is in slavery with her children.***

Paul says that Hagar's case refers to the earthly Jerusalem, which is to say, the synagogue, which bears people into slavery, because those to whom it gives birth are captive to sin.

***26 But the Jerusalem above is free, and she is our mother.***

This Jerusalem, which Paul calls our mother, is the rule of the Lord's mystery by which we are born again into freedom, just as it is free. This

[53] Ex 24:8.

is why it is called heavenly, because heaven is its dwelling place, and those to whom it gives birth will be there with her, as the Lord says: *Father, I desire that they also, whom you have given me, may be with me where I am.*[54] This is also life, because those who believe and are born again by it are gifted with immortality. So it is said of the Lord, that what is made in him is life. *For as the Father has life, so he has given life to the Son, and the life was the light of men.*[55] This life and light is the mother of believers.

***27For it is written,***
***"Rejoice, O barren one who does not bear;***
***break forth and shout, you who are not in travail;***
***for the children of the desolate one are many more***
***than the children of her that is married."***[56]

Paul says that this earthly Jerusalem has a husband and gives birth according to the flesh, but he calls the heavenly Jerusalem, which he says is our mother, infertile, because it does not give birth according to the flesh nor does it suffer the pains of childbirth. Instead, it gives birth without suffering in a spiritual way and rejoices that the one who was barren—and where did this barrenness come from if not from Adam, whose barren life brought him death?—now has many more children than the woman who has a husband and who gives birth according to the flesh. Christians are far more numerous than Jews, as it says in Revelation: *And I saw a great multitude, which no one could number, from every tribe and nation.*[57]

***28Now we, brethren, like Isaac, are children of promise.***

This means that they are not children of the flesh but of God, because Isaac was born as a type of the Son of God. Paul wants the Galatians to realize that they had become children of God but had turned away and become children of the flesh. If they repent though, they are [true] children of God.

***29But as at that time he who was born according to the flesh persecuted him who was born according to the Spirit, so it is now.***

It was not only Ishmael who was born according to the flesh. Esau was too, because he was also a type of the Jewish people. Malachi the prophet wrote of him: *Jacob have I loved but Esau have I hated.*[58] Esau persecuted Jacob, who was born as a figure of the Christian people and was called Israel, which means "a man who sees God." Likewise, Paul also meant that the Jews persecute Christians because of their jealousy. This is why they tried so hard to lead the Galatians astray by their worldly cleverness.

***30But what does the scripture say? "Cast out the slave and her son; for the son of the slave shall not inherit with the son of the free woman."***[59]

These are the words of Sarah, the type of the heavenly Jerusalem, who gave birth to Isaac according to the promise. She wanted the son of the maid—that is to say, the Jewish people who had been cast down because of their unbelief, for they are slaves to sin and the forgiveness of sins has not been given to them—cast out so that the son of that free heavenly Jerusalem, which is the new people of the kingdom of heaven, might be the heir instead.

***31So, brethren, we are not children of the slave but of the free woman.***

When we were bound to sin we were children of the maid, but when we received the forgiveness of sins we were set free by Christ.

[54]Jn 17:24. [55]Jn 5:26; 1:4. [56]Is 54:1. [57]Rev 7:9. [58]Mal 1:2-3. [59]Gen 21:10.

## Galatians 5

***[1]For freedom Christ has set us free; stand fast therefore, and do not submit again to a yoke of slavery.***

Paul tells us to stand in the grace we have received so as not to fall back into our previous ways and lose the gift of freedom which we have obtained.

***[2]Now I, Paul, say to you that if you receive circumcision, Christ will be of no advantage to you.***

At this point, Paul demonstrates the force of revealed truth and its authority, saying: *I, Paul, say to you,* that is: "I, the teacher of the Gentiles, whose work you are in Christ, say to you quite clearly that Christ will be of no advantage to you if you are circumcised." The Lord himself said: *The law and the prophets were until John, since then the kingdom of heaven is preached.*[60] Before the new preaching began, it was necessary to be circumcised. But now that the law of faith has replaced it, we must do what the plain truth requires, which is that on the authority of the Lord the preacher, the old must not be mixed with the new. He says: *No one sews a piece of unshrunk cloth on an old garment; if he does, the patch tears away from it, the new from the old, and a worse tear is made.*[61] Thus not only will circumcision not be of any advantage to a believer, it will actually stand in his way. It is worse to become a slave after having been free than to be born into slavery.

***[3]I testify again to every man who receives circumcision that he is bound to keep the whole law.***

Some people can keep the law to some extent without being circumcised, and there were many Romans in Judea who did just that. This is why the apostle Paul says to King Agrippa of Judea: *I know, King Agrippa, that you believe the prophets. I know you do.*[62] There was also the centurion whose servant was on the point of dying, who sent a message to Jesus, asking him to come and heal that servant, to whom the Jews bore witness when they said to Jesus: *He is worthy of your assistance because he loves our people and even built our synagogue himself.*[63] There is nobody who has been circumcised who must not keep the whole law, for he is bound to it by the fact that the law was given to those who are circumcised. Paul said this because the Galatians were so full of themselves that they claimed that they could bear all the burdens of the law.

***[4]You are severed from Christ, you who would be justified by the law; you have fallen away from grace.***

The Galatians had been full of grace, but they rejected it and so lost it all. Paul said this because after they had accepted the gift of God's grace they had chosen to be circumcised.[64] The righteousness of the law is dependent on keeping what has been given in it. Thus whoever wants to be justified by the law after believing in Christ loses his grace, because the gift of God amounts to this, that the works of the law have come to an end and that believers are justified before God.

***[5]For through the Spirit, by faith, we wait for the hope of righteousness. [6]For in Christ Jesus neither circumcision nor uncircumcision is of any avail, but faith working through love.***

What Paul is saying is clear; the hope of justification is in faith by the Spirit and not through

[60]Lk 16:16. [61]Mt 9:16; Mk 2:21. [62]Acts 26:27. [63]Lk 7:4-5. [64]Instead of this sentence, some manuscripts read: "This is a rhetorical device, because after saying that Christ is of no advantage to them, he adds that they have been separated from him altogether."

the works of the law. By faith we serve God spiritually, by the devotion of our minds and the purity of our hearts. This is why the Lord said to the Samaritan woman: *God is spirit, and those who worship him must worship in spirit and in truth.*[65] For this reason, neither uncircumcision nor circumcision is of any value, but only faith in love is required for justification. Faith must be accompanied by brotherly love if the believer is to be perfect. Finally, the Savior answered the scribe who asked him what the most important commandment was, as follows: *You shall love the Lord your God with all your heart and with all your soul and your neighbor as yourself. On these two commandments hangs the whole law and the prophets.*[66] Everything else is excluded and imperfect, because perfection is contained in these two commandments.

***7You were running well; who hindered you from obeying the truth?***

Paul testifies that their progress in the work of faith had been good, but they had been prevented by the wickedness of evil men from finishing the race with the effectiveness which comes from perseverance. This is why he calls on them to repent so that in future they would not believe any of those people who, in an attempt to persuade them to keep the works of the law, suggested to them that they did not have to obey the truth of the gospel.

***8This persuasion is not from him who calls you.***

It is true that the Jews were acting in their human wisdom in trying to subject them to the yoke of the law, and not with the judgment of God, who was calling them by the apostle to his grace.

***9A little leaven leavens the whole lump.***

Paul says this because the slightest addition to the law of faith corrupts that faith and makes it fruitless and unacceptable. Paul put this in so that the Galatians would not think that they could keep the grace of faith pure and still observe some of the law's commands.

***10I have confidence in the Lord that you will take no other view than mine; and he who is troubling you will bear his judgment, whoever he is.***

Paul says this hoping that he can trust the Galatians in these matters, because they had embarked upon the way not automatically but by avoiding error. Therefore he was confident that once the true pathway was pointed out to them, it would be easy for them to return to it.

The reward for someone who manages to convert a person who has fallen into error is spelled out by the apostle James in his epistle: *Whoever brings back a sinner from the error of his way will save his soul from death and cover a multitude of sins.*[67] In the same way, someone who forces a person who is walking in the right way to deviate from that path will obtain damnation, whoever he is. Paul has added this because of those who defended their own merit on the ground that they were the children of Abraham according to the flesh. Those who boasted of this said to Jesus: *We are the children of Abraham.*[68]

***11But if I, brethren, still preach circumcision, why am I still persecuted? In that case the stumbling block of the cross has been removed.***

It is clear what Paul is saying. He was considered an enemy by the Jews who did not stop persecuting him because he taught that circumcision was no longer valid. In the end, when the Jews forced the issue and laid in-

[65]Jn 4:24. [66]Mt 22:37, 39-40. [67]Jas 5:20. [68]Jn 8:33.

numerable false charges against him, Paul realized that he had no chance of a fair trial and so appealed to Caesar.[69]

The preaching of the cross was a scandal to the Jews because it nullified the sabbath and circumcision. However, if Paul had accepted circumcision there would have been no scandal and we would have lived in peace with the Jews. They said of the Savior: *This man is not from God because he does not keep the sabbath.*[70]

***[12]I wish those who unsettle you would mutilate themselves!***

This is what Paul said in 1 Corinthians: *Whoever does not love the Lord Jesus, let him be accursed.*[71] They belonged to the same tainted flock and shared the same condemnation (i.e., that they should be cut off from the mercy of God), as those who took the Galatians away from the grace of God. Paul curses them not only spiritually but also in the flesh. Because they forced the Galatians to be circumcised, they themselves would be cut off, so that the pain of their body might be increased.

***[13]For you were called to freedom, brethren; only do not use your freedom as an opportunity for the flesh, but through love be servants of one another.***

They were called to freedom because when they were still bound in sin they received the forgiveness of their wrongdoings and were set free by the grace of God. Paul says this because he was afraid that the flesh would seize the opportunity to take it away. This was why the false apostles wanted them to be circumcised, so that they would come under the restrictions of the law. Paul therefore warns them not to give them any opportunity by agreeing to what they say. He exhorts them saying that they should not love each other carnally but in the Spirit and so be subject to one another.

***[14]For the whole law is fulfilled in one word, "You shall love your neighbor as yourself."***[72]

This is written in Leviticus and is what is said above, that the perfection of salvation works itself out in love, for as the apostle John says: *Whoever does not love his brother does not love God.*[73]

***[15]But if you bite and devour one another take heed that you are not consumed by one another.***

It is clear that disagreement among the brethren is inimical to love. Therefore Paul urges them to be peaceful and to grow in good works. Disputes generate contention, the result of which is the destruction of life.

***[16]But I say, walk by the Spirit, and do not gratify the desires of the flesh.***

After telling them to stay away from the law of works with its carnal precepts, Paul now instructs them to avoid the vices of the flesh. The person who walks in the Spirit is the one who runs away from sins.

***[17]For the desires of the flesh are against the Spirit, and the desires of the Spirit are against the flesh; for these are opposed to each other, to prevent you from doing what you would.***

Paul posits two laws, as he does also in his letter to the Romans, which are contrary to one another.[74] One of these is the law of God, the other is the law of sin. The latter is in the flesh because it lusts after sin by taking delight in visible things, and with these opposed to him, the average person does things which he does not want to do. The divine

[69]Cf. Acts 25:10-11. [70]Jn 9:16. [71]1 Cor 16:22. [72]Lev 19:18. [73]Cf. 1 Jn 4:20. [74]Cf. Rom 7:14-25.

law clamps down on this and drives out the law of sin by advising people to follow the strength of their nature and not be captivated by wicked things. The law of sin, on the other hand, works insidiously and afflicts people with temptations, so that they reject the commandments of the divine law. Therefore when a person submits to the law of God, the law of sin counterattacks by trying to persuade him not to do what the divine law commands. But the law of God works against this by calling him back and telling him not to do what the law of sin suggests, which the person concerned does not find absurd because he knows that it is in his nature to do what the law of God commands, and in the end he is glad when he does it. But if he does what the law of sin suggests, he is ashamed and horrified afterwards. Therefore the commands of the law of the Spirit are to be kept and those of the flesh are to be avoided. Even his conscience accuses him if he agrees to the law of sin, because it knows how terrible what it suggests is.

***18But if you are led by the Spirit you are not under the law.***

It is clear that anyone who is led by the Holy Spirit will not go astray. The law rules over those who err, as it says elsewhere: *The law is not laid down for the just.*[75]

***19Now the works of the flesh are plain: fornication, impurity, licentiousness, 20idolatry, sorcery, enmity, strife, jealousy, anger, selfishness, dissension, party spirit, 21envy, drunkenness, carousing, and the like. I warn you, as I warned you before, that those who do such things shall not inherit the kingdom of God.***

All these things and others like them are parts of the law of sin, which the apostle calls the works of the flesh, because these errors come from the world as does the flesh. All sins originate from outside us and come through the flesh, not the Spirit, so it is not absurd to call them the works of the flesh.

***22But the fruit of the Spirit is love, joy, peace, patience, kindness, goodness, faithfulness, 23gentleness, self-control; against such there is no law. 24And those who belong to Christ Jesus have crucified the flesh with its passions and desires.***

Paul did not say that love is a work of the Spirit but rather one of its fruits. As he mentioned above, the law of the Spirit bears fruit which leads to the inheritance of the kingdom of heaven. Paul calls those who are devoted to Christ christs, that is to say, anointed ones. These people crucify the flesh, that is the world, when they condemn the things out of which errors arise. The apostle John said the same thing: *Do not love the world or the things in the world. If anyone loves the world, love for the Father is not in him. For all that is in the world is the lust of the flesh and the lust of the eyes.*[76] Therefore the person who does not love the world or what is in the world is the one who crucifies the flesh. Vices like idolatry, sorcery, heresies, jealousy, hatred, anger and so on cannot be ascribed to the human body, but they are called carnal because they belong to the world, as I mentioned above. Note that there were no more than ten things which the apostle called fruits of the Spirit, because he wanted the whole thing to parallel the tables of God's covenant, in which no more than ten commandments were handed down.

***25If we live by the Spirit, let us also walk by the Spirit. 26Let us have no self-conceit, no provoking of one another, no envy of one another.***

[75]1 Tim 1:9. [76]1 Jn 2:15-16. Ambrosiaster reads this slightly differently from the Greek text.

Paul says this because if we live well and honorably, we shall also have good habits. To live in the Spirit is to live a blameless life, and we are walking in the Spirit if we strive for peace. This gives birth to love. There is no point trying to win something which has no reward, which happens when someone goes after arguments and jealousy, knowing that these things produce disagreements and disputes. Paul says: *The Lord's servant must not be quarrelsome.*[77] The person who behaves like that makes the fruits of a good life barren and loses the hope promised to those who live a pure life. A good and pure life is characterized by good habits, and its benevolence will be richly rewarded.

## Galatians 6

***1Brethren, if a man is overtaken in any trespass, you who are spiritual should restore him in a spirit of gentleness. Look to yourself, lest you too be tempted. 2Bear one another's burdens, and so fulfil the law of Christ.***

Now Paul addresses those who were stronger, telling them not to think that, puffed up with their good life, they could reject someone who had been led astray by sin and throw him out. He gives them the following advice. People like that are to be gently challenged to put matters right, because if they are sharply attacked by a superior they will not put up with the rebuke and will start to defend themselves so as not to be ashamed and appear to be worse than they really are. Lift a person out of argument and willfulness and you will have him in your power, for humility is the best means of humbling the proud. In order to ensure that this would be done with all gentleness, Paul added: *Lest you too be tempted.* With this in mind they would not reject the sinner, knowing that they too were capable of sinning. The law of Christ wants everyone to be saved, and for this reason Paul says that whoever counsels a sinning brother and persuades him to return to the right way is fulfilling the will of Christ.

***3For if any one thinks he is something, when he is nothing, he deceives himself. 4But let each one test his own work, and then his reason to boast will be in himself alone and not in his neighbor.***

It is true and obvious to everyone that if we consider our own actions and thoughts we shall not think that we are superior to anyone else nor will we judge others easily. Anyone who boasts of being something special is wrong, because he does not realize that it is by being humble that we grow. Such a person does not have in view the words and deeds of the Savior who, although he was Lord of all, humbled himself in order to give us a model of how we should live if we want to grow, and if we exalt ourselves we shall be brought low. Whoever tries to look good in front of other people is acting out of the stupidity of a puffed-up heart. He claims that he appears to be righteous when he rejects and despises sinners, like the Pharisee whom the Lord describes.[78] Is it not true that someone who hankers after the glory of this world is really stupid? Is such a person not wanting to obtain a reward for his righteousness in this life because he has no hope of one in the future? Why? Because he is not righteous in what he does, but merely invents a kind of righteousness based on a false premise. Whoever really wants to be righteous should put others before himself. Each person knows his own faults better than those of other people.

***5For each man will have to bear his own load.***

In conclusion, Paul wants these proud people to realize that no one is blamed for someone

[77]2 Tim 2:24. [78]Cf. Lk 18:9-14.

else's sin, as long as he disagrees with it, and so no one should hesitate to link up with a sinner or get alongside him in order to help him.

***6Let him who is taught the word share all good things with him who teaches.***

Paul says that those who are hearers ought to share everything they have with their teachers. Of course, if the latter teach one thing and do another, there should be no sharing with them. Instead they should object to them, because the law is a better guide than the individual person. The latter will only harm himself and not you, who do what you are taught.

***7Do not be deceived; God is not mocked, for whatever a man sows, that he will also reap.***

Nobody doubts that God cannot be fooled, but everyone receives from him what he deserves.

***8For he who sows to his own flesh will from the flesh reap corruption; but he who sows to the Spirit will from the Spirit reap eternal life.***

Paul is talking here about those carnal vices which have a way of creeping into the body. Whoever corrupts his body ought to realize that he will have to live with the consequences later on. Whoever does what is not allowed corrupts his body.

A Christian person is made up of spirit and flesh, but in comparison with the Holy Spirit he is all flesh. Therefore when he submits to the Spirit he refrains from doing what is contrary to the Spirit's wishes and sows spiritual seed so that he may reap eternal life. By the witness of the Spirit he will receive immortality as his reward, for just as the person who dishonors his body and corrupts it will inherit not eternity but corruption, so the one who keeps himself spotless will obtain eternal life. Eternal life is to live without punishment and to have glory. If someone who is in difficulties in this life says that he is dead, how much more will he say this when he is cut off from God and suffering the fires of torture!

***9And let us not grow weary in well-doing, for in due season we shall reap, if we do not lose heart.***

Paul says this because the person who is keen on sowing will also be keen on reaping and will get a corresponding reward. Therefore he exhorts us to be ready to do good and not to put up with laziness, because we are sure to receive great rewards for small things and eternal blessings for earthly effort, at the time that God has promised.

***10So then, as we have opportunity, let us do good to all men, and especially to those who are of the household of faith.***

The Gentiles have time to do what is wrong. As people without God, how can they do what is right? After they become Christians, however, they have time to do good to everyone, and so the good works done after their conversion contribute to the reward promised to them. For this reason there is some time allotted to us in this life for us to act righteously and show an example to the Gentiles.

It is true that we should be even more ready and willing to do good to our brethren, because we belong to one another. This is the sort of thing which is profitable—not circumcision, which leads nowhere.

***11See with what large letters I am writing to you with my own hand.***

Paul reinforces the authority of his letter here. When he says: *I have written with my own hand,* he means that his words must be obeyed. When a letter is handwritten it cannot be said that it is false. Those who had been led astray might try to explain away this letter by saying that it had been falsified or that it did not come from the apostle, because they did not want to be rebuked.

***[12]It is those who want to make a good showing in the flesh that would compel you to be circumcised, and only in order that they may not be persecuted for the cross of Christ.***

To make a good showing in the flesh means to please other people. Those whom Paul calls the false apostles preached Christ in such a way as to teach that the law must also be kept, because they wanted to live happily with Jews and not offend them. The apostle was never afraid to speak the truth and was always prepared to demonstrate both to himself and to them what he taught. Thus he says: *I am willing not only to be imprisoned but also to die at Jerusalem for the name of the Lord Jesus Christ.*[79]

***[13]For even those who receive circumcision do not themselves keep the law, but they desire to have you circumcised that they may glory in your flesh.***

This is much the same as what he said to the apostle Peter: *If you as a Jew live like a Gentile, why do you force Gentiles to become Jews?*[80] In the same way, these false apostles did not keep the law themselves, but lived [and associated with Gentile Galatians, forcing them to circumcise themselves in order to keep the Jews happy. In this way they were softening the attitude of the Jews toward themselves, so that they would not believe that they were living like Gentiles.][81] Thus the ruin of the Galatians was the way they avoided being persecuted by the Jews. Paul says this so that they would understand that they were playing around like idiots and fools who took pride in their troubles.

***[14]But far be it from me to glory except in the cross of our Lord Jesus Christ, by which the world has been crucified to me, and I to the world.***

Just as the false apostles were ashamed of suffering for the name of Christ and did all they could to avoid them by their hypocritical behavior, because they thought there was nothing in it for them, so the apostle gloried in his sufferings because he knew that they would bring him a great reward. His fellow apostles thought exactly the same, as it is written in the Acts of the Apostles: *Then having been beaten the apostles went out of the council rejoicing, because they had been considered worthy to suffer reproach for the name of Christ.*[82] Whoever puts all his hope in Christ will glory in his cross. The world is crucified to him because he is sure that the love of the cross of Christ is life, and the love of the world seems like death. Therefore they have died to one another, the world to the apostle and the apostle to the world, because the apostle desires nothing in the world and the world finds nothing of its own which it recognizes in the apostle, as the Lord says: *Look, the prince of this world is coming and he will find nothing in me.*[83]

***[15]For neither circumcision counts for anything, nor uncircumcision, but a new creation. [16]Peace and mercy be upon all who walk by this rule, upon the Israel of God.***

Our rebirth is a new creation. It is this which gives an advantage to those who persevere, because the peace of God is upon them. The

[79]Acts 21:13. [80]Gal 2:14. [81]An alternative version reads: "they wrongly insisted on circumcision, so that they would appear to be defenders and lovers of the law, since it was accepted that whoever followed its righteousness and did not overlook the commandment which was given because it pointed to life, would be defending and keeping the law." [82]Acts 5:40-41. [83]Jn 14:30.

person who is at peace with God will not be afraid of any enemy, because he is safe in the protection and mercy of God which is promised to and dwells in the Israel of God, not in the Israel of man. Unbelieving Jews are Israel according to the flesh. Paul pointed out that there are two groups of people upon whom the peace and mercy of God rests, believing Jews and faithful Gentiles.

***17Henceforth let no man trouble me; for I bear on my body the marks of Jesus.***

Paul does not want there to be any more trouble which would force him to write again. Instead he wants the Galatians to put matters right so that they may have rest after such great struggles once their errors have been removed. If they showed themselves to be more resistant and unwilling to change their ways, he wanted them to stop acting that way, and so he held up his works and their effectiveness before them, by which they could hope for reward and profit.

Paul says this in annoyance, because he sees that the sufferings which he has endured for the sake of believers have had no effect on them. Because of the consistency and trustworthiness of his teaching Paul was not afraid to suffer beatings and imprisonment for Christ. For the love of believers he suffered and had the scars of his beatings on his body, which did nothing to make him preach less faithfully to them, as did the false apostles, who had deceived the Galatians. Therefore he did not want to be bothered by anyone who was not equally dedicated to this cause. The marks, that is, the scars from his beatings, were a witness to believers of what they suffer, which makes them worthy of the future promise.

***18The grace of our Lord Jesus Christ be with your spirit, brethren. Amen.***

Paul does not say that it was the grace of the law, but the grace of the Lord Jesus Christ which is with the spirit of those whom he calls spiritual brethren (for not all the Galatians had gone astray).

# AMBROSIASTER
## *Commentary on Ephesians*

### Preface

The apostle Paul did not win the Ephesians to the faith but stated that he had suffered many terrible things for their sake, as he said: *What do I gain if, humanly speaking, I fought with wild beasts at Ephesus?*[1] Since he realizes that his struggle for them has resulted in their spiritual growth, he rejoices in them and encourages them by writing from his custody in Rome to go on to better things. He is understood to have come from Jerusalem in custody but under bond, since he was living out of prison in his own hired house.[2]

### Ephesians 1

***1Paul, an apostle of Christ Jesus by the will of God,***

***To the saints who are also faithful in Christ Jesus:***

Paul writes in his usual way and testifies that he is an apostle of Christ Jesus by the will of God. He writes not merely to the believers but also to the saints, who are true believers if they have been sanctified in Christ Jesus. A good life is profitable and called holy if it is lived in the name of Christ. Otherwise it would be impure because it would become an insult to the Creator.

***2Grace to you and peace from God our Father and the Lord Jesus Christ.***

Paul says that the grace of God is with the saints and believers. He calls God our Father because all things have been created and restored by him, and Christ our Lord, because he redeemed us by offering himself for us.

***3Blessed be the God and Father of our Lord Jesus Christ, who has blessed us in Christ with every spiritual blessing in the heavenly places,***

God has blessed us not with an earthly but with a heavenly blessing which is not corruptible but eternal, because the glory of Christians is not on earth but in heaven and in Christ. Every gift of God's grace is in Christ, so that if anyone thinks that he can reject Christ and still be blessed by God, he should realize that he is wrong. Nevertheless, God is blessed in one way and human beings are blessed in another. The same term is used for both, but the meaning must be understood in relation to the subject. For example, God is said to make things and so are human beings. But God makes things by his will without any effort, whereas human beings make things by using their hands, their impulses, their labor and their sweat. God is blessed when he is extolled with suitable praises. But God blesses human beings when he gives them the gift of his grace, not according to their merits but according to his mercy, by which their glory is perfected. Paul did not say: "Who has blessed us with a spiritual blessing" in order to show that the perfect blessing of the heavenly places is given to those who believe in Christ, so that they may be filled with heavenly glory, lifted

[1]1 Cor 15:32. [2]Cf. Acts 28:30-31.

up above the powers of the heavens, because Christ says: *Where I am, there my servant will be also.*[3]

***[4]even as he chose us in him before the foundation of the world, that we should be holy and blameless before him.***

God foresees everything and knew who would believe in Christ, as Paul says to the Romans: *Whom he foreknew he also called, not only from the Jews but also from the Gentiles.*[4] Therefore those whom God is said to call are the ones who persevere in the faith. These are the people whom he chose before [the foundation of] the world in Christ, so that they might be spotless before God in love, that is, that the love of God might establish a holy way of life in them. No one is more obedient to someone else than the person who submits in love.

***[5]He destined us in love to be his sons through Jesus Christ, according to the purpose of his will,***

Paul says that God has decreed that those who believe in Christ will be adopted as children of God and that Christ, the true Son of God, will be their head.

***[6]to the praise of his glorious grace which he freely bestowed on us in the Beloved.***

Paul says that it was God's plan that the grace given to human beings should redound to the praise of his glory, because our salvation is God's glory. God has given us grace because we have believed in Christ his Son. It is because he loves his only-begotten Son that he bestows his grace on those who love him.

***[7]In him we have redemption through his blood, the forgiveness of our trespasses, according to the riches of his grace [8]which he lavished upon us.***

Paul proclaims a double grace, because God has redeemed us by his blood and has not imputed our sins to us. In other words, he has redeemed us and set us free as well. He adds to this grace, because after the benefits mentioned above he includes the gift of wisdom and understanding of spiritual things.

***[9]For he has made known to us in all wisdom and insight the mystery of his will, according to his purpose which he set forth in Christ [10]as a plan for the fulness of time, to unite all things in him, things in heaven and things on earth.***

It pleased God, who cannot withdraw his counsel, to show forth the mystery of his will in Christ at the time when he wanted him to be revealed so that the creation might recognize him. His will was this, that he should become more favorable toward all those who were in error, whether in heaven or on earth, when he manifested Christ as his gift to believers, so that those who accepted the faith of Christ would not have their sins imputed to them. Every creature in heaven and on earth is restored to its original state when it learns to acknowledge Christ. When someone comes to understand the mystery of Christ and is immersed in the faith of the one God, he is brought back from the error into which he had fallen and knows for sure that his Creator is the one God and Lord. This is why he says in the Revelation of John: *I saw Michael and his angels fighting in heaven with the dragon and his army.*[5] This hostility arises partly out of error and partly out of the presumption which comes from the tyranny which the devil has usurped.

***[11]In him, according to the purpose of him who***

[3]Jn 12:26. [4]Rom 8:29; 9:24. [5]Rev 12:7.

***accomplishes all things according to the counsel of his will, [12]we who first hoped in Christ have been destined and appointed to live for the praise of his glory.***

What Paul says is that the dispensation of the preaching has been appointed by God to those Jews who believed in Christ, because no Gentile was chosen to be an apostle. It was right for the preachers to be chosen from among those who had previously been waiting for the salvation which had been promised to them in Christ.

***[13]In him you also, who have heard the word of truth, the gospel of your salvation, and have believed in him, were sealed with the promised Holy Spirit, [14]which is the guarantee of our inheritance until we acquire possession of it, to the praise of his glory.***

The praise of God's glory occurs when many are won to the faith, just as a doctor's reputation grows if he cures a lot of people. Thus it is part of God's glory that he called the Gentiles, so that they might receive the blessing of his salvation through the faith promised to the Jews. As a sign of their redemption and future inheritance they have the Holy Spirit given to them after baptism. Having been redeemed they are appointed heirs if they persevere in their regeneration, so that faith brings them forgiveness to start off with, and a holy life which perseveres in faith earns the crown.

***[15]For this reason, because I have heard of your faith in the Lord Jesus and your love toward all the saints, [16]I do not cease to give thanks for you, remembering you in my prayers,***

Since, according to the decree of God by which he declared that the Gentiles would share in the promises made to the Jews, the Ephesians heard the Word of God and accepted the faith of Christ, loving all the saints as the Lord commanded, for this reason Paul gives thanks to God for their conversion and their love, because he has been pleased to incorporate the Gentiles into the same body as the Jews.

***[17]that the God of our Lord Jesus Christ, the Father of glory, may give you a spirit of wisdom and of revelation in the knowledge of him, [18]having the eyes of your hearts enlightened, that you may know what is the hope to which he has called you, what are the riches of his glorious inheritance in the saints,***

It is obvious that Paul says that he is praying for them to recognize the hope of their faith in their heavenly reward, because when they fully understand what the fruit of believers is they will become all the more eager to practice their religion. The future blessing is already visible in that if they are this devout before knowing about the glory of the promise, they will certainly be even more eager when they realize [that although it is said that Christ is from God and therefore is called God, he is not like our God, whom Paul called the Father of glory because he is the source of all light.][6]

***[19]and what is the immeasurable greatness of his power in us who believe, according to the working of his great might [20]which he accomplished in Christ when he raised him from the dead and made him sit at his right hand in the heavenly places, [21]far above all rule and authority and power and dominion, and above***

[6]An alternative reading of this is: "that he calls God the Father of glory and the God of Christ, because the Father of Christ is the true God and the God of creation. The Lord himself said: *I am going to my Father and to your Father, to my God and to your God* [Jn 20:17]. Therefore he is the Father of all glory, because all glory, power and honor come from him. He is also the Father of Christ, but in a different way, because he is the true Son and God of all, but Christ is not God in this way, because Christ is God from God. The God of all is a source of fear, as he says in the prophet Malachi: *If I am God, where is my fear?* [Mal 1:6]."

***every name that is named, not only in this age but also in that which is to come;***

Paul claims that the example of the salvation and glory of believers is found in the resurrection of the Savior, because it is by that that believers know what has been promised to them. In the same way those who will be with Christ are exalted above the heavens, as Christ himself says: *Father, I desire that where I am, they may be with me also and may see my glory.*[7] He says this on account of the incarnation of the Son of God, who became a man and is said to be above all the heavens and above every creature, sitting at the right hand of God, having the name of God by nature, not by adoption, so that those who crucified him might know that he is the Son of God. The honor which the Father gave him by his birth was manifested when he was born as a man, suffered and having overcome death rose again, ascending to the place above all the heavens from which he had descended. This is why it was said: *Truth has risen from the earth.*[8] The Father has given all judgment to the Son, which is why he is said to be seated at the right hand of God, like a judge. Finally, Christ himself said to his disciples: *So far you have asked nothing in my name; ask, and I shall do it.*[9] This is also why he said to the Jews: *In a little while you will see the Son of Man sitting at the right hand of power and coming with the clouds of heaven.*[10] On the basis of what he declared would happen he began to act as a judge.

***22and he has put all things under his feet and has made him the head over all things for the church, 23which is his body, the fulness of him who fills all in all.***

Paul says that the Father has subjected all things to the Son, so that because everything was made through him he should be the head and Lord of all things. He subjected all things to him when he gave birth to him before all things, so that what did not then exist might come into being through him. When Paul says "the whole church," he is including all things in heaven and on earth, which will become part of him in the new man, when they confess that he is the one through whom they were made by God.[11] They are subjected to him as the members are to the head from which they derive their origin, so that all things may be fulfilled in all. When they return to the confession of the one God and bow the knee to Christ, he is fulfilled in all so as to become all, because they are from him. He is in them for this reason, because they exist by his power. Those who turn away from God appear to empty him [of power]. This is why Paul says elsewhere: *That all things may grow in the increase of God.*[12]

## Ephesians 2

***1And you he made alive, when you were dead through the trespasses and sins 2in which you once walked, following the course of this world, following the prince of the power of the air, the spirit that is now at work in the sons of disobedience.***

Paul says that those who follow the errors of this age are dead. Whoever turns away from confessing the one God is considered to be dead because he does not remain in the root from which he derives his origin.

Paul indicates that the prince of power, that is, the devil, has corrupted the mind of this age so that it has turned away from the one God and taken up belief in many gods. In this way the devil has made them accomplices of his conspiracy, because they have fallen into the same ungodliness by denying the one God. He

[7]Jn 17:24. [8]Ps 85:11. [9]Jn 16:24. [10]Mt 26:64. [11]Ambrosiaster reads this verse somewhat differently from the English text given here. He thought it should read: "He subjected all things under his feet and made him head over the whole church." [12]Col 2:19.

says that the prince of this error is the spirit of the air, in order to show that he has taken over that part of the universe in order to exert his power there. The air is one thing and the prince is another, but because he rules in the world (or in the air), he is called the spirit of the air.

***3Among these we all once lived in the passions of our flesh, following the desires of body and mind, and so we were by nature children of wrath, like the rest of mankind.***

Paul means unbelief when he refers to the desires of the flesh. The lust of the flesh is to take delight in visible things, for example, to call the elements (which God established to govern the world), gods, when this name ought to be reserved for the one God from whom all things come. God shares none of his power with these things, and therefore he does not share his name with them either. However, this name is not denied to Christ, because just as they share a common nature, so too they have the same name. The difference between the Father and the Son is that the Father receives nothing from anyone, whereas the Son receives everything by being begotten of the Father, so that the Son is not inferior to the Father in power, substance or name. This is why he says: *Everything which the Father has is mine, and everything of mine is the Father's.*[13] Thus it is neither unworthy nor contradictory if Christ is called God, but he is from God the Father, so that the uniqueness of the one God may be preserved.

If anyone thinks that Paul means something else when he talks about the lust of the flesh, let him realize that the apostle led a clean life, because he acted according to the righteousness of the law without any problem. It is because he persecuted the faith of Christ that he says: *We once lived in the passions of our flesh.* Every sin is called "flesh" but especially unbelief, which is the mother of all wickedness. Good works and purity are of no use to anyone who is an unbeliever, because his unbelief taints everything else. This is why Paul added: *We were children of wrath like others.* When an evil will is subjoined to nature it becomes a nature of wrath, which means that it is subjected to retribution. It is not the substance which had changed but the will which is evil. What follows from this is that attributed to the nature, as it says in Isaiah: *Wicked seed.*[14] To explain why the seed is wicked, Isaiah added the following: *You have turned away from the Lord and incited the Holy One of Israel to anger.* So a nature which turns away from God is called a wicked seed. To turn away from the author is to degenerate, and because it presents a bad example to others, the seed is evil, and brings forth bad fruit. But if it returns to its author, the nature will be good, according to the apostle, who was changed when he acknowledged his creator and was called *a chosen vessel.*[15]

***4But God, who is rich in mercy, out of the great love with which he loved us,***

The true riches of mercy are that it was freely preached to those who were not looking for it, as Isaiah says: *I have made myself known to those who were not looking for me.*[16] To abound in mercy is to grant it to those who have not asked for it. The love of God for us is such that because he made us he does not want us to perish, since he loves what he has made. Nobody hates his own work.

***5even when we were dead through our trespasses, made us alive together with Christ (by grace you have been saved),***

When we were cut off from God we were dead,

[13]Jn 16:15. [14]Is 1:4. [15]Acts 9:15. [16]Is 65:1.

but by his grace he has called us back, that is to say, he has given us new life in Christ. Since he made us through him, he has also remade us through him in himself, that is, made us members of him. He is our head. At God's behest we recognize him as the author of our life, as the apostle Peter says: *You have killed the author of life.*[17] To this gift God adds the Gentiles, indicating that we have been saved by the grace of Christ.

***6and raised us up with him, and made us sit with him in the heavenly places in Christ Jesus,***

Paul says what I mentioned above, that the saints, even the Gentile ones, will be where Christ their head is.

***7that in the coming ages he might show the immeasurable riches of his grace in kindness toward us in Christ Jesus.***

[Paul says that the immortal gift of God will appear in the age to come when believers will begin to receive their reward.][18] *What eye has not seen nor ear heard, nor has entered into the heart of man, which God has prepared for those who love him.*[19] The superabundant riches are such that the mind cannot investigate them because they are given only to believers.

***8For by grace you have been saved through faith; and this is not your own doing, it is the gift of God—9not because of works, lest any man should boast. 10For we are his workmanship, created in Christ Jesus for good works, which God prepared beforehand, that we should walk in them.***

It is true that we must render all thanks to God who has given us his grace to recall sinners to life even when they are not looking for the true way. Therefore there is no reason for us to glory in ourselves, but rather in God, who has regenerated us to a heavenly birth through the faith of Christ, so that tested by the good works which God has appointed for those who are already born again, we may deserve to receive the things promised.

***11Therefore remember that at one time you Gentiles in the flesh, called the uncircumcision by what is called the circumcision, which is made in the flesh by hands—12remember that you were at that time separated from Christ, alienated from the commonwealth of Israel, and strangers to the covenants of promise, having no hope and without God in the world.***

Paul warns the Gentiles to remember what they once were—for they were carnal and without hope, having no part in the promise made to the Jews in Christ, for Christ had been promised to the Jews and not to the Gentiles—so that they would be all the more eager to give thanks to God in Christ, who by his mercy made them partakers of spiritual things when they were still carnal. Note that he refers to the *circumcision made with hands* in order to indicate that there is another one which is not made with hands.

***13But now in Christ Jesus you who once were far off have been brought near in the blood of Christ.***

Paul is still praising the gift and grace of God for which he wants us to go on giving thanks as we are bound to do. He recalls that we have been brought near to God by the blood of Christ, so that God might show how great the love which he has for us is. He allowed his Son to die for us so that we might persevere in his

[17]Acts 3:15. [18]An alternative reading of this is: "Paul means that in the age to come the immortal gift of God will appear in the reward of believers." [19]1 Cor 2:9.

faith and not succumb to any of the afflictions laid on us for his sake, knowing that he deserves more from us than anything that can be inflicted on us by our enemies. Even though he is our Lord and lacks for nothing, he offered himself up for us, not for his benefit but for ours. It is possible that we, as his servants, might be persuaded to die for him even if that were to be of no particular benefit to us, but how much more so when not only his but also our death offers us a reward.

***[14]For he is our peace, who has made us both one, and has broken down the dividing wall of hostility,***

The passion of the Savior has made peace between the circumcision and the uncircumcision. The Savior has dissolved the enmity which stood like a partition dividing the circumcision from the uncircumcision and the uncircumcision from the circumcision by decreeing that no Jew should reproach a Gentile because of circumcision nor should a faithful Gentile detest a Jew on the basis of uncircumcision, that is, of paganism, but that both should be renewed and follow the faith of the one God in Christ. Everything which the Savior taught he confirmed when he rose from the dead.

As for the dividing wall of partition between the law of works and the Gentile way of life, Paul indicated that it was just a temporary structure and not a firm and solid wall. The Gentile way of life was not a fixed thing because it was just a human invention, nor were circumcision, the new moons, or the observance of the food laws and sacrifices stable and fixed either. Even they had been given with the intention that they would cease at the coming of Christ. God had indeed given them, but only for a time. However, the preaching of the faith is firm and will not be superseded.

***[15]by abolishing in his flesh the law of commandments and ordinances, that he might create in himself one new man in place of the two, so making peace,***

This is what I briefly mentioned above, namely, that Christ nullified the law which had been given to the Jews in circumcision, new moons, food laws, sacrifices and the sabbath, that is to say that he ordered it to come to an end because it was burdensome, and so he made peace. This is why the apostle Peter said in the Acts of the Apostles: *Why do you put a yoke on the neck of your brethren which neither our fathers nor we have been able to bear?*[20]

***[16]and might reconcile us both to God in one body through the cross, thereby bringing the hostility to an end.***

By taking away the enmity, Christ first of all reconciled the peoples to each other and then made peace between them and God, so that people of the same nature who had been made enemies by their error might be made members of one new body, whose head is Christ.

***[17]And he came and preached peace to you who were far off and peace to those who were near; [18]for through him we both have access in one Spirit to the Father.***

The meaning here is the same. Christ has killed the enmity in himself, because he has died for everyone, both Jews and Gentiles. The death of the Savior benefits everyone. He condemned death, which held everyone in its grip, when he rose again from the dead and thereby demonstrated the hope which believers have in him. He then commanded the preaching by which everyone would be called before God the Father in the unity of the Spirit. The

[20]Acts 15:10.

discord would be demolished, so that both the Jews, who are said to be near because the promise was made to their ancestors, and the Gentiles, who are said to be far away because they did not accept the law of God given by Moses, received the faith of Christ when the old way of worship was taken away, and by that were made one.

***19So then you are no longer strangers and sojourners, but you are fellow citizens with the saints and members of the household of God,***

Paul warns them to be mindful of God's benefits because when they were still far away from the knowledge and fear of God, they were united to him by his mercy in order to become partakers with those who were near, once they were made fellow citizens of the children of God. Just as any nation which wanted to follow the peace of the Romans was accepted when they gave gifts and became Roman citizens, like the inhabitants of Tarsus—which is why the apostle called himself a Roman citizen[21]—so whoever allies himself with the Christian faith becomes a fellow citizen of the saints and a servant of God.

***20built upon the foundation of the apostles and prophets, Christ Jesus himself being the cornerstone,***

This means those who are grounded on the Old and New Testaments. What the apostles preached the prophets had predicted, even though Paul says to the Corinthians: *God first put apostles in the church and then prophets.*[22] However, these prophets were different. In that passage he was expounding the order of the church, whereas here he is talking about its foundation. The prophets set out the plan but the apostles added the foundation. This is why the Lord said to Peter: *On this rock I will build my church,*[23] which means: "On this confession of the catholic faith I establish believers in life." David also planned to build the house of God and designated the site for it, but it was Solomon who actually built it.

***21in whom the whole structure is joined together and grows into a holy temple in the Lord; 22in whom you also are built into it for a dwelling place of God in the Spirit.***

The meaning here is an extension of what the Lord said: *On this rock I will build my church.* The Savior took two peoples into himself and made them one in the Lord, just as the cornerstone contains two walls which are fixed in the one house. Believers are the covering of the temple, living in the Spirit in order to become heirs of the heavenly dwelling place.

## Ephesians 3

***1For this reason I, Paul, a prisoner for Christ Jesus on behalf of you Gentiles—***

Now that he has shown the dispensation of the divine mercy which had existed before the foundation of the world for the salvation of the Gentiles, Paul declares that by God's provision he has been sent by Christ as an ambassador of this gift. He says that he is bound to it for the sake of Christ, giving the impression that he is in chains or in prison as if he were guilty of preaching Christ. After his resurrection, the Lord sent his apostles to preach in his place and directed Paul toward the conversion of the Gentiles. Thus God said to him: Go, *I am sending you far away to the Gentiles.*[24] Paul was using God's words when he said: *[Peace] to you who are far away and peace to you who are near.*[25]

***2assuming that you have heard of the steward-***

[21]Cf. Acts 22:25. [22]1 Cor 12:28. [23]Mt 16:18. [24]Acts 22:21. [25]Eph 2:17.

***ship of God's grace that was given to me for you,***

Paul wants the Ephesians to know that it was by God's decision that he was sent by Christ to preach the mystery of God's grace to the Gentiles.

***[3]how the mystery was made known to me by revelation, as I have written briefly. [4]When you read this you can perceive my insight into the mystery of Christ,***

Paul is referring to the revelation of the mystery of God which had been shown to him, about which he recalls having written briefly already. What he means is that he wrote about it in moderation, so that they would be able to grasp the wisdom of the apostle in the sacrament of Christ.[26]

***[5]which was not made known to the sons of men in other generations as it has now been revealed to his holy apostles and prophets by the Spirit; [6]that is, how the Gentiles are fellow heirs, members of the same body, and partakers of the promise in Christ Jesus through the gospel.***

Paul asserts that this was made known by God in the time of Christ because it was not then clear that the Gentiles would one day be partakers of the grace promised in the law. He says that it was made known to the holy preachers and prophets, that is, to the apostles and expositors of the law, not to the ancient prophets. Although Gentiles were previously admitted to the law, they had to be circumcised, and although the prophets knew that one day the Gentiles would share in the gift of God—something which they stated in several places—this remained hidden because they would be partakers of the future grace of God, without circumcision, sabbaths, new moons and other such things, since they would accept the faith of Christ and be saved apart from the law. This is what Paul means when he says that in the Spirit *the Gentiles are fellow heirs, members of the same body, and partakers of the promise in Christ*. Whoever worships God in the Spirit has no need of the law.

***[7]Of this gospel I was made a minister according to the gift of God's grace which was given me by the working of his power.***

Paul asserts that the gift of God has been made known by the preaching of his ministry, which God planned for the Gentiles according to the working of his power. The working of his power is that he overcame death by raising Christ from the dead, in whom he saved everyone. The dispensation of the gospel is that by which the will of God is made known, that he has decided to save the Gentiles apart from the works of the law.

***[8]To me, though I am the very least of all the saints, this grace was given, to preach to the Gentiles the unsearchable riches of Christ,***

Paul humbles himself when he calls himself the least, because he knows that humility is the way to grow. He says that the grace given to him is so great that this gift, which had been unknown to previous ages, has been given to him, so that he can declare it to the Gentiles. How can someone who had been called *a chosen vessel* even before being baptized possibly have appeared as the least of all saints?[27] Paul says that he has been chosen to preach the gift of God in the unsearchable riches of Christ, which God was pleased to bestow on the Gentiles when they were still without hope, so that

[26]Note that Ambrosiaster translates the word "mystery" as "sacrament" here as elsewhere. He uses the two words virtually synonymously.
[27]Acts 9:15.

they might be saved by faith without works. It is obvious that nobody would send a magnificent and enormous gift by way of an unworthy emissary. In showing how much he has earned from God he humbles himself so that his merit might increase.

***[9]and to make all men see what is the plan of the mystery hidden for ages in God who created all things;***

Paul repeats his assertion that he has been sent by God to teach the Gentiles about the mystery which was in God, from whom all things come, that through him they might learn and understand that Christ is always in God and with God, and that he has planned to save the Gentiles without circumcision and the other commandments of the law. The Jews were found to be unworthy to have such a great and highly qualified teacher. They believed in Christ, but in such a way that they went on keeping the law, something which God detests. As the apostles said to their fellow apostle Paul: *You see, brother, how many thousands of believers there are in Judea, and all of them are zealous for the law.*[28] Thus it came about that the chosen vessel was sent to the Gentiles so that they might have the full hope of their faith, looking for nothing from the law but trusting in Christ alone. When the mystery of Christ was made known, the gift given was such that it was able to bring about perfect salvation. Just as the greatest rewards are bestowed when great sacrifices are made, so people are blessed with such a wonderful gift because of their joy and gladness when so magnificent a mystery is made known, and it is enough to ensure their salvation.

***[10]that through the church the manifold wisdom of God might now be made known to the principalities and powers in the heavenly places.***

God thought so highly of Paul that he gave him not only as a teacher to the Gentiles but also so that through him the truth of Christ would impress the spirits in the heavenly places, who are the principalities and powers. The powers are those who are more powerful than the other spirits, and the principalities are so called because they rule over the powers. They are meant to recognize, through the church which has been drawn to life in so many different ways, the mystery of the one God which dwells in Christ and so turn away from their error. It happens that the preaching of the church is of benefit to them as well and that they renounce their allegiance to the devil's tyranny, by which he has armed himself by ungodly presumption against belief in the one God. This meaning is set down in Psalm 24, where the God of the universe is revealed as Lord when the Spirit of God says through David: *The earth is the Lord's and the fullness thereof, the whole world and all who dwell therein.*[29] And in what follows: *Lift up the gates of your prince, and be lifted up you everlasting doors, and the king of glory will go in. Who is the king of glory? The Lord of hosts, he is the king of glory.*[30] It is said to these princes who are in error in the heavenly places, and to the devil's servants on earth, that they should take away the gates of their prince, that is, the devil, from their minds, through which gates the error of worshiping many gods has entered. They are temporal, because all error is limited to time; *the way of the ungodly will perish.*[31] They are therefore advised by the exhortation of righteousness to erect eternal gates, because truth endures for ever and ever. This is why it says in Psalm 118: *This is the gate of the Lord, the righteous will enter through it.*[32] It is clear that those who are justified by faith go to heaven, into the kingdom of God, which the prophet Daniel says will never be corrupted when he proclaims elsewhere: *Another, incor-*

[28]Acts 21:20. [29]Ps 24:1. [30]Ps 24:7-10. [31]Ps 1:6. [32]Ps 118:20.

*ruptible kingdom will arise.*[33] The ungodly go to hell because of their unbelief. Therefore the king of glory is Christ who conquered death and rose again, appearing as the Lord and king of glory. By the power of his might, by which he subjugated hell, it is manifested that he is the Son of God, who preached the kingdom of the one God in heaven and on earth to the condemnation of the devil's tyranny.

***11This was according to the eternal purpose which he has realized in Christ Jesus our Lord, 12in whom we have boldness and confidence of access through our faith in him.***

Paul says that God revealed Christ at the time when he planned to make known his mystery for the salvation of the human race, so that knowledge of that mystery might bestow salvation on human beings, so that he might grant this grace to believers as a kind of dedication of the kingdom of Christ. Even if it is unfinished as yet, it still seems new to a creation which does not know it.

***13So I ask you not to lose heart over what I am suffering for you, which is your glory.***

By revealing the hope which is in the mystery of Christ, Paul warns them in case they have to suffer the tribulations which are inflicted on the saints by unbelievers. It contributes to their glory if they, the pupils, are not put off by the tribulations of their teacher but instead are strengthened in the hope that the sufferings of believers will be vindicated by the glory of the age to come. The test of believers is seen in the degree to which they rely on the hope of their faith.

***14For this reason I bow my knees before the Father, 15from whom every family in heaven and on earth is named, 16that according to the riches of his glory he may grant you to be strengthened with might through his Spirit in the inner man,***

Paul says that because he is worthy to summon the Gentiles to recognize the mystery of God's goodness, he prays on bended knee that God who is rich will also grant that by his will they may be strengthened in the Spirit. In other words, he prays that carnal misfortunes which are inflicted on them by unbelievers will not upset them, but that they will remain firm in the hope of a reward for this in the future.

***17and that Christ may dwell in your hearts through faith; that you, being rooted and grounded in love,***

Paul asks that they may be strengthened in the inner man so as not to doubt but to believe more deeply that Christ dwells in them. They have not seen him with their eyes, but the Spirit given to them by the gift of God has given them the assurance that Christ is alive, that he is the Son of God and that he dwells in our hearts by faith, so that when we have his faith in our hearts it is as if we see him. He encourages us to be certain of his help by not deserting us. He is always present with us because of his faith, which he sees in us, especially since his Spirit, which is also the Spirit of God the Father, is given to us in order to protect us on his behalf if we accept him, and to reveal things which are hidden. By his presence we do not doubt that Christ himself dwells in us. He is the other comforter, distinguished from the Son in terms of his person but not of his nature, because he receives from him and proceeds from God the Father.[34] There is a unity of nature in them because they belong to each other. This is why the Lord says: *All that the Father has are mine and all mine are the Father's.*[35]

[33]Cf. Dan 2:44. [34]Jn 15:26. [35]Jn 16:15.

***[18]may have power to comprehend with all the saints what is the breadth and length and height and depth,***

Paul says that the Spirit of Christ dwelling in us grants that we may be grounded in the love of God, bound to him by his blessings, and that we may be able to understand, with all the saints (who are the apostles and prophets) that the incomprehensible and immeasurable God towers over everything by the power of his majesty.

When he says *the breadth and length and height and depth,* he means that just as in a ball the length is as great as the breadth and the height is as great as the depth, so also in God all these things are equal in the immensity of his infinity. A ball is defined in time and space, but God not only fills all things, he goes beyond them as well. He is not limited by anything but contains everything in himself, so as to be the one and only ineffable and infinite being. It is impossible to thank him too much when in his greatness he was pleased through Christ to visit the human race, which was subject to sin and death.

***[19]and to know the love of Christ which surpasses knowledge, that you may be filled with all the fulness of God.***

After the infinite and incomprehensible knowledge of God the Father and the ineffable mercy of Christ, Paul also wants us to know the love which is far above knowledge (and here it is human knowledge which must be understood), for the love of Christ surpasses human knowledge. Who can understand the nature of this mystery of love, that God should be born as a man for the sake of the human race and die for us—the Lord for his servants, the Creator for his creatures, the godly for the ungodly? Why did he love us like that? What did he want from us, when he lacks for nothing himself? Is this not a love beyond human understanding? What human being could possibly show such love to anyone else, since God is not our equal and for this reason stands far above human thoughts? Paul wants us to know that our minds cannot grasp or perceive the depths of Christ's benefits toward us. We must therefore always be completely submissive and devoted to him, and because we can never pay our debts to him in any way, we must persevere in his faith until death. He has done for us what is worthy of him, for the sake of the honor of his majesty, so that we might serve him as much as we can.

Because faith is not fully complete in the Father alone, nor is it perfect in the Son alone, Paul added this verse to show that both in confession and in thanksgiving the honor reserved for the Father and the Son is the same. Everything which has been made by the Father must also be believed to have been made and restored by the Son, so that the fullness of the Godhead might be seen in the confession of believers. The Christian will lack nothing when he acknowledges that God the Father is incomprehensible above everything, and confesses that the love of Christ is ineffable and far above human knowledge.

***[20]Now to him who by the power at work within us is able to do far more abundantly than all that we ask or think, [21]to him be glory in the church and in Christ Jesus to all generations, for ever and ever. Amen.***

This refers to the person of the Father, because he knows best what is useful for us, what we ought not to ask for, when we should be given it and how much is required. By his providence and power he governs the lives of believers. Glory is due to him in Christ Jesus, because it is through him that he offers everything to us and because the honor of the Father is seen in the Son and in the church, that is to say, in the people whom he has been pleased to adopt for himself. The glory of the

Father is found in the brilliance of the children, as the Lord says: *Let your light so shine before men, that they may see your good works and glorify your Father who is in heaven, for ever and ever. Amen.*[36]

## Ephesians 4

***[1]I therefore, a prisoner for the Lord, beg you to lead a life worthy of the calling to which you have been called,***

Paul exhorts them to walk rightly in the precepts of the Lord so that they may come to the glory promised to them. Just as a skilled doctor makes the sick swear that they will look after themselves properly in order to recover their health, so the teacher of the Gentiles urges them to do things which are worthy of their faith in order to obtain the things which are promised to the saints, because he knows that success in this matter will reflect well on him.

***[2]with all lowliness and meekness, with patience, forbearing one another in love, [3]eager to maintain the unity of the Spirit in the bond of peace.***

Now Paul forbids dissension and urges the Ephesians to strive for love, so as not to lose the spirit of unity and peace which will enable them to put up with one another in patience. Modesty engenders success, because if they tolerate one another and point things out gently to one another, they will be corrected in the right way and peace will dwell in them. Then they will deserve to be called children of God, because the Lord said: *blessed are the peacemakers, for they shall be called children of God.*[37] Disturbance and tension lead to contention, which usually tries to defend even things which it knows to be wrong, so as not to appear to give way. Thus arises discord which destroys the bonds of peace.

***[4]There is one body and one Spirit, just as you were called to the one hope that belongs to your call,***

Paul added this for the sake of peace and harmony. The church is a single body, and so the people in it ought to think the same way, because what they believe is the same.

***[5]one Lord, one faith, one baptism, [6]one God and Father of us all, who is above all and through all and in all.***

Paul continues to advocate unity. Since it is unity that we are called to, we should not have any disagreements. If there is only one Lord, that is, Christ (as he himself said in the Gospel: *For you have one master, the Christ*)[38] and *one faith, one baptism, one God and Father of us all, who is above all and through all and in all* believers, the mind of the people should also be one, because the things which Paul lists are part of that unity and so they agree in everything. Paul also said that God the Father, who is dependent on no one for what he is, *is above all and through all.* He is *through all* because everything comes from him, and he must be above all because everything else derives from him. He is also *in all* of us, that is, us who are believers. He is in us by confession, because we believe in him and because he has given us his Spirit, by whom he is in us without any doubt. He is not in pagans, because they deny that he is the Father of Christ.

***[7]But grace was given to each of us according to the measure of Christ's gift.***

Now Paul goes on to counter the thought that the diversity of spiritual gifts given to people

[36]Mt 5:16. A note is added explaining the meaning of "amen" as "truth for ever." [37]Mt 5:9. [38]Mt 23:10.

might go against the principle of unity. He says that this is not so, because in these gifts there is a difference of function, not of nature. He says that each person is given the measure of grace which the Lord has been pleased to attribute to him. His gift is not without a measure of equity, because he assigns to each according to his abilities, so that he may drink what he needs to quench his thirst.

**[8]*Therefore it is said,***
***"When he ascended on high he led a host of captives,***
***and he gave gifts to men."*[39]**

This is a quotation from Psalm 68. Christ began to bestow these gifts after his triumph. He had already defeated death by being exalted on the cross, as he said himself: *When I am lifted up from the earth, I will draw all men to myself.*[40] He robbed hell when he stole the captives who were imprisoned there, either because of the sin of Adam or because of their own sins, and who accepted him. He then ascended into heaven and took them with him. Some of them rose from the dead and appeared in their bodies as a witness to the defeat of death, so that those who would probably not have believed in the resurrection of Christ would be convicted by the resurrection of people whom they knew were dead, for they saw people whom they knew had once been alive.[41] They had been led into captivity against their will and as strangers, but the Savior led only those who were willing to follow him. It is because his appearance provoked those who wanted to be set free that it is said to have captured them.

**[9]*(In saying, "He ascended," what does it mean but that he had also descended into the lower parts of the earth?***

It is true that it is said that he descended in order to ascend, and not like other people who descended in order to remain there. They were kept in hell because of their sentence. That sentence could not bind the Savior though, because he conquered sin. He triumphed over the devil and for that reason descended into the heart of the earth, so that by showing himself there he could preach to the dead, that as many of them who wanted could be set free. It was impossible for Christ not to ascend, because he had descended with the express purpose that by the power of his might death would be trampled on and he would rise with the captives for whose sake he had allowed himself to suffer.

**[10]*He who descended is he who also ascended far above all the heavens, that he might fill all things.)***

This is what the Lord says: *No one has ascended into heaven but he who descended from heaven, the Son of Man.*[42] The same thing is found in the psalm which says: *Its rising is from the end of the heavens, and its circuit to the end of them.*[43] First of all he descended to the earth where he was born as a man. Later he died and descended to hell, from which he rose again on the third day, and before any mortals he ascended into heaven in order to show that the death of creation had been undone.

**[11]*And his gifts were that some should be apostles, some prophets, some evangelists, some pastors and teachers,* [12]*to equip the saints for the work of ministry, for building up the body of Christ,***

By apostles Paul means bishops, and by prophets he means expositors of the Scriptures.[44] It may be true that in the early days there were

[39]Ps 68:18. [40]Jn 12:32. [41]Cf. Mt 27:52-53. [42]Jn 3:13. [43]Ps 19:6. [44]In interpreting this verse, Ambrosiaster tries to equate the offices listed by Paul with those which existed in the late fourth-century church.

prophets like Agabus and the four virgins, as is recorded in the Acts of the Apostles,[45] but this was in order to support the beginnings of the faith. Nowadays it is interpreters [of Scripture] who are called prophets. The evangelists are deacons, as Philip was.[46] Although they are not priests, they are free to evangelize without their own pulpit, just like Stephen and the above-mentioned Philip.[47] The pastors may be readers, who instruct the people with readings, because *man shall not live by bread alone, but by every word of God.*[48] The teachers are the exorcists because in the church they are the ones who restrain and beat the unruly. They are also the ones who used to teach children their lessons, a custom which is found among the Jews and which was inherited by us, but which has become obsolete through neglect. Among these people, who came after the bishop, it is further to be understood that there were those who were said to prophesy because they expounded the hidden meaning of Scripture, particularly because they brought out the words of future hope, which is not the function of the presbyterate. All the orders are found in the bishop, who is the chief priest, that is to say, the prince of the priests, as well as the chief prophet, evangelist and so on, in order to fill the offices of the church's ministry.

However, once churches were established all over the place and offices set up, the system changed from what it had originally been. At the beginning they had all preached and baptized on whatever day and at whatever time was convenient. Philip did not fix a day or a time for the eunuch's baptism, nor did he assign a period of fasting beforehand.[49] Paul and Silas did not waste any time in baptizing the jailer and all his household,[50] nor did Peter have clerks or set a day when he would baptize Cornelius with all his household. He did not do it himself in fact, but ordered the brethren from Joppa who had gone up with him to Cornelius to do so.[51] Up to that time too, no one had been ordained, apart from seven deacons.

It was to allow the people to grow and multiply that at the beginning everyone was allowed to evangelize, to baptize and to expound the Scriptures in the church. But when the church became established in every place, congregations were formed and rectors and other officials were appointed, with the result that after that no clerk who was not ordained would dare perform a function which was not appointed or assigned to him. Thus the church began to be governed by a different order and system, because if everyone could do it, there would have been chaos and the whole thing would have looked vulgar and improper. This is why nowadays deacons do not preach in public nor do they (or laymen) baptize, nor are believers anointed on any day whatsoever, unless they happen to be sick.

Therefore not everything written by the apostle coincides with the order of things which now exists in the church, because the apostolic writings describe what happened at the beginning. For example, Paul calls Timothy, whom he had made a presbyter, a bishop, because at first presbyters and bishops were the same thing, and when he eventually left the scene Timothy succeeded him. Even today in Egypt presbyters perform confirmations if the bishop is not present. But because succeeding presbyters were not fit to hold the chief offices, the system was changed by judicious foresight, so that it would not be his order but his merit which would create a bishop who would be elected by the judgment of many priests. This was done in order to prevent some unworthy person from claiming the office and becoming a scandal to many. In the law priests were Levites born into the tribe of Aaron.[52] But now everyone belongs to the priestly tribe, as the apostle Peter says: *For we are a royal and*

[45]Cf. Acts 21:9-10. [46]Cf. Acts 8:5. [47]Cf. Acts 6:5. [48]Mt 4:4. [49]Cf. Acts 8:38. [50]Cf. Acts 16:33. [51]Cf. Acts 10:48. [52]Cf. Ex 28:43.

*priestly nation,*[53] and therefore anyone can become a priest.

Paul says that church order is designed so that the entire human race will be on the same page in the unity of their confession, so that although they are different in dignity they are all one in Christ, having Christ as their head, who is the author of life.

***[13]until we all attain to the unity of the faith and of the knowledge of the Son of God, to mature manhood, to the measure of the stature of the fulness of Christ;***

Paul says that this order will continue until all those who are predestined to life are united in faith and acknowledge Christ. Paul exhorts the Ephesians to grow so that they may come to a mature faith, which is this: Christ is full and perfect God and is not to be measured in human terms, but recognized in the fullness of his divinity as perfect God. When he talks about mature manhood he is not thinking in terms of age and physical stature, but by what he says here, that he wants us to be perfect in the full understanding of the divinity of the Son of God.

***[14]so that we may no longer be children, tossed to and fro and carried about with every wind of doctrine, by the cunning of men, by their craftiness in deceitful wiles.***

Paul wants us to be rooted and grounded in the doctrine of the catholic faith, which the apostle Peter confessed by God's revelation. He does not want us to be blown about or to go astray because of the pestilential attacks of different heresies which have been invented by men and which open the door to error which creeps in by the wiles of the enemy and poses as truth. Falsehood's technique is to introduce error in the guise of truth. And not only in the guise of truth, but also so that now that we have become believers, we should not be weak and doubtful and turn away from the hope promised to us, as we once wandered quite innocently through various errors before we were converted. Paul reminds us that now that we are Christians we must be grounded, because there is no ambiguity in our faith, which is backed up by the power of miracles.

***[15]Rather, speaking the truth in love, we are to grow up in every way into him who is the head, into Christ,***

Paul says that this is the truth, that we should look up to the love of Christ by which he loved us and gave himself for us and submit everything to him, knowing that he is the source of life for all things which are put under him as members are under the head. So if others out of error or malice deny that Christ is the head of all things (for they were made through him by the Father's will), we who adhere to the catholic faith must act with all care and devotion to bring credit to that faith and not harm, persevering in it so that the babblings of a depraved mind which fight against the truth may be suppressed.

***[16]from whom the whole body, joined and knit together by every joint with which it is supplied, when each part is working properly, makes bodily growth and upbuilds itself in love.***

Paul teaches us why he had said that Christ is the head of all things. He says that the whole body comes from him, by which he means the entire chorus of archangels and principalities, princes and powers exists because of him. Even though each individual one of these has its own identity and there are thousands of them, as the Lord himself said,[54] Paul calls them all together

[53]1 Pet 2:9. [54]Cf. Mt 26:53.

one body because they all exist by one and through one. Just as they are all members of the one body, so they are also distinct in function and honor. The whole creation was made by God through Christ in such a way that there is a kind of hierarchy arranged right up to the firmament and coming down from the cherubim and seraphim, the powers which sit under the throne of God, and the angels, whom the Lord himself calls the holy ones,[55] so that the whole thing can be seen to be joined together according to their merits. I say their merits, not merely the ones belonging to their functions but also those belonging to their natures. The fact that Paul says that all things are joined together does not mean that they all have the same nature, but rather that, in the body, they all make distinct members because of their functions, not because of their nature, so that in all these things it is not the members but the natures themselves which make the differences and that there may be a unity of confession in them. What Paul is trying to do is give a coherent explanation of creation, and in a sense the body is one since the confession of all the members is the same, so that it may hold together in the love of the Creator for its own benefit. It is rebuilding itself as the temple of the Lord, because it had been destroyed by the madness and fury of the devil.

***[17]Now this I affirm and testify in the Lord, that you must no longer live as the Gentiles do, in the futility of their minds; [18]they are darkened in their understanding, alienated from the life of God because of the ignorance that is in them, due to their hardness of heart;***

Once the Creator has been manifested and the pattern revealed which the creation ought to follow in the faith of its God as far as it can, Paul testifies to the Ephesians in the Lord that they must not act or think otherwise than they have been taught to do, so that they will not end up like the Gentiles who neither accept the faith nor conform to the behavior which the law mandates, but have a darkened mind which prevents them from contemplating the truth of divine light. Instead they go after vain things like idolatry, and are restrained by the devil from walking in the way of the one God so that he can make them share in his own damnation.

***[19]they have become callous and have given themselves up to licentiousness, greedy to practice every kind of uncleanness.***

Paul means that the Gentiles have a blinded heart because they have no hope of a future resurrection. Like people who do not think they have any future, they ruin their lives with the most disgusting behavior and are unwilling to submit themselves to the law of faith which prohibits loose living on account of the hope of a future life, which they think is ridiculous. They claim the right to dishonor themselves and go after strange things with an avid desire, as if there were no life after this transitory one.

***[20]You did not so learn Christ!—[21]assuming that you have heard about him and were taught in him, as the truth is in Jesus.***

It is clear that Christians have not learned that there is nothing to hope for after death, but that there is hope for everyone. For believers there is a promise of life, and for unbelievers death, which is eternal punishment. Either way, life and death are both taught in Christ, because the person who follows him will rise with him to life, and the one who distances himself from him will be bound by him in hell and condemned by him as the judge. Since there are some in the church who claim the name of Christ but do not follow his truth,

[55]Cf. Mk 8:38.

Paul says: *as the truth is in Jesus,* so that if they are so taught they will then appear to have learned Christ, to have heard him and to have been taught in him. Christ teaches what he is, how much he ought to be believed, what the hope in him is and what believers [in him] ought to be like. Whoever has learned Christ knows that he rose again from the dead in order to be a model for believers, and so there is great hope after death for those who love God.

**[22]*Put off your old nature which belongs to your former manner of life and is corrupt through deceitful lusts,***

Whoever has heard Christ has learned to turn away from his previous life which Paul calls the old man, because that earlier time was one of ignorance. A man who follows his original vices is quite properly called old, but if he walks in newness of life he is cut off from his previous error, whether it is one of act or thought, and is called uncouth, not in the substance of his flesh or soul, but in his mind and way of life. The old man, on the other hand, is called corrupt because his mind is defiled and his life is wicked.

**[23]*and be renewed in the spirit of your minds,* [24]*and put on the new nature, created after the likeness of God in true righteousness and holiness.***

It is righteous and true to live an upright life. A person who lives an upright life is one who is devoted to his Creator and walks in his will, of which the Gentile world is ignorant. Such a person is born again in the Spirit of his mind and is said to have put on the new man, who is Christ. A person puts on Christ when he is renewed by Christ through faith and imitates the life which Christ has handed down, so that he may appear to have been created according to the will of God. Whoever has been created in him comes to understanding in him, because the truth and righteousness of God is not known to the Gentiles. When people who believe in God acknowledge their Creator and keep his commandments, they are born again in righteousness and truth.

**[25]*Therefore, putting away falsehood, let every one speak the truth with his neighbor, for we are members one of another.***

Because we have been created in righteousness and truth and have been born again in baptism so that we may dwell in him, we are commanded to lay aside falsehood and put on the truth, so that we will not act deceitfully with a brother. Since we are members of one body, we ought to behave toward one another in truth.

**[26]*Be angry but do not sin; do not let the sun go down on your anger,* [27]*and give no opportunity to the devil.***

Since no one can be forbidden from getting angry (because with anger the motive is natural, born of causes which contribute to the perfecting of the sinner), Paul says that a person may be angry, but warns that he should not sin because of it. When we get angry we often lose our temper and find ourselves sinning even when we are disputing with sinners. The more we sin the more we burden the sinner beyond what he deserves. Therefore Paul teaches that our anger should be moderated and that no one should claim to be more righteous when dealing with a sinner than he really is. Some people sin when they are subjected to punishments far beyond anything they can bear, and someone who might have been put right is instead deprived of life because of the sin of the person who is angry with him. This is why Solomon said: *I do not want to be too righteous, for there is a man who dies in his righteousness.*[56]

[56]Eccles 7:16.

We should be imitators of God, who has a balanced righteousness. Although it is just for the wicked to be punished, God puts up with them in his patience, and so some of them are put right. He tolerates us his servants when we sin and is slow to punish anyone.

Paul wants anger to pass and not be retained in the heart. It should die with the day on which it arose, because if it remains in the mind it will give the devil an opportunity to boast. An angry mind is bound to think wrongly, which is what the devil wants. He finds a mind ready to do evil and creeps into it in order to deceive a man made for life by his actions. What a man thinks, the devil does.

***28 Let the thief no longer steal, but rather let him labor, doing honest work with his hands, so that he may be able to give to those in need.***

Paul exhorts the new man not to go back to his previous vices and sins because he wants his new behavior to remain, and it will be no use saying that anything is new as long as the old man is revealed in bad works. Therefore not only is a Christian ordered not to adopt incompatible habits, but he must also, by his own labor, minister to the needs of the suffering, so that by being given to good works he can repay what he had previously stolen and start to lay up treasure for himself in the future. What is so great, or of what merit is it, to deal with things which do not belong to you? A person gains merit when he gives to the poor out of his own resources.

***29 Let no evil talk come out of your mouths, but only such as is good for edifying, as fits the occasion, that it may impart grace to those who hear.***

All good things ought to be seen in a servant of God, and his purity should not be sullied in any way. What is the use in living a clean life if you have a filthy mouth, when the Lord says that everyone will be justified or condemned by his own words? No one can believe that a person who speaks badly is living a good life, for bad talk leads to many evils. A person may be speaking badly if he swears, if he detracts from what is good, if he speaks deceitfully and if he lies. These things cause horror, whereas good and sober speech gives grace and sets an example for the hearers, so that they will honor God in the words of the one who is built up in the faith of Christ.

***30 And do not grieve the Holy Spirit of God, in whom you were sealed for the day of redemption.***

When we behave well, the Holy Spirit given to us rejoices in us, seeing that his promptings are bearing fruit in our lives, just as it is said of the Lord: *So there is joy in heaven over one sinner who repents.*[57] The Holy Spirit rejoices at our salvation, not for his own sake, because there is no lack of happiness in him, but rather because if we were not obedient to him he would be upset about not having any effect on us, because he wants us to be part of life. He is not upset because he is suffering, since he cannot suffer, but when Paul says that he is upset, he means that this is for our sake. He deserts us because we hurt him by ignoring his commands. His grief is our unworthiness which prevents us from being called children of God. He is the Holy Spirit, who makes us children of God by dwelling in us.

***31 Let all bitterness and wrath and anger and clamor and slander be put away from you, with all malice,***

Paul reminds us that everything which might present a danger to our minds must be taken

[57]Lk 15:10.

away. Anger produces indignation, indignation produces clamor like the voice of a madman, which is foreign to a servant of God. Through clamor blasphemy creeps in, which can never be a good thing. This all points to a bitter life which leads to death. Therefore all these things are to be avoided. The fear of God must control us and help us to get what happens to us in perspective. But because some people can suppress anger and clamor in their mind and nurse wickedness until they find some opportunity to get revenge, Paul added that these things should be taken away along with all wickedness. Not only is it wickedness to blaspheme, but it is also wicked to pretend to be at peace with someone to their face and [at the same time] harbor hatred in the mind.

***32and be kind to one another, tenderhearted, forgiving one another, as God in Christ forgave you.***

By using the example of God the Father, Paul exhorts the Ephesians to be kindhearted and merciful to one another, as the Lord said: *Be merciful so that you may be like your Father who is in heaven.*[58] If the Lord took pity on his servants through his Son, how much more should the servants show mercy to one another and forgive, if one of them sins against another! These are the commands of the one who has shown mercy [on us]. If someone shows contempt for this, God will undoubtedly revoke the sentence by which he gave him mercy. The end result will be just what the Lord said in the Gospel about the man who received mercy from his Lord and was then found to be unfaithful in his responsibilities.[59]

## Ephesians 5

***1Therefore be imitators of God, as beloved children.***

This is what he said above. By this exhortation we are commanded to be imitators of God the Father, so that if we obey we shall be considered children of God and most beloved. The child the Father likes best is the one who imitates his good works.

***2And walk in love, as Christ loved us and gave himself up for us, a fragrant offering and sacrifice to God.***

Just as Paul wants us to be imitators of God the Father in kindheartedness and mercy, so he wants us to be imitators of Christ his Son in love, so that just as he loved us and gave himself for us, so we might also give our lives for one another. The apostle John also said that we should give our lives for our brethren following Christ's example.[60] Therefore, if Christ's death is a sweet savor to God, it means that he freely accepted it. If that is true, can we say that those who crucified him according to God's will did not commit a sin? Of course not. Christ is said to have offered himself to God, since he allowed himself to be killed unjustly because he was persevering in the will of God his Father. Someone who is justly killed by offering himself to the devil is doing the devil's will and so deserves to be killed. Since Christ was sticking to the will of God, he upset the devil, and so the devil killed him because he offered himself up to God in the course of fulfilling righteousness. In his sacrifice, righteousness and truth are signified. God looked on this, and this is why his sacrifice was accepted. Therefore someone who is killed undeservedly pleases God, not because he is killed but because he has maintained his righteousness up to his death. God accepted this death [as the price] for life, which is why it is called a sweet savor to God. Paul also said to the Romans that God gave him up for us all.[61]

We must now inquire how God gave him up

[58]Lk 6:36. [59]Cf. Mt 18:23-35. [60]Cf. 1 Jn 3:16. [61]Cf. Rom 8:32.

or how he offered himself up to God, because this seems to be a verbal contradiction. God is said to have given him up when he allowed him to be killed, just as the Lord said to Pilate: *You would not have any power against me if it had not been given to you.*[62] The power was given, but not to someone who did not want to have it. Pilate was allowed to do what he wanted, and this is what it means to say that God gave him up. It may not look like it, but that is what God did. If he had not wanted to allow it, Christ would not have been killed. He wanted him to be killed therefore, but by people who wanted to do it without being forced to. They killed him willingly, and for that reason they are not immune from punishment, because they were allowed to do what they wanted to do anyhow. The condemnation is in the fact that they wanted to do it. God allowed it to happen because he knew that it would be against the devil and of benefit to many. It was right that the enemy should be allowed to do this, because, being ignorant of the future, he thought he was doing something to his advantage when it was really against him. By paying the price of his lack of foresight he was tortured by regret for what he had done. Whether Christ offered himself up or whether God gave him up makes no difference, because they have a common will.

***3But fornication and all impurity or covetousness must not even be named among you, as is fitting among saints.***

What Paul says here is clear. How great a sin is greed, which we like to conceal, when compared with fornication and impurity! We think of it as a fault of little consequence when it is really a serious sin. People in whom something forbidden is found cannot be holy.

***4Let there be no filthiness, nor silly talk, nor levity, which are not fitting; but instead let there be thanksgiving.***

Because there are some people who think there is nothing wrong with telling dirty jokes or speaking in a silly way, Paul prohibits it, for God's servants should always be seen to be sober and modest. Foolish talk is a sin. This is why Solomon said: *A fool does evil things as a joke.*[63] In the Gospel, the Lord says that *Every careless word which people have uttered, they will account for on the day of judgment.*[64] Nothing that can be discovered which might be said to bring shame on someone will go unpunished. Therefore these things do not lead to salvation. This is why Paul urges us to say and do things which are useful to us and further the praise of God, in whose law we ought to meditate day and night, as it is written in the first psalm.[65] The servants of God can be distinguished by their behavior and morals, even if they say nothing, because as truth differs from falsehood, so the servants of God differ from the servants of the devil.

***5Be sure of this, that no fornicator or impure man, or one who is covetous (that is, an idolater), has any inheritance in the kingdom of Christ and of God.***

Paul shows why these things must be taken away, because whoever is like this will have no part in the kingdom of heaven, which belongs to the Father and the Son. In order to show how serious a matter greed is, Paul calls it idolatry, and there is no greater sin than that. Let us consider why greed is called idolatry. Idolatry usurps the honor of God and glorifies the creature, who in the name of deity attracts what belongs to the creator alone, and idolaters claim that it is a part of him. Greed is equated with it because a miser also usurps and reserves for himself what belongs to God. What God has allowed for the common use of

[62]Jn 19:11. [63]Prov 10:23. [64]Mt 12:36. [65]Cf. Ps 1:2.

everyone greed denies when it hoards things for itself so that no one else can use them. It does this so that things will become very expensive and the poor will not be able to survive. If nothing was hoarded, the abundance of everything would make them cheap. Finally, in ancient times there was neither greed nor love. Therefore it is right to compare it with idolatry because it harms many and is hostile to the Creator as well. God wants and commands those whom he has created to support the poor, but greed goes against that. Consider whether it could exist without the devil.

***6Let no one deceive you with empty words, for it is because of these things that the wrath of God comes upon the sons of disobedience. 7Therefore do not associate with them,***

Empty words are vain and vanity is the worship of idols. It does not come from God but from error. Paul teaches this so that no one will agree with their words. They are always shouting, and by the deception of falsehood they hold out the custom of antiquity in opposition to the faith, judging that it is better to rely on the interests of the present rather than on the hope of the future. Therefore revenge will come upon them from heaven, and they will know that what they did not want to believe is true. Paul teaches that the servants of God should steer well clear of such vanity so as to avoid sharing in the penalty of those who do such things.

***8for once you were darkness, but now you are light in the Lord; walk as children of light***

The darkness is ignorance, because nobody can see in the dark. Ignorance is the Gentile condition of unbelief, from which they have been rescued by the grace of God and drawn to the faith. They have become light, that is, truth, because in the light things are revealed for what they are. Finally, pagans who celebrate their mysteries in the dark are closed up in caves with their eyes covered. Those who become Christians and know the truth are called children of light, because God is light and they have accepted his faith in truth.

***9(for the fruit of light is found in all that is good and right and true),***

Paul says this so that the Ephesians will live in a way which will make them worthy to be called children of the light. The works of the light are done openly and without fear, but the works of darkness are done in secret because they are unlawful. Every sin is afraid to appear openly.

***10and try to learn what is pleasing to the Lord.***

By the magnificence of holiness and goodness it can be worked out what works are pleasing to God. He himself said: *Be holy even as I am holy, your Lord God.*[66] And the Lord said: *Be merciful like your Father.*[67] These are the things which are pleasing to God. In holiness there is purification, and in mercy there is full and perfect righteousness.

***11Take no part in the unfruitful works of darkness, but instead expose them. 12For it is a shame even to speak of the things that they do in secret;***

Paul warns us not to be corrupted by consenting to the acts of evil people, which produce no good and lead to what is evil. Not only does he want the Ephesians to stay away from evil deeds, but he also wants them to condemn the evil acts which are done shamefully in secret. Such sins will be revealed if they are criticized, and the children of light will be admired by

[66]Lev 19:2. [67]Lk 6:36.

those who are rightly condemned because they will not be able to contradict them. Instead they will respect them even more.

***13but when anything is exposed by the light it becomes visible, for anything that becomes visible is light.***

It is true that sins become visible when they are exposed, because as long as a sinner is not rebuked he is not really aware that he is sinning. There is no ambiguity in the open, nor can something which is an open crime be excused. Just as it is impossible to deny that it is daytime when the sun is shining, so when sin is revealed it will be exposed as false.

***14Therefore it is said,***
***"Awake, O sleeper, and arise from the dead, and Christ shall give you light."***

Sleep refers to that stupidity of the mind which is cut off from the true way. This separation is a kind of death, from which we are urged to rise, so that by repenting we may acknowledge the truth, which is Christ. Unbelievers and wicked people are submerged in mud having lost any hope of life, which is why they are urged to rise up and come out of it, and have a part in Christ, so that they may pass from darkness to light and from death to life.

***15Look carefully then how you walk, not as unwise men but as wise, 16making the most of the time, because the days are evil.***

Since he had already ordered God's servants to condemn unbelief and the vices of this life, he now adds that these things should be criticized because of the scandal they cause, so that believers may be able to live wisely among unbelievers, especially at a time when unbelievers are in control. On the assumption that the king will be an unbeliever, if a Christian sees that he is a restless and angry opponent, he should retreat into the background so as not to provoke him to blasphemy and violent persecution, and should speak out only when the opportunity arises.

Someone who finds himself among powerful unbelievers must not keep silence or deny the truth when he is asked about it, even if he is afraid of the consequences of a dispute between them. However, he is to avoid this as much as possible because there is no point sowing seeds among thorns. The wise person will know how to answer each one as the occasion arises. There are some people who may be unbelievers but who are not so intractable that they cannot bear to listen to the words of faith. On the other hand, there are also people who are so determined in their unbelief that not only is it impossible to discuss matters of faith with them, it is even impossible to do so [with others] when they are present. If such a person starts shouting and blaspheming, many people will be scandalized. This is why Paul and Barnabas, when they heard people blaspheming against them, tore their garments and went away.[68]

***17Therefore do not be foolish, but understand what the will of the Lord is.***

The Lord Jesus told [his followers] to strive for peace[69] and [Paul] the chosen vessel says: *If possible, so far as it depends upon you, live peaceably with all.*[70] He also says to Timothy: *The Lord's servant must not be quarrelsome but kindly to everyone.*[71] It is God's will that what his servants do should be done with modesty. Disturbance, noise and argument generate enmity with animosity. Paul therefore adds these remarks because of what he said earlier, that he wants God's servants to rebuke the misdeeds

[68]Cf. Acts 18:6. [69]Cf. Mt 5:9; Mk 9:50. [70]Rom 12:18. [71]2 Tim 2:24.

of sinners. It is because such rebukes are liable to give rise to dissension and quarreling that they are to criticize sinners with moderation and meekness so that they will not be provoked and start an argument. Paul therefore says that these things must be done carefully in order to ensure success.

***18And do not get drunk with wine, for that is debauchery; but be filled with the Spirit,***

Sober people are more likely to be able to criticize others properly. Good behavior makes a sinner afraid, and the person who is being criticized will not be able to retort back when he knows that his critic leads a blameless life. Where there is drunkenness there is also extravagance, and extravagance leads to debauchery. For this reason it is better to be sober so that the norms of good behavior are preserved.

***19addressing one another in psalms and hymns and spiritual songs, singing and making melody to the Lord with all your heart,***

The Holy Spirit loves a well-ordered life. If we live well we shall be filled with him, as Paul reminds us, so as to be able to confess and extol God's gift in different kinds of song, because the praise of God is sung by every tongue. The person in whom the Spirit dwells is always meditating on spiritual things which are not merely on his lips but spring from the heart, as the ancient saying of the Lord through the prophet reminds us: *This people honors me with their lips but their heart is far from me.*[72]

***20always and for everything giving thanks in the name of our Lord Jesus Christ to God the Father.***

***21Be subject to one another out of reverence for Christ.***

We are told to give thanks to God for all his gifts. He has even been pleased to adopt us through Christ his own Son. Through him we have come to know God and have learned to worship him in the Spirit, because God is Spirit.[73] We must submit to one another because of the fear of Christ, who commanded us to act in humility.

***22Wives, be subject to your husbands, as to the Lord. 23For the husband is the head of the wife as Christ is the head of the church, his body, and is himself its Savior. 24As the church is subject to Christ, so let wives also be subject in everything to their husbands.***

Wives are told to be subject to their husbands by natural law, for the man is the source of the woman. For that reason, Paul says that women must be subject to their husbands as they are to the Lord. This is why Sarah called Abraham her lord. The man is the head of the woman just as Christ is the head of the church. The church originated with Christ and is therefore subject to him, and in the same way, woman derives from man and must be subject to him. Nevertheless, there is a difference between the two cases, in that a woman is of the same substance as her husband whereas the church can only participate in Christ in name, not in nature.

***25Husbands, love your wives, as Christ loved the church and gave himself up for her, 26that he might sanctify her, having cleansed her by the washing of water with the word, 27that he might present the church to himself in splendor, without spot or wrinkle or any such thing, that she might be holy and without blemish. 28Even so husbands should love their wives as their own bodies. He who loves his wife loves himself.***

72Is 29:13. 73Cf. Jn 4:24.

Women are told to be humble and respect their husbands, and men are ordered to love their wives to the extent of giving their lives for them out of love. They must be concerned for their love and discipline, so that their wives may be godly and holy women.

By natural reason, a woman is a part of her husband's body, and for this reason a man loves himself when he loves his wife. Thus if he commits fornication he sins against himself, because the two are one flesh. The persons do not divide the substance so as to create a new nature for each person, but coexist in a common nature.

***29For no man ever hates his own flesh, but nourishes and cherishes it, as Christ does the church,***

Paul exhorts husbands to love their wives following the Savior's example, so that just as Christ nourishes and cherishes his own work, so a man should nourish and cherish his wife, because she is his flesh.

***30because we are members of his body.***

This must be understood spiritually. Paul said that we are members of Christ's body, because he is the head of the whole church. He is called the head because we originate from him. The whole body lives because of him, and his members constitute a complete spiritual creation as long as they bow the knee at his name.

***31"For this reason a man shall leave his father and mother and be joined to his wife, and the two shall become one flesh."***[74]

In order to recommend the principle of unity Paul gives an example of it. Just as a man and wife are one by nature, so Christ and the church are understood to be one by faith.

***32This mystery is a profound one, and I am saying that it refers to Christ and the church;***

Paul indicates that in the union of man and woman there is a great sacrament of mystery. He does not contradict this but brings out another instance which tallies with the above-mentioned mystery and which he knows contributes to the advancement of the human race. This is the mystery of the Savior and the church. Just as a man must leave his father and mother and cling to his wife, so the church must leave every error and cling and submit to its head, who is Christ.

***33however, let each one of you love his wife as himself, and let the wife see that she respects her husband.***

Because man and wife share a common nature, the man is told to love his wife as he loves himself. The wife, on the other hand, who is an inferior person because of her origin though not because of her nature, is subject to her husband and is told to respect him.

## Ephesians 6

***1Children, obey your parents in the Lord,***
***for this is right. 2"Honor your father and***
***mother"***[75] ***(this is the first commandment with***
***a promise), 3"that it may be well with you and***
***that you may live long on the earth."***[76]

The law is given to children that they must obey their parents because they derive their existence from them. It is therefore just that they should show respect to the people from whom they originate.

This promise is contained in Exodus. If parents are honored then all will be well and people will live to a greater age. But how is it that Paul calls this the first commandment,

[74]Cf. Gen 2:24. [75]Ex 20:12. [76]Deut 5:16.

when it is well known that the first commandment says the following: *You shall have no other gods before me.*[77] The second one goes: *You shall not make for yourself any image of what is in heaven above or in the earth below.*[78] The third one is: *You shall not take the name of the Lord your God in vain.*[79] The fourth one says: *You shall observe my sabbaths.*[80] The fifth one is: *Honor your father and mother, et cetera.*[81]

But because the first four commandments refer directly to God, they are understood to belong to the first table of the law. The other commandments, about honoring parents, not killing, not committing adultery, not stealing, not bearing false witness and not coveting anything which belongs to one's neighbor all refer to other people. These six commandments therefore belong to the second table of the law. It is the first of these which says: *Honor your father and mother.* It is for that reason that Paul said: *This is the first commandment with a promise,* because he wanted to distinguish between those commandments which refer to God and those which refer to other people.

***4Fathers, do not provoke your children to anger, but bring them up in the discipline and instruction of the Lord.***

If the law is to be kept, children must honor their parents. But another law is given to parents by the apostle, which is that they are to treat their children in such a way that they will not reject the commandments of the law, for if they have been brought up in the fear of the Lord they will be able to keep what is commanded. However, if parents provoke their children they will not keep the way of the law, and it will look as if the parents are forcing them to become sinners, because angry people never recognize what they ought to do. Therefore parents ought to teach their children by showing them an example of moderation, so that the children will choose what is best for them. Parents ought to remember that they were once children themselves and did not want to be provoked by their own parents. Children should also remember that they will one day be parents, and they will not want their own children to disobey them. So each of them should treat the other in the way that they want to be treated themselves.

***5Slaves, be obedient to those who are your earthly masters, with fear and trembling, in singleness of heart, as to Christ;***

It may be that our religion is higher than any other and the only one with any power, because it promises believers the kingdom of heaven, but this is no reason for us to adopt a haughty attitude toward other people. We are all obliged to fulfill our responsibilities in whatever situation or position we currently find ourselves in, so as to encourage the minds of unbelievers to worship God when they see that that is just and humble. Masters will see that their servants have improved and are more reliable in the services they render, and servants will experience the kindness of their masters. Both will then eagerly desire the faith of the one who governs human affairs with such peaceful forms of control. If a servant has a dependent of his own, he will not want to be disrespected by him, and therefore he should not disrespect his own master. He must treat his servant in the way that he wants his master to treat him, and in that way he will be able to please God.

***6not in the way of eye-service, as men-pleasers, but as servants of Christ, doing the will of God from the heart, 7rendering service with a good will as to the Lord and not to men, 8knowing that whatever good any one does, he will receive the same again from the Lord, whether he is a slave or free.***

[77]Ex 20:3. [78]Ex 20:4. [79]Ex 20:7. [80]Ex 20:8. [81]Ex 20:12.

For the sake of the fear of God, Paul wants just and faithful service to be given to other people. The person who sticks to the rules in his duties toward his earthly master is the one who serves God, whom he will hear on the day of judgment bearing witness to righteous deeds and giving everyone else their due. Such behavior may even contribute to the conversion of the masters. When they see that by the grace of God their slaves have become loyal servants, something which they know is difficult, they may be able to join in the praise of God's glory.

***9Masters, do the same to them, and forbear threatening, knowing that he who is both their Master and yours is in heaven, and that there is no partiality with him.***

Earthly masters should recognize that God is the common Lord of everyone and therefore should demand only such service as they would be prepared to perform if it were demanded of them. In this matter, the measure they give is the measure they will get.[82] The Lord is a just judge who decides according to the cases, not according to the status of the persons involved.

***10Finally, be strong in the Lord and in the strength of his might.***

After all the warnings and exhortations, after the principles of doctrine faithfully handed on and the revelation of the dispensation of the mystery, Paul wants them to be strong in their faith by trusting in the power of God. If they know that the hope of the promise is sure, they will be ready to serve God by putting up barriers against the waves stirred up by the impudence of the enemy. He brings down a storm on the servants of God, but he is the one who is shipwrecked.

***11Put on the whole armor of God, that you may be able to stand against the wiles of the devil.***

The armor of God is a steady faith, which is the only thing that always defeats Satan.

***12For we are not contending against flesh and blood, but against the principalities, against the powers, against the world rulers of this present darkness, against the spiritual hosts of wickedness in the heavenly places.***

The apostle is sure that the sufferings which are inflicted by apostate servants of God are actually controlled by the devil, who is too high and mighty for us to resist [in our own strength]. Paul therefore tells us to put on the armor of God against them, because it is only by his power that all the devil's machinations will be overcome and destroyed. The people whom Paul calls the rulers of this darkness, evil spirits who dwell in heavenly places, in the firmament of the world, are only puppets of the devil. It is those who are in charge of ignorance and unbelief who are the masters of evil and rulers of darkness. The rulers of darkness are understood to lead people astray because they are the masters of unbelief.

***13Therefore take the whole armor of God, that you may be able to withstand in the evil day, and having done all, to stand. 14Stand therefore, having girded your loins with truth, and having put on the breastplate of righteousness, 15and having shod your feet with the equipment of the gospel of peace; 16besides all these, taking the shield of faith, with which you can quench all the flaming darts of the evil one. 17And take the helmet of salvation, and the sword of the Spirit, which is the word of God.***

Because we are at war against the most vicious enemies who are skilled in all manner of wickedness, we must be on our guard with all

[82]Cf. Mt 7:2.

caution and care, so that however they tempt us, we may be armed and ready for them. We must be vigilant in prayer and expect God to give us the victory, because God will help those whom he sees acting like that. In warfare of this kind a sober mind and a pure conscience are absolutely essential, because it is not being waged against carnal evils but against spiritual ones. Against earthly enemies the body is strengthened by liquor and the mind is inflamed by strong drink which give them the courage to resist. But resistance against spiritual evils must be spiritual, and our weapons must be sobriety and abstinence, so that filled with the Holy Spirit we might defeat unclean and aberrant spirits. We gird our loins with truth if we are prepared to resist error. Everyone who wants to be effective protects himself in this way, so that by removing hindrances he can function more effectively.

***18Pray at all times in the Spirit, with all prayer and supplication. To that end keep alert with all perseverance, making supplication for all the saints, 19and also for me, that utterance may be given me in opening my mouth boldly to proclaim the mystery of the gospel, 20for which I am an ambassador in chains; that I may declare it boldly, as I ought to speak.***

If we live a good life the Holy Spirit dwells with us and we can receive what we ask for. To pray in the Spirit always means to offer prayer to God with a clean conscience and a pure faith. The person who prays in the flesh prays with a corrupt mind and will sin again, not accidentally or incidentally, but deliberately. However, he can avoid sin as long as he lives if he perseveres in prayer, so that his mind is always firmly fixed and focused on the law of God and he meditates day and night on the things which God loves. People who are like this are able to pray for the saints.

It is not unworthy if *the members care for one another*,[83] nor will it appear arrogant if loyal disciples intercede on behalf of their teacher in order to assist him to lay aside every hindrance and use his freedom to preach, as he was commissioned to do by the Author. Paul did not want to be pressured by the force of his tribulations into blunting the sharp edge of his teaching by softening it in the face of such opposition. He therefore encourages them to pray for him in two ways, first that his mind might be filled with the Spirit so that he might be bold to proclaim the fullness of the mystery, and second that he might be given the boldness to do so. God willingly hears that kind of prayer.

When God sees that his mission [given] in his apostle is being despised, he will be outraged and will not refuse to act in the defense of his own cause. If it is both custom and law not to inflict harm on human ambassadors, by what presumption and audacity is not only suffering but also death inflicted on the ambassadors of God! This is why Paul says: *Because of this embassy I am in chains*. He was not allowed to speak freely but reported the words of God in subjection and necessity, being subject to chains, beatings and death. He was even stoned and fought wild beasts at Ephesus.[84]

***21Now that you also may know how I am and what I am doing, Tychicus the beloved brother and faithful minister in the Lord will tell you everything. 22I have sent him to you for this very purpose, that you may know how we are, and that he may encourage your hearts.***

It was through Tychicus that the Ephesians found out what the apostle was doing and vice versa. As far as the apostle was concerned, there was no doubt that what he was doing was God's will, but the Ephesians had to know that

[83]1 Cor 12:25. [84]Cf. Acts 14:19; 1 Cor 15:32.

he was acting against unbelievers and their tricks. As far as the Ephesians were concerned, Paul wanted to find out if they were growing in their faith or not. To ensure that they would obey and listen to the words of Tychicus, Paul commends him, calling him a most beloved brother and faithful servant of God.

**23*Peace be to the brethren, and love with faith, from God the Father and the Lord Jesus Christ.***

Paul wants that peace which is the gateway of love to be with the brethren, and love with faith also, so that having entered by peace they may dwell in the love which comes from faith. This is the faith of God the Father and of his Son our Lord Jesus Christ.

**24*Grace be with all who love our Lord Jesus Christ with love undying.***

Paul foresees that in time to come there will be many who will lose hope in the faith of the Lord Jesus Christ when he says that eternal grace will dwell with those who love Christ in the right way and think about him according to God's will. Those who say that he is worthless will lose the grace which has been given to them.

# AMBROSIASTER
## *Commentary on Philippians*

### Preface

The apostle brought the word of faith to the Philippians. He had been warned in a dream, as the Acts of the Apostles says, to go to them and open their ears, so that they might receive the word of God.[1] He stayed with them for many days and taught them the doctrine of the Lord. After his departure they did not turn away to some other teaching, as the Galatians had done, but remained true to their faith and did not welcome false apostles. In his letter, Paul congratulates them and rejoices at the attitude of their hearts. By praising them, he is implicitly criticizing others, for the Corinthians had gone away and followed false apostles after his departure, although they too had listened to him for a long time. For this reason, the Philippians were rightly praised.

### Philippians 1

***[1]Paul and Timothy, servants of Christ Jesus,***
***To all the saints in Christ Jesus who are at Philippi, with the bishops and deacons:***

Paul does not mention that he is an apostle because he is writing to people who already recognize that. He therefore passes over his dignity because it was clear to them. However, he does mention his status [as a servant], because whoever confesses Christ as Lord is a free man and is saved.

He writes as he usually does to the saints, but this time it is to the saints in Christ Jesus, that is to say, those who confess that Jesus Christ is both God and man. Photinus denied that he was God, and Mani denied that he was a man, so they were both unclean. Paul was not writing to people who suppress the truth by their own lies.

He specified that he was writing to the Philippians and mentioned the bishops and deacons. These were with Paul and Timothy, who were also bishops, and he included the deacons who ministered to them. He was writing to the lay people [at Philippi], because if he were writing to bishops and deacons there he would have mentioned them by name. In particular, he would have written to the [one] bishop who was standing in for him, as he wrote to Titus and Timothy, and not to two or three of them.

***[2]Grace to you and peace from God our Father and the Lord Jesus Christ.***

It is clear that the Father is God and that Christ Jesus is our Lord. Does this somehow make Christ appear to be more our Lord than the Father is? Only from the human perspective, because there is perfect harmony between God the Father and Christ the Lord. In this world Christ would be more our Lord than the Father is only if either he was Lord of the Father or the Father had begotten him with a different status than his own. However, God has begotten in such a way that those whom he has begotten are still in his power, so that even those who are freeborn are his servants. When he handed them over to his Son, he made them the Son's servants as well, so that Christ

[1]Acts 16:9-10.

would be their Lord. As he says: *Father, those whom you have given to me were yours, and you have given them to me,*[2] so that they might be servants of the one God in the Father and in the Son.

***[3]I thank my God in all my remembrance of you, [4]always in every prayer of mine for you all making my prayer with joy, [5]thankful for your partnership in the gospel from the first day until now.***

First of all, Paul gives thanks to God who by his grace gives all good things to those who believe in him. He remembers them in all his prayers with great joy because they have become his colleagues in the gospel, just as the apostle Peter says elsewhere: *That you may be partakers of the divine nature.*[3] Paul foresaw their devotion and their faith established on these very principles, and he always rejoiced in them, knowing that there would be many more like them in the future.

***[6]And I am sure that he who began a good work in you will bring it to completion at the day of Jesus Christ. [7]It is right for me to feel thus about you all, because I hold you in my heart, for you are all partakers with me of grace, both in my imprisonment and in the defense and confirmation of the gospel.***

Sure of the goodness and righteousness of God, and not doubting their faith, Paul confesses that, aided by the help of God, they would persevere in their faith until the day of the Lord, when those who endure to the end will be rewarded. He had no reason to think anything else of them, because he knew from experience that they had always remained firm in their devotion to God. He saw that their determination was so consistent and unflagging that he knew that they were worthy to share in his joy. People who have the same faith ought to rejoice in the hope of future immortality and glory.

***[8]For God is my witness, how I yearn for you all with the affection of Christ Jesus.***

He calls God as witness to his love [for them]. When somebody attaches great importance to a thing, he testifies in order to make it credible. By doing this, Paul is also stirring up a desire in them toward him, because those who feel wanted will respond in kind. Therefore it is Paul's desire to have them all as colleagues in the understanding of the mystery of the divinity and incarnation of the Lord Jesus Christ, not out of human longing but in the love of Christ, not by the affections of the flesh, but by the affections of the Spirit.

***[9]And it is my prayer that your love may abound more and more, with knowledge and all discernment, [10]so that you may approve what is excellent, and may be pure and blameless for the day of Christ, [11]filled with the fruits of righteousness which come through Jesus Christ, to the glory and praise of God.***

With God's help Paul wants to instill in them a pattern of Christian discipline. For them to be securely grounded in the faith, they must know what the sacrament of their belief is and be able to distinguish what is beneficial from what is not. In that way they will supplement the Lord's teaching with their good works, bearing the fruit of immortality in an abundance of all good things, so that he may appear among them as the glorious teacher of the Gentiles.

***[12]I want you to know, brethren, that what has happened to me has really served to advance the gospel, [13]so that it has become known***

[2]Jn 17:6. [3]2 Pet 1:4.

***throughout the whole praetorian guard and to all the rest that my imprisonment is for Christ; [14]and most of the brethren have been made confident in the Lord because of my imprisonment, and are much more bold to speak the word of God without fear.***

***[15]Some indeed preach Christ from envy and rivalry, but others from good will. [16]The latter do it out of love, knowing that I am put here for the defense of the gospel; [17]the former proclaim Christ out of partisanship, not sincerely but thinking to afflict me in my imprisonment.***

The Philippians did not need this explanation, but Paul went though everything step by step because of his concern that no one should be in any doubt. Since he has already said that they shared in his joy, his preaching outlines what would help them. He speaks to them as people who were dear to him, so that his sufferings for Christ might make an impression on them all. By this humble approach he demonstrates that he is glorious, so that those who love him may have reason to be joyful. If it is clear that he is in chains for Christ's sake, his reputation will be all the greater.

*In every camp and among everyone else.*[4] This means: "throughout Judaism and among all the churches of the Gentiles." Judaism comes first, because the promise was made to it, as the Lord said: *For salvation is of the Jews.*[5] Paul says that many of the brethren have followed his example and been bold to preach the word of God with confidence. His persistence has encouraged many not to be afraid to evangelize in the light of the apostle's example, because God is present to defend those who love him. There were, however, other false brethren who preached the Word of God not with confidence nor in the love of God, but out of the strife of jealousy, because they were envious of him. However, most of the brethren were proclaiming Christ sincerely, even if their motives varied. Some did it out of good will, purely for the glory of God alone, whereas others did it out of love for the apostle, knowing that God would protect them. On the other side, Paul referred to two kinds of people who were not preaching sincerely. Some were jealous of the apostle and were doing it in a spirit of contention, whereas others were cleverly pretending to preach Christ in order to stir up opposition to the apostle, as if he were the founder of a sect who had attracted many to his conspiracy. Jealousy of the apostle grew in direct proportion to the numbers who appeared to be teaching his doctrine.

***[18]What then? Only that in every way, whether in pretense or in truth, Christ is proclaimed; and in that I rejoice.***

***[19]Yes, and I shall rejoice. For I know that through your prayers and the help of the Spirit of Jesus Christ this will turn out for my deliverance, [20]as it is my eager expectation and hope that I shall not be at all ashamed, but that with full courage now as always Christ will be honored in my body, whether by life or by death. [21]For to me to live is Christ, and to die is gain.***

Paul's first joy is in those brethren who preached Christ out of good will, and then he goes on to say that he rejoices in the fact that by the deceit of people who opposed him, it had turned out that Christ was being preached in order to torment him and make him jealous. He says that what they planned for his death turned out instead to contribute to his life. It was his life that Christ should be preached to all, and that he was even prepared to die if by so doing that could be accomplished, because he knew that a great reward might be given to him for such dedication and effectiveness. There was always

[4]This is how Ambrosiaster understood the meaning of v. 13. [5]Jn 4:22.

some unforeseen wickedness being cooked up against him which he did not know about.

In order to counteract the malice of those who plotted against his life under the cover of deception, Paul testifies that he is armed with the protection of God. With the help of those who he says share with him in his joy because of their common readiness and the support of the Holy Spirit, who was opening ways for the preacher against the will of those people, giving grace and confidence to his words, he would be able to put down the rebellions which have arisen. Therefore he says that he is in no way confounded in the doctrine of Christ, because it is the great hope of the promise and because there is nothing in it which is sordid, dishonest or false, as is the case among the pagans. Its sincerity is perfectly clear. This is why he persists and does not give in to his opponents, so that Christ may be magnified in his body, whether he is killed or whether he escapes death with no more than a beating. We can gauge the quality and depth of his hope in Christ when we realize that he was prepared not only to be beaten and afflicted for his sake, but to die for him as well. Paul says that his life is Christ, whether in the present or in the future, just as John the Evangelist testifies when he says: *What is done in him is life and the life was the light of men.*[6] Paul gave up his mortal body for this life in order to get it back in eternity, and for this reason he thought it was worth dying for Christ.

***22If it is to be life in the flesh, that means fruitful labor for me. Yet which I shall choose I cannot tell. 23I am hard pressed between the two. My desire is to depart and be with Christ, for that is far better. 24But to remain in the flesh is more necessary on your account. 25Convinced of this, I know that I shall remain and continue with you all, for your progress and joy in the faith, 26so that in me you may have ample cause to glory in Christ Jesus, because of my coming to you again.***

What Paul says is clear. If he is placed in the flesh there must be some reason why he is alive and he makes the best of it. He does not know what to choose because he is torn between two things. He has a desire to die and go to be with Christ because he thinks it is much better to be in the presence of God and enjoy the things which have been chosen and promised to him. But he says that so far he has to remain in the flesh for the instruction of believers.

Although he says that it is much better to die and be with Christ, he nevertheless states that he knows he must remain in the flesh for the benefit of believers, so that their glory may abound in the Lord and contribute to the praise of the apostle when they see him again. The Philippians are growing in knowledge and are more fully grounded in their faith. How much love he had for the believers, when, instead of choosing what he says was much better, he preferred what was best for the many. He was certain that whatever contributed to the salvation of many others would please the Lord.

Who would not abandon all the cares of the present out of a desire to go up to the third heaven? Who would not lay aside everything out of a desire for the paradise above? Who would not give up human speech for the sake of the hidden words [of God]? Who would not have chosen peace and quiet after so many sufferings? But because Paul made love for everyone his priority, he did what would benefit the brethren.

***27Only let your manner of life be worthy of the gospel of Christ, so that whether I come and see you or am absent, I may hear of you that you stand firm in one spirit, with one mind***

[6]Jn 1:3-4. Ambrosiaster links the end of v. 3 with v. 4 in an unusual way.

***striving side by side for the faith of the gospel, [28]and not frightened in anything by your opponents. This is a clear omen to them of their destruction, but of your salvation, and that from God.***

Paul wants them to live in a way which is worthy of the Lord's teaching, so that he would not regret his desire to remain in the flesh. He wants them to be of one mind in their faith and devotion in the face of their opponents, so that he will hear the same things about them in his absence as he saw when he was with them. He wants them to keep the faith and not to fear the threats or terrors of their adversaries in any way, knowing that whatever they suffered for Christ would contribute to their salvation, and that those who persecuted them were headed to damnation.

***[29]For it has been granted to you that for the sake of Christ you should not only believe in him but also suffer for his sake, [30]engaged in the same conflict which you saw and now hear to be mine.***

Although he praises the grace of God in them all, he nevertheless says that it contributes to their praise that God has allowed them to suffer for Christ, because he only permits or grants this to those who love Christ. Thus he said: *It has been granted to you for the sake of Christ,* because it has been granted by God the Father to those who love Christ that they should suffer for him in order to increase their merits, and by following the example of their teacher they should fight with every confidence to triumph over unbelievers.

## Philippians 2

***[1]So if there is any encouragement in Christ, any incentive of love, any participation in the Spirit, any affection and sympathy, [2]complete my joy by being of the same mind, having the same love, being in full accord and of one mind. [3]Do nothing from selfishness or conceit, but in humility count others better than yourselves. [4]Let each of you look not only to his own interests, but also to the interests of others.***

Paul said that "If there is true encouragement of hope in Christ among us, by which we console one another in the comfort of a common love, if there is any participation in the Holy Spirit through whom we are joined in one new body, if there are affections, that is to say, if I am in your mind as you are in mine, if there are mercies, that is, if there is a feeling of godliness in love, fulfill my joy." He indicates that the things which he lists must be demonstrated in practice if what he commands afterwards was to be done, so that they would be of one mind, humble in spirit, not provoking one another but rejoicing in love, making the apostle's joy in them complete. Therefore he reminds them that if they are not keeping these things and are not approved of by others, they should do so because they do not want to be disapproved of by other people, and then they will be perfect. No doubt there were those among them who disagreed, and who were restless and longing for vainglory, wanting to argue and win debates by the sharp cleverness of their minds, which does not bring reward but leads to disputes and breaks [the bonds of] love. What kind of congregation would it be that contained only gold and silver vessels, and had no wooden or clay ones? However, by learning to do good, such vessels could become gold and silver ones, because vice is not a thing of nature but of the will.

***[5]Have this mind among yourselves, which is yours in Christ Jesus, [6]who, though he was in the form of God, did not count equality with God a thing to be grasped,***

Christ was always in the form of God because he was the image of the invisible God.[7] But here the apostle is talking about the Son of God when he had become incarnate and been made man, saying: *Have this mind in you, which was also in Christ Jesus,* that is, in God and man. *Who although he was in the form of God,* lived among human beings and appeared by his acts and deeds to be God. The form of God is exactly the same as God. He is called the form and image of God so that it will be understood that although he is not God the Father, he is what God is. Therefore *he did not count equality with God a thing to be grasped,* because he knew that for him to be in the form of God was not something he had stolen, as he said: *I and the Father are one.*[8] And in John's Gospel he says: *For not only did he break the sabbath, but he said that God was his own Father, making himself equal with God.*[9] Therefore he equated himself with God as of right, whereas someone who makes himself equal to another person to whom he is inferior would say that that was robbery.

**[7]*but emptied himself, taking the form of a servant, being born in the likeness of men.* [8]*And being found in human form he humbled himself and became obedient unto death, even death on a cross.***

Christ therefore knew that he was in the form of God, which made himself equal with God. But in order to teach the law of humility, not only did he not refuse to let the Jews seize him, but *he* also *emptied himself,* that is to say, he withdrew his power from use, by being humbled he might appear to be weakened by a loss of power. *Taking the form of a servant,* he was held and bound and beaten, being made obedient to the Father right up to the cross. He knew he was the Father's equal, but rather than claim that equality he submitted himself. Paul teaches us to imitate this patience and humility, so that not only will we not claim precedence over our peers but that we will also defer to them, following the example of our Author. Yet it is not said that he received the form of a slave on the grounds that he was humbled like a sinner. Slaves are created by sin, like Ham the son of Noah, who was the first person to earn the name of a slave. Nor do I think, as some do, that he received the form of a slave simply by becoming a man. Look what Paul says: *Have this mind in you that was in Christ Jesus,* that is, in God and man. Even before his incarnation he could be called either Christ or Jesus, because the names Son of Man and Son of God both mean exactly the same thing. But what does Paul say elsewhere about Christ before his birth? *The rock was Christ,* and *Let us not tempt Christ as some tempted him.*[10] Therefore, when Scripture wants to indicate that Christ was God and man, it uses one or other of these names, either Jesus or Christ. For the Son of God was born as a man, yet he was in the form of God, so that although he seemed to be a man, he did the works of God. In the deeds he performed he was seen to be God when he was thought to be only a man. His works demonstrated the form, since given that his works were not like the works of a man, he was understood to be God because he was in the work or form of God.

What is the form of God other than the evidence that he appears as God when he raises the dead, gives the deaf their hearing, cleanses lepers and so on? Why would he be said to have become like a man, if he were no more than a man? And by what logic would he have been found in the likeness of a man, if he were not also God, and if he had not always appeared in the power of God before allowing himself to be humbled and then found in the likeness of a man after having been weakened? He appeared on the mountain like God, and when he walked on the sea he was seen and understood to be not only a

[7]Cf. Col 1:15. [8]Jn 10:30. [9]Jn 5:18. [10]1 Cor 10:4, 9.

man but God as well. Finally, what did those who were in the ship say? *Truly this man is the Son of God.*[11] Once this power ceased he appeared once more as a man. Therefore Paul says *in the likeness* in order to indicate that Christ was also God. He said it was because of weakness that God was made like human beings. He explains this in what he adds next, as follows: *He humbled himself, being made obedient even unto death, the death of the cross.* It was in this way that he was found in the likeness of a man. He held back his power so that it would not appear in him. Instead, he appeared like a man and died, though he did not know what death was.

***9Therefore God has highly exalted him and bestowed on him the name which is above every name, 10that at the name of Jesus every knee should bow, in heaven and on earth and under the earth, 11and every tongue confess that Jesus Christ is Lord, to the glory of God the Father.***

Paul shows what and how much humility earned, so that we will suppress our pride and seek it more. This is why Solomon said: *God resists the proud but gives grace to the humble.*[12] It is also why the Lord said: *Whoever exalts himself will be humbled, and whoever humbles himself will be exalted.*[13] Humility is when somebody does not claim what he knows is owed to him. The Pharisee was said to be exalting himself when he said things about himself which were true, and for that reason he was humbled.[14] Christ however went further, because although he was God, he became flesh and deferred to human beings.

Now let us see how the name which is above every other name was given to Christ, as if the Son of God was lacking something or was imperfect, because whoever lacks something is imperfect. If he was in the form of God, equal and on the same level with God, how was this given to him? Paul says it was given to him because he humbled himself and appeared as a man, emptying himself and *becoming obedient even to death.* But if he was born perfect, what was he lacking? Whoever says that the Son who was born of God the Father was not perfect is an Arian,[15] because Paul shows that before his passion he was equal to God the Father, as I mentioned above. Because of this it is clear that he was born perfect, and appears to have obtained everything in his nativity. He was born in the fullness of divinity in order to do all the things which he did, so that he must have received the gift before doing what he was born to do.

It appears that the gift of God the Father was to be the Son, so that his name would be above every other name, that is to say, he was God. The name of God by nature and not merely by designation is above every other name. This is why *at the name of Jesus every knee shall bow in heaven and on earth and under the earth,* just as Paul says to the Romans elsewhere: *From whom is Christ according to the flesh, who is God over all and blessed for ever.*[16] What these all are he reveals in this letter when he says: *In heaven and on earth and under the earth.* There is no room for anything else to exist!

Some people think that this name which is above every other name was given to him as a man, but that makes no sense. If Christ the Son of God is also a man, he cannot have been a God who became a man, but remained God and somehow lacked what he had. If he lacked what belongs to God because he was a man, then the Son of God as God would have given to himself whatever he lacked as a man. This is absurd. Why would the Father be said to have given, when the one who had become a man was missing nothing? Could the divinity

[11]Mt 14:33. [12]Prov 3:34. [13]Lk 14:11. [14]Cf. Lk 18:11-12. [15]A follower of Arius (256-336), who taught that Christ was inferior to God and whose doctrine was condemned at the first council of Nicaea in 325. [16]Rom 9:5.

of the Son not have supplied what was missing to his body and soul? Perhaps it is because all things are from God the Father that he is said to have given them. But if everything comes from the Father, why is it not said that he gave everything to his Son when he generated him? Although he made the Son equal to himself, order requires that everything should be done in the name of the Father. The Father has granted to the Son that after the cross everything would be saved in the name of the Son. Finally the Lord spoke to the Father about his disciples as follows: *Father, those whom you have given me I have kept, for they were yours and you gave them to me.*[17] And to his disciples he said: *So far you have asked nothing in my name. Ask and you will receive.*[18] When he was born he received this, so that it would become clear after the cross what he had received from the Father when he was born. He received a name from the moment when he began to be known by the creation. It is recognized that he received it on account of what he did before he actually did it. Thus before the cross he said: *All things have been granted to me by my Father.*[19] Therefore how can this refer to the body when the name of God was given to the body? It is clear that Christ was both God and man and it is not right for God to be changed into flesh, nor can flesh be transformed into what God is.

But perhaps he was God by adoption, and this is the slant here. Christ would then start off being part true God and part adopted, or else being two gods. But Scripture tells us something different. It says that this was given to the one who emptied himself, who took on the form of a slave, who was made in the likeness of man and who obeyed the Father. If a man obeyed God the Father, what is so special about what the apostle said? But Paul says that this is extraordinary because he obeyed, even though he was equal with God. What would there be to praise by saying that he was made in the likeness of a man, when every man is made in that likeness? This cannot be. No one is made in the likeness of someone unless he is different before being made in the likeness of whoever it is. He was made like a man by a [divine] act and not by his [natural] substance.

Who is it who emptied himself? A man. Therefore he had [a human nature]. How did he receive it? How could a man, a weak creature, empty himself? Could someone who was in the form of God have been a man? But perhaps the man in the form of God was the Son. Come now, in what form was he the Son of God? If he was a man in the form of God, and for that reason was the Son of God, he was already perfect before his passion. Therefore he could not have received anything after his passion. But let us examine what is written about him: *For which cause he highly exalted him and gave him a name which is above every other name, that at the name of Jesus every knee should bow, in heaven and on earth and under the earth, and every tongue confess that Jesus is Lord in the glory of God the Father.*

Let us now examine these words and note the force of the rhetoric. It is certain that the name which is above every other name is the name of God. But if he does not have this name by nature, it is not above every other name. The name would then be no more than a designation given in words and would say nothing about the quality of his nature, nor would creation bow the knee to an adopted God, but only to one who was not a fellow creature. How can it be that a man should be in the glory of God the Father? Even if a man were to be adopted as God, he could still not be in the glory of God the Father. The name suits him because he is born of God.

To be in the glory of God the Father is to differ in no way from God, because there is one glory of the Father and the Son through

[17]Jn 17:12, 6. [18]Jn 16:24. [19]Mt 11:27.

their common substance and power, for this is the unity of nature. What, I ask, is the contradiction, if the Son is said to have received the gift from the Father, when everything the Son has comes from the Father, from whom all things are believed to come? We therefore say that his nature is the substance of God, because it is from that that Christ was born.

**[12]*Therefore, my beloved, as you have always obeyed, so now, not only as in my presence but much more in my absence, work out your own salvation with fear and trembling; [13]for God is at work in you, both to will and to work for his good pleasure.***

Paul testifies that God helps those who make a good effort. He always refers every grace back to God, so that it is ours to will but God's to perform. For who will overcome *the principalities and powers, the rulers of the darkness, the spiritual forces of evil in the heavenly places,*[20] whom we have as our enemies because of their jealousy, other than God alone? They are angry that we are called children of God. What Paul is encouraging is nothing new; he is only saying in his usual way that they should be subject to the gospel by making sure that they behave well. Good behavior leads to salvation.

**[14]*Do all things without grumbling or questioning, [15]that you may be blameless and innocent, children of God without blemish in the midst of a crooked and perverse generation, among whom you shine as lights in the world, [16]holding fast the word of life, so that in the day of Christ I may be proud that I did not run in vain or labor in vain. [17]Even if I am to be poured as a libation upon the sacrificial offering of your faith, I am glad and rejoice with you all. [18]Likewise you also should be glad and rejoice with me.***

In order that the Philippians might enjoy the fruits of their faith and works Paul commands them to do everything which pertains to Christian discipline without hesitation or grumbling, because if something is done haphazardly or without devotion, it will not have the desired result but fall into condemnation. But they were to act like spotless children of God in all innocence. They were to be mindful of their profession [of faith] and act in a way which corresponded to that, and appear among unbelievers in their life, behavior and morals as bright as the sun and the moon are sublime in their splendor among the stars. Just as the stars are obscured when the sun appears, so the unrighteous and unbelievers seem vile and deformed in the presence of believers and righteous people. When the Son of God returns, the apostle will be glorified, because his plantation has produced such fruits. At that time his labor and effectiveness will not appear to have been in vain. Thus he says: *Even if I am poured out as a libation on the sacrifice and service of your faith, I rejoice.* Paul means that it is a matter of rejoicing to him if he had been oppressed by unbelievers, because by this means he has united them to himself, for he knows that his death will have that effect. It is a great sadness if someone suffers for other people for nothing. Paul testifies that he must rejoice in them and that they must join with him in doing that, so that the people and their great teacher might share a common joy.

**[19]*I hope in the Lord Jesus to send Timothy to you soon, so that I may be cheered by news of you. [20]I have no one like him, who will be genuinely anxious for your welfare. [21]They all look after their own interests, not those of Jesus Christ. [22]But Timothy's worth you know, how as a son with a father he has served with me in the gospel. [23]I hope therefore to send him just as soon as I see how it will go with me;***

[20]Eph 6:12.

***[24]and I trust in the Lord that shortly I myself shall come also.***

These things are clear and need no interpretation. Paul indicates that after this letter he will send Timothy through whom he will be reassured about what is going on with them, for he was of the same mind as the apostle. This is the sign that he is truly concerned about them, not like some who, wanting to recommend themselves, neglected the discipline and behavior of their brethren and did not preach with a devout mind, but for their own gain. And because Timothy was a gifted man, Paul says that they knew his worth, because he was with him as a most dear son, serving the gospel of Christ. Paul calls Timothy his son, because he had been ordained by him. He is sending him on ahead and will shortly go to them himself.

***[25]I have thought it necessary to send to you Epaphroditus my brother and fellow worker and fellow soldier, and your messenger and minister to my need, [26]for he has been longing for you all, and has been distressed because you heard that he was ill. [27]Indeed he was ill, near to death. But God had mercy on him, and not only on him but on me also, lest I should have sorrow upon sorrow.***

All these things are clear. Paul indicates that he will send Epaphroditus to them with this letter. Against his wishes the people [of Philippi] had been distressed because of his illness. When they saw him they would be relieved at seeing him returned to health, and Epaphroditus could also lay aside the concern which he had when he saw them again. He was their apostle, appointed as such by the apostle, when he sent him to them for their encouragement, and because he was a good man, the people longed to see him. Why was it that this Epaphroditus was sick almost to the point of death when he was a companion of the apostle, who raised the dead? Did the apostle not pray for him and intercede for his immediate healing? However, signs like that were done for the sake of unbelievers. Epaphroditus's illness was not detrimental to him but beneficial. Believers are tested in many different ways. Some are tried by illness, others by the loss of loved ones, others by fines and others by tribulations, and if they stay firm in their need and do not look for help from elsewhere, their merits will be increased.

The apostle did not refuse to pray for him, but there was something better for him, and he asked for that instead. Why is it that in another letter Paul tells people not to be sad when their brethren pass away, when in this one he says that he would be sad if Epaphroditus had died? When Paul said that he would have sadness if Epaphroditus had died, he was speaking about the sadness which he had because he was ill, for Epaphroditus was necessary for the churches. To the Thessalonians he said: *see that you are not sad for those who have fallen asleep, as others are who have no hope.*[21] He said that he would have been sad if Epaphroditus had died because he needed his comfort and assistance, not because he would have been weeping over someone who was lost.

***[28]I am the more eager to send him, therefore, that you may rejoice at seeing him again, and that I may be less anxious.***

Paul indicates that Epaphroditus and the people of Philippi loved each other, and that when they saw him again they would be excited and the apostle would rejoice, because it reassured him to think that he was sending Epaphroditus back to see his beloved ones again.

***[29]So receive him in the Lord with all joy; and honor such men, [30]for he nearly died for the***

[21]Cf. 1 Thess 4:13.

***work of Christ, risking his life to complete your service to me.***

Although the love of Epaphroditus and the Philippians for each other was undiminished, he is nevertheless commended by the apostle in order to make him even more beloved, especially because of those who may have been less affectionate toward him, because there are differences like that in every congregation. This is why he recalls Epaphroditus's struggle, and how he did not hesitate to die for the work of the gospel. This means that he was not frightened by the threats and pressures of unbelievers, but that he persisted in his encouragement of the believers, so as to fill in what was missing in what they had received according to the dispensation of the apostle. The man who did not keep his soul back from death and burial now sacrifices it in this present life, as the Lord said: *Whoever wants to save his soul will lose it.*[22] This loss is burial, because according to the world, whoever gives his soul for Christ's sake loses it, although he will save it for the future.

## Philippians 3

***[1]Finally, my brethren, rejoice in the Lord. To write the same things to you is not irksome to me, and is safe for you.***

Paul shows how concerned he is for their welfare when he says that he is impatient to write and tell them what they need to know for their benefit.

***[2]Look out for the dogs, look out for the evil-workers, look out for those who mutilate the flesh.***

These are the names Paul gives to the people who were jealous of the Gentiles and tried to lead them astray by using twisted arguments to persuade them to be circumcised. In order to show that they must by all means be avoided and rejected, Paul teaches that they are like dogs who surround them first and then mutilate their flesh by their savage bite.

***[3]For we are the true circumcision, who worship God in spirit, and glory in Christ Jesus, and put no confidence in the flesh. [4]Though I myself have reason for confidence in the flesh also. If any other man thinks he has reason for confidence in the flesh, I have more:***

It is clear that believers circumcise their own hearts and that by removing the cloud of error they see and acknowledge the God of creation. This is what it means to serve God in the Spirit and to glory in the Lord Jesus Christ, who gave the law of the Spirit, so that the glory of the flesh may be made void. Nevertheless the apostle was confident that he could have gloried in the flesh had he wanted to, but because he knew that such glory was empty he rejected it.

***[5]circumcised on the eighth day, of the people of Israel, of the tribe of Benjamin, a Hebrew born of Hebrews; as to the law a Pharisee, [6]as to zeal a persecutor of the church, as to righteousness under the law blameless. [7]But whatever gain I had, I counted as loss for the sake of Christ.***

Paul discounted whatever pertained to the worship of the law, to the keeping of its righteousness, to the learning of the heresy of the Pharisees and to the zeal of his ancestral tradition in persecuting the church. Those who, like him, were Jews by birth had been his colleagues in all those things, but what appeared to be profitable from the human point of view turned out to be a loss in comparison with Christ.

Why should it be a loss, unless the time for

[22]Mt 16:25.

keeping the law was now over? All these things were useless and hindrances, which prevented him from receiving grace, because they are carnal, whereas our worship is spiritual. Paul says he is of the tribe of Benjamin in order to exalt his tribe over those who traced their origin to those patriarchs who were sons of Jacob's concubines or those who were converts to Judaism. This is why he says: *I have more, being circumcised on the eighth day of the people of Israel.* He shows that he is first among the Jews, but that he rejects this for the sake of the hope promised by Christ.

The Hebrews are so called because of Abraham. The word has been slightly changed in its sound so that it is now Hebrew rather than Abrew. Compare this with the Latin *medidies* which was the ancient form, but being too hard to say, it got changed into *meridies.*[23] If they derive from Abraham, their name must also come from Abraham and not from Heber, who lived six generations before Abraham. If the human race began to be reformed in Abraham, and if he is the father of faith, then both the name and the language of the Hebrews must come from him. At first the language had no name, but when it was given one, it came from him. There is no reason at all why it should have taken its name from Heber. Abraham was a Chaldean and the Chaldeans do not speak Hebrew.

***8Indeed I count everything as loss because of the surpassing worth of knowing Christ Jesus my Lord. For his sake I have suffered the loss of all things, and count them as refuse, in order that I may gain Christ 9and be found in him, not having a righteousness of my own, based on law, but that which is through faith in Christ, the righteousness from God that depends on faith; 10that I may know him and the power of his resurrection, and may share his sufferings, becoming like him in his death, 11that if possible I may attain the resurrection from the dead.***

Earlier Paul spoke about the race of Abraham, the law and its righteousness and the merits of those who observe it, and considers that all such things are a loss when compared to the promises of the Savior. Now he adds that not only these things but everything else as well is *loss because of the surpassing worth of knowing Jesus Christ my Lord.* After the law and its righteousness, what can these things be, except that acknowledging Christ is put before the life and soul of the body itself? If, as he says to the Colossians, *all the treasures of wisdom and knowledge are hidden* in Christ,[24] these other things, whatever they are, are to be regarded as of no value as far as attaining to the excellence of the wisdom and knowledge of Christ is concerned. The righteousness which comes by faith and not from the law, which is given by the grace of God on the basis of acknowledging Christ, is sufficient for salvation. The recognition of the mystery of his incarnation, passion and resurrection is the perfection of life and the treasure of wisdom. Where there is wisdom there is life, and there is no life where there is stupidity. As Solomon put it: *The foolish man does evil as a joke.*[25] Whoever understands that it was for his sake that Christ became a man, suffered and rose again after defeating death will despise and reject everything else to follow him, by whose protection he sees himself delivered from death, and will look for ways of repaying him, and see if he can do anything on his behalf which might earn him a greater reward at the promised resurrection.

***12Not that I have already obtained this or am already perfect; but I press on to make it my own, because Christ Jesus has made me his own.***

[23]The word means "midday." [24]Col 2:3. [25]Cf. Prov 10:23.

Because throughout the letter Paul testifies that he rejoices in them and praises their obedience and their faith, he now declares openly and in his own person that they must strive to add to their good works by fulfilling what is lacking in their righteousness. He says this so that they will not be puffed up and congratulate themselves as being already worthy. If someone as gifted as the apostle Paul was with such a great dignity, confesses that he is still imperfect, how much more should the Philippians understand that they must go on working in order to obtain the merits of justification. This is why Paul says: *I press on to grasp it because I have been grasped by Christ Jesus.*[26] When he was still an unbeliever, Paul was tossed about in his mind by error, which took him far away from the way of the Lord. Then the mercy of God seized him on the way as one running away from the grace of Christ, when he was going to upset and afflict the church. The result was that he learned to accept the grace which he had rejected and to know that for such a blessing it was worth even dying. He also realized that he was not standing in the way of believers but only of himself if he did not believe and instead persecuted the message of salvation by his ignorance. It was in that way that he was grasped, that is to say, he was commandeered by the foreknowledge of God and found. He learned the mystery of Christ and throughout his life did everything he could to increase his merits so as to grasp the intended reward, by attributing everything to the one whom he had learned was killed for his sake.

***13Brethren, I do not consider that I have made it my own; but one thing I do, forgetting what lies behind and straining forward to what lies ahead, 14I press on toward the goal for the prize of the upward call of God in Christ Jesus.***

This is what Paul said above. He indicates that he labored to improve himself every day by constantly stretching himself to tackle greater challenges. Forgetting what was past, he chose what was better, not because past things were bad but because they were less able to earn merit. He was heading toward what was better in order to reach the goal of the heavenly reward. He declared in all seriousness that the cause of such an admirable and invisible reward was something worth fighting for.

***15Let those of us who are mature be thus minded; and if in anything you are otherwise minded, God will reveal that also to you.***

Earlier Paul had said that they were not mature, but this was according to the standard of what was promised, since there was always room for improvement. In comparison with others, who paid less attention to divine matters, those who walked the way of perfection with due circumspection could indeed be considered mature. This is what Paul wants to say here, so that things might only get better. If the Philippians need any more encouragement to improve their behavior, they should remember that it is God's gift and not be proud of their own achievements.

***16Only let us hold true to what we have attained.***

In order to prevent the appearance of pride and the thought that this did not come from God, Paul adds that it was all revealed by God, saying: *Let us hold true to what we have attained.* In other words, we have not attained to anything in our life of faith apart from what the rule of doctrine lays down. All that we have is what is simple and straightforward in the truth of the gospel.

[26]This is a more precise translation of the verse which is made necessary here because of what Ambrosiaster goes on to say about it.

***17Brethren, join in imitating me, and mark those who so live as you have an example in us.***

Paul wants the Philippians to be careful not to be deceived by the subtlety of wicked men. They should note how each one of them lives and teaches, so that they will associate only with those in whom they recognize their master's teaching.

***18For many, of whom I have often told you and now tell you even with tears, live as enemies of the cross of Christ. 19Their end is destruction, their god is the belly, and they glory in their shame, with minds set on earthly things.***

The people Paul refers to here are the same as the ones who led the Galatians astray. They went about deceiving people and undermined churches by preaching the worship of Judaism in the name of Christ, as if Christ was promised in and through that. He recalls them with sadness and tears, because they got in the way of the salvation of believers by raising questions about what food should be eaten and what not, as if salvation lay in food or the stomach was God, whom they thought they could please by eating only clean food according to the law and by being proud of their circumcised private parts. This way of thinking is worldly, but the person who thinks spiritually glories in faith, hope and love. In that situation there is no room for greed or gluttony, which is why he said: *Their god is the belly.*

***20But our commonwealth is in heaven, and from it we await a Savior, the Lord Jesus Christ, 21who will change our lowly body to be like his glorious body, by the power which enables him even to subject all things to himself.***

Those who mind spiritual things are said to live in heaven even though they are still here on earth, in the same way as the wicked principalities and powers, although they are themselves in the firmament [of heaven], are nevertheless alive and well here on earth. The acts of Christians are therefore in heaven, where the hope of their salvation, which is Christ, also is. Every believer is waiting for him to come and transform the body of flesh, so as to cover what is of the earth with spiritual clothing and make it like his glorious body at the coming of his majesty, *according to his working,* that is to say, according to his power, *by which he can subdue all things to himself.* This means that the power of the Lord will be manifested by the resurrection of the dead and their transformation into glory, when he subdues all principalities and powers and is revealed as the God and Lord of all things.

## Philippians 4

***1Therefore, my brethren, whom I love and long for, my joy and crown, stand firm thus in the Lord, my beloved.***

Paul tells them to stand firm in the same faith, because their perseverance is his joy right now and will be his crown in the future. If the disciples are victorious in the struggle the teacher will be worthy of a crown.

***2I entreat Euodia and I entreat Syntyche to agree in the Lord. 3And I ask you also, true yokefellow, help these women, for they have labored side by side with me in the gospel together with Clement and the rest of my fellow workers, whose names are in the book of life.***

Paul urges Euodia and Syntyche to be wiser with the help of those whom he mentions, whom he declares are all named in the book of life because of the merit of their faith, so that they may continue in the works of the gospel and grow both in the knowledge and in the wisdom of God.

***4Rejoice in the Lord always; again I will say, Rejoice.***

Paul is happy with their works and faith, and in order to encourage their eagerness he prays that they will grow in their endeavor and rejoice in the Lord always. He even repeats this in order to show that he rejoices in them with true affection.

***5Let all men know your forbearance. The Lord is at hand. 6Have no anxiety about anything, but in everything by prayer and supplication with thanksgiving let your requests be made known to God. 7And the peace of God, which passes all understanding, will keep your hearts and your minds in Christ Jesus.***

Now Paul wants others to benefit by their example. Since their forbearance was widely known, that is to say, their reasonable behavior, their works will shine out and there will be no lack of people who will copy their good deeds so as to receive merit not only for their own acts but for those of others too, just as it is said that they will eat the fruits of their own labors. When he looks for further fruit from their own works it is for a good purpose, because the labors which they have achieved will benefit those who will begin to do good works by copying their example.

Paul says: *The Lord is at hand. Have no anxiety about anything.* That is, he teaches them that they must be prepared and keep watch in prayer and supplication, giving thanks to God. They must put away all earthly concern and keep what God has promised them before their eyes, and for that reason give him thanks. When the Lord is at hand earthly concerns must cease. Why would anyone bother about something which is about to perish?

Paul goes on to say: *Let your requests be made known to God.* This report to God is to be given with dedication and the vigilance of prayer. Then, they will be armed with his peace, *which passes all understanding,* says Paul, and *will keep your hearts in Christ Jesus.* Paul said this because whoever has peace with God will not be afraid of any opponent. Everyone who loves God is safe in God's peace in Christ Jesus. Who would not be afraid of someone whom he knows is a friend of God?

***8Finally, brethren, whatever is true, whatever is honorable, whatever is just, whatever is pure, whatever is lovely, whatever is gracious, if there is any excellence, if there is anything worthy of praise, think about these things. 9What you have learned and received and heard and seen in me, do; and the God of peace will be with you.***

In conclusion, Paul explains what was still required for the imitation of perfection, so that those things will not fall into disrepute but will appear worthy of praise, because those who think and do them, following the model of the apostle, have the peace of God with them. Our God is truly a God of peace who exhorts us to peace, but not because there is any doubt about his own power, nor because he is afraid of appearing weak. He even forgives sins which have been committed against him, when he could perfectly well have pushed us not toward peace but into subjection against our will, by the terror of his power at work and his ineffable greatness. This, however, is the way of the world's peace, not of God's, for his very nature is peace.

***10I rejoice in the Lord greatly that now at length you have revived your concern for me; you were indeed concerned for me, but you had no opportunity.***

Paul now shows that his cheerfulness has become greater because the Philippians had had their attention drawn back to the apostle after a period in which they had grown neglectful of him, and putting their minds to it, they had gone back to their earlier work, sending him their fruits to be stored in the heavenly barn, where neither moth nor rust destroys them.[27]

***[11]Not that I complain of want; for I have learned, in whatever state I am, to be content. [12]I know how to be abased, and I know how to abound; in any and all circumstances I have learned the secret of facing plenty and hunger, abundance and want. [13]I can do all things in him who strengthens me.***

Paul testifies that he is not rejoicing in their work for his own sake but for their benefit, because with God's help he is perfectly content. He neither regrets poverty nor glories in abundance, because he knows that abundance often makes people proud whereas the acceptance of poverty earns heavenly riches. Nevertheless he says that their work for him is a blessing because it has helped meet the needs of many.

***[14]Yet it was kind of you to share my trouble.***

*This verse is not in Ambrosiaster's text.*

***[15]And you Philippians yourselves know that in the beginning of the gospel, when I left Macedonia, no church entered into partnership with me in giving and receiving except you only; [16]for even in Thessalonica you sent me help once and again. [17]Not that I seek the gift; but I seek the fruit which increases to your credit.***

Paul recalls these things so that by hearing in memory and praise that they are his work, they will not doubt that God will accept them and therefore will apply themselves all the harder to this matter.

***[18]I have received full payment, and more; I am filled, having received from Epaphroditus the gifts you sent, a fragrant offering, a sacrifice acceptable and pleasing to God.***

Paul is not wasting his breath when he tells them what must be done, and he encourages them because he knows that they have been more neglectful or less generous than they had been in the past, and by reminding them of their previous works he wants them to realize that they were doing less than they had done before. He was not disapproving of their action but merely indicating that they had been more devoted in this work in the past. Nevertheless he is still grateful to them and says that what they have done is acceptable to God like a fragrant sacrifice.

***[19]And my God will supply every need of yours according to his riches in glory in Christ Jesus.***

Paul has drawn attention to himself here by saying *My God,* because he expects God to meet their needs in the abundance of the greatness of his goodness in the glory of Christ Jesus, just as God had already supplemented Paul's merits. The glory of Christ Jesus is when, by the grace of God, the desires of Christians are fulfilled according to the teaching of the gospel.

***[20]To our God and Father be glory for ever and ever. Amen.***

Here Paul does not set himself apart but says along with everyone else: *To our God and Father be glory.* He is God because of his fear and Father because of his honor and also because he is the source of all things. As he himself said in the prophet Malachi: *If I am your God, where is my fear? And if I am your Father, where is my honor?*[28]

***[21]Greet every saint in Christ Jesus. The brethren who are with me greet you.***

Paul greets those who sanctify themselves in Christ Jesus, so that they may be worthy of

[27]Cf. Mt 6:20. [28]Mal 1:6.

the Christ who said: *Be holy, for I am holy, the Lord your God.*[29] The greeting of the brethren brings consolation all round, as if he were showing pictures of those mentioned.

**[22]*All the saints greet you, especially those of Caesar's household.***

Paul indicates that he has a special affection for those of Caesar's household. He shows that they are also stronger than the above-mentioned brethren because he calls them saints.

**[23]*The grace of the Lord Jesus Christ be with your spirit.***

Since questions arise about the person of the Savior, Paul here prays that our spirit will be protected by his grace because he wants to reinforce the reality of his divinity.

[29]Lev 19:2.

# AMBROSIASTER
## *Commentary on Colossians*

### Preface

After the preaching of Epaphras and Archippus, false apostles had tried to seduce the Colossians by corrupting the straightforward devotion of their minds with philosophical disputations, so that they would not renounce the principles of the elements by which human life is more or less governed. Therefore the apostle exhorts and admonishes them by letter not to think that there is any hope anywhere outside Christ, and thus be deceived.

### Colossians 1

***1Paul, an apostle of Christ Jesus by the will of God, and Timothy our brother,***
***2To the saints and faithful brethren in Christ at Colossae:***
***Grace to you and peace from God our Father.***
***3We always thank God, the Father of our Lord Jesus Christ, when we pray for you,***

Paul starts the letter in the usual way, writing to the Colossians because he continues to send letters to those who are holy and faithful brethren, and he prays that the grace of God will dwell in them through Christ.

***4because we have heard of your faith in Christ Jesus and of the love which you have for all the saints, 5because of the hope laid up for you in heaven. Of this you have heard before in the word of the truth, the gospel 6which has come to you, as indeed in the whole world it is bearing fruit and growing—so among yourselves, from the day you heard and understood the grace of God in truth, 7as you learned it from Epaphras our beloved fellow servant. He is a faithful minister of Christ on our behalf 8and has made known to us your love in the Spirit.***

Since God thought it worthy to entrust his Son to them, Paul gives thanks to him in his prayers, and also because of the love which the Colossians had for the saints. They were confident that because of this love they had a sure hope in God, who they were sure would reward those who believe and love each other because of Christ, whose name had gone out to all the Gentiles so that many more of them might be brought to faith in him.

Paul encourages them in a cheerful mood to grow and produce living fruit as the other Gentiles do, so that by the fact that they have received God's grace they might increase both in number and in achievement by adding to their faith those who will become their brethren in Christ. Epaphras, who ministered the grace of Christ to them on the apostle's behalf, has borne witness that many have been attracted by the example of their good works. They imbibed that grace like a spiritual drink in the love of the Lord, which is not in the flesh but in the Spirit.

***9And so, from the day we heard of it, we have not ceased to pray for you, asking that you may be filled with the knowledge of his will in all spiritual wisdom and understanding, 10to lead a life worthy of the Lord, fully pleasing to him, bearing fruit in every good work and increasing in the knowledge of God.***

Hearing of their devout and eager willingness in matters concerning the faith of Christ, the apostle prays for them, that when they have understood the will of God they might more readily express the devotion, which they had learned when they heard the faith of Christ, by some corresponding work, so that such confident dedication of mind and strength of faith might not lose the fruit of their labor by doing something without the proper consultation and advice. Whatever was done with a devout mind and in wisdom would be freely accepted by God.

***11May you be strengthened with all power, according to his glorious might, for all endurance and patience with joy, 12giving thanks to the Father, who has qualified us to share in the inheritance of the saints in light. 13He has delivered us from the dominion of darkness and transferred us to the kingdom of his beloved Son,***

Paul wants their work to increase with knowledge, so that they would not be ignorant of the hope of their faith. The Colossians will be firm and stable if they pay attention to what has been promised in return for faith and [recognize] how great the power of the glory of God's majesty is in its patience, because it preserved the human race for a long time, although it not only turned away from the Creator in its own irreverence but also persecuted those who love him. Paul wanted them to be equally patient and to put up with the insults and curses of unbelievers, or if pressure was placed upon them, to wait for the judgment of God, not doubting him but rather rejoicing in the life promised, giving thanks to God, who has been pleased to call and admit the Gentiles to the promise made to the Jews, which is light eternal, that is, everlasting truth.

We have been delivered from the state of darkness, that is, freed from hell where were we held by the devil, as much because of our own sin as because of the transgression of Adam, who is the father of all sinners, and transferred by faith to the heavenly kingdom of God's Son, so that God might show us how great his love for us is, when taking us from the depths of hell he has admitted us into heaven with his true Son. All believers who are single-minded in their devotion are admitted to heaven by an angel who leads us on the right when we go out of this world,[1] something which had not been granted before death had been overcome.

***14in whom we have redemption, the forgiveness of sins.***

God has brought us into the kingdom of his Son, through whom he has redeemed us and set us free. The forgiveness of sins makes us free, so that once we have been delivered from our debts we can no longer be bound. Without faith in Christ nobody gets out of hell, because someone who is bound by his sins cannot go out through the gates of hell.

***15He is the image of the invisible God, the first-born of all creation;***

The image of the invisible God cannot be visible, since if it were it would not be an image. What is invisible cannot be portrayed, nor can the visible see the invisible. Either there is a body which can be seen or a figure or some unformed substance which the eye can pick out; whatever the case, there is still a body of some kind. But God is completely different from all such things, and how can he have a visible image? This is said here so that it might be understood that the Son is the same kind of being as the Father. He comes from him and is no different from him in the divinity of his

[1]The image here is that the right hand is the hand of power and security, whereas the left hand was the hand of deceit and weakness.

nature. He is said to be the Father's image and likeness, so that unbelievers will not think that he is a different god, since he is included under the same name. He is therefore called the true Son, so that people will believe that he comes from God the Father himself.

But because of misunderstanding it was added that he should be called the image of God, so that when he appears, whether in human form or in fire, as he did to Moses,[2] he would not be understood as being the Father but the Son, and by the fact that he is called the Father's image it would not be believed that there was any distance between them. This is why Jesus says to Philip: *Philip, whoever sees me sees the Father. How can you say, Show us the Father? Do you not believe that I am in the Father and the Father is in me?*[3] This is the unity and consubstantiality of the Father and the Son. They are in one another, so that whoever sees the Son sees the Father also.

Now let us consider how the Father is seen, so that we may understand in what way Philip might see the Father when he sees the Son. Certainly they saw the Son by understanding the works of God, and not with their physical eyes. What the Son did he attributed to the Father, in order to show the unity of their power. In the same way the Son was also seen by Jacob, which is why he got the name Israel, that is, a man who sees God.[4]

For these reasons therefore Christ is called the image of the invisible God. He is understood to be what by the intellect he appears to be—God. The Father has never appeared at any time, as it says in the Gospel: *No one has ever seen God.*[5]

*The firstborn of all creation.* Paul testifies that Christ was born, not created, as the Son before the whole creation, in order to distinguish his birth from the making of creation. To clarify this he adds what follows.

**[16]*for in him all things were created, in heaven and on earth, visible and invisible, whether thrones or dominions or principalities or authorities—all things were created through him and for him.***

Paul not only indicates how magnificent and glorious Christ was in God, because he was born before anything else was made, but he also says that all things were created in him, which means that the power to do anything is in him and comes from him, since everything is made through him. He is the head of all creation, because it derives its existence from him. The things that were made by him are said to have been made through him. He was born in order to make the creation, that is, to have made it in him and through him. His birth was of no benefit to himself, but to us, because there was no need for someone who was already in everything to be born. How is it that he is the only Son of God, and how does he know that God the Father is unbegotten? Christ was in God and came forth from God, so that there should only be one God. So it is that when the Son was born the Father did not decrease nor did the Son gain anything. In order to explain more clearly what and how great the power of the Son was, Paul shows what comes through him—thrones, dominions, principalities and powers—so that no one would ever think that there was anything less in him than there was in the Father.

**[17]*He is before all things, and in him all things hold together.***

He is before all things because he alone was born from God the Father, out of the unbegotten substance of God. All the rest came into being by the power which he has by his generation from the Father, not because they all share a common substance but because by God's will

[2]Cf. Ex 3:2. [3]Jn 14:9-10. [4]Gen 32:28. [5]Jn 1:18.

they came into being out of nothing by the action of the Son. Everything holds together in him because without him they are nothing, unless perhaps they had been subtracted from him by some devious error and were bound for perdition.

***18He is the head of the body, the church; he is the beginning, the first-born from the dead, that in everything he might be pre-eminent.***

The head of the church is Christ, but only if everyone in heaven and on earth feels that they are one and can be the church, that is, of one faith. If not, they are cut off from the head of the whole body, that is to say, they are separated from their Creator and go mad in some kind of delirium and vanity.

Since all things were made through him, the things which had fallen away because of some sort of neglect had to be reformed again by him. There would have been some injury done to him if his work had been restored by someone else. This is why, just as he was born before everything else, so he rose again from the dead before everyone else and his original life was given back to him. He was born of God before all things, so that he could create everything which did not yet exist. Then again, he was born by taking flesh from a virgin in order to wipe away sin, which had entered the world through the virgin Eve. Therefore he was born, died and rose again so that what he originally made he could later recreate when it had become dead through error, so that he might always be first and head of all life.

***19For in him all the fulness of God was pleased to dwell,***

The fullness is in him and remains in him, because he can always do everything. There are no exceptions which cannot be dealt with by him. He is able to do and to reform everything; he can raise up the fallen and restore the dead to life. This is why he said: *Just as the Father has life in himself, so he has given it to the Son to have life in himself.*[6] And: *Just as the Father raises the dead and gives them life, so the Son gives life to whom he wills, nor does the Father judge anyone, but he has given all judgment to the Son.*[7] What could be more just than that the Father should give judgment to the Son over those things which he made through him, so that all the fullness of the Godhead might dwell in him because he has all power in himself, as we have already said. This means that he is perfect God, because whoever does not have all these things in him is not God.

***20and through him to reconcile to himself all things, whether on earth or in heaven, making peace by the blood of his cross.***

This is what I mentioned above, because in order to restore all the things which he had made through him after they had started to fall out with one another, and also with their Author, because of a certain error—this error still exists in the earthly heaven—God humbled him by incarnating him, so that having become a man he might show and teach how those things which are in the firmament and on the earth might be reconciled to their Creator. In order to complete this work he allowed himself to be killed for the sake of human beings, so that those whom he had taught when they were in the heavenly places could not, on leaving them, be held captive by the second death. As a result, his teaching enjoyed the fruit of its original purpose, and everything made by him once more dwelt in him as in the Author, as Peter says in the Acts of the Apostles.[8]

***21And you, who once were estranged and hostile in mind, doing evil deeds, 22he has now***

[6]Jn 5:26. [7]Jn 5:21-22. [8]Acts 3:15.

***reconciled in his body of flesh by his death, in order to present you holy and blameless and irreproachable before him,***

Paul recalls what the gift of God to the Gentiles was like in order to show that they had to give thanks, and a great deal of thanks, to God. When they were still hostile to the plans by which he had decided to visit the human race through his servant Moses, whose doctrine and power they did not accept because they were too devoted to their idols, and therefore to their own evil works (for they worshiped the things which they had made), the mercy and providence of God called them in order that they might receive God's grace free of charge. They were to return to him with a clean conscience, so that on the day of judgment, as long as nothing of their old error was still to be found in them, they would be incorporated into their Creator who had become a man in order to benefit the human race by overcoming death in his flesh.

***23provided that you continue in the faith, stable and steadfast, not shifting from the hope of the gospel which you heard, which has been preached to every creature under heaven, and of which I, Paul, became a minister.***

***24Now I rejoice in my sufferings for your sake, and in my flesh I complete what is lacking in Christ's afflictions for the sake of his body, that is, the church,***

Paul says that he rejoices in the tribulations which he suffers because he sees the effect he is having on the faith of believers. Tribulation is not pointless when it gains the one on whose behalf it is suffered for [eternal] life. Paul says that sufferings which were inflicted on Christ, whose teaching they persecuted, both to burden unbelievers with the cruelty of their ungodliness and to preach love to those who believe in God, whose Son even suffered afflictions for our sake. At this point he wants it to be understood why he is writing to the Colossians [when he says]: *Provided that you continue in the faith,* so that they would know that Christ's sufferings would benefit them if they remained faithful.

From the beginning Paul declared how great and how infinite the power of the greatness of Christ was in order to teach that hope should be placed in him alone, because everything is his and nothing can live without him either in heaven or on earth. He is before all things and everything holds together in him because he holds the headship in everything, so that if anyone thinks he owes worship to one of the elements, angels or powers, he will know that he is wrong. Christ is the only Son of God, the head of all principalities and powers, whose gospel has been preached in all the world, starting with Moses who said to the Jews: *The Lord your God will raise up for you a prophet like me from among your brethren. You will heed him. It will be that whoever does not hear that prophet will be cut off from the people.*[9] This is why the Lord said: *Moses wrote about me.*[10] Therefore he is the only one to be listened to and worshiped, nor is anyone else to be compared with him, because whoever holds the head has the rest of the body under his control. Anyone who humbles himself before one of his subjects is completely wrong, because without the head he is only a stump of the whole body which is needed for life.

***25of which I became a minister according to the divine office which was given to me for you, to make the word of God fully known, 26the mystery hidden for ages and generations but now made manifest to his saints.***

Paul confidently states that through Christ God has made him a minister of the gospel

[9]Deut 18:15, 19. [10]Jn 5:46.

among the Gentiles, so that the mystery begun by the Lord might be completed by a good and faithful servant, something which was unknown to past ages.

[27]***To them God chose to make known how great among the Gentiles are the riches of the glory of this mystery, which is Christ in you, the hope of glory.*** [28]***Him we proclaim, warning every man and teaching every man in all wisdom, that we may present every man mature in Christ.***

Paul asserts that the mystery which was hidden in past ages has just been revealed, that is, shown forth in the time of the apostles, which was that the Gentiles too were to be admitted to the faith of Christ, who was promised to the Jews, without the circumcision of the flesh. Before the preaching of this faith it was commanded that Gentiles had to be circumcised if they wanted to accept the law, but now by the mercy of God they are commanded to be received in the faith just as they are. The Jews thought it was unworthy that Christ, in whom their hope lay, should make even Gentiles partakers of his glory.

Paul says that true wisdom lies in the Lord's teaching, once Christ is acknowledged. The apostle testifies that he himself takes great care to instruct everyone in that wisdom, so that he may present them to God as mature in the understanding of Christ, confessing the mystery of his birth from God and his birth from Mary and of all his work in heaven and on earth.

[29]***For this I toil, striving with all the energy which he mightily inspires within me.***

Paul says that he struggles for this purpose against unbelievers with the help of signs of power, so that unbelief may be conquered by such means and suppressed. Whoever dared to object to his words by employing some subtlety of diabolical cleverness would be covered with shame and forced to give way to [the evidence of his] power.

## Colossians 2

[1]***For I want you to know how greatly I strive for you, and for those at Laodicea, and for all who have not seen my face,*** [2]***that their hearts may be encouraged as they are knit together in love, to have all the riches of assured understanding and the knowledge of God's mystery, of Christ,*** [3]***in whom are hid all the treasures of wisdom and knowledge.***

Paul testifies that he is no less concerned for those whom he does not see in the flesh than for those to whom he preaches directly. He wanted them to know that they were loved by him, though he did not see them, just as much as those among whom he was [were loved]. His intention was to nourish their minds in love, so that they would be ready as a result of the letter to receive the knowledge of the sacrament of God in Christ, realizing that the riches of wisdom and knowledge were to be found when it was acknowledged that Christ was to be worshiped in the fullness of his deity.

The entire mystery of the sacrament of God is in Christ. He is the one in whom every creature must put his hope if he is not to perish, for all power is in him. Whoever knows him will also have a knowledge of everything else, whatever that may be, nor must anyone other than him be worshiped, because the strength of all powers is in him and they all derive from him. Although he is one, he can do all things, for which reason he is also called the head of all things, since all things are seen to exist through him. It is therefore quite right to say that all the treasures of wisdom and knowledge are hidden in him. The whole principle of knowledge of every creature, whether heavenly or earthly, must be in him who is the head of them all, whether angels, the sun, the moon, the stars or other things. Every skill of knowledge is in the Author of these things, so that the person who acknowledges him needs nothing else, neither wisdom nor power, because he has acknowledged the one in whom perfect power and perfect wisdom is found.

Whatever anyone might think that he can find somewhere else he will find fully and abundantly in him. Who was wiser than Solomon? Who was more discerning than Daniel? God gave them a wisdom beyond that of others in order to show unbelievers that he was the Author of wisdom. For example, Nebuchadnezzar admired Daniel for his wisdom and said to him: *Truly your God is the living God who reveals secret things.*[11] Unbelievers deny that all wisdom and knowledge can be found in Christ because they do not read about astrology in the Gospels or about geometry in the apostle, or about arithmetic or music in the Prophets. These things are disregarded by us since they do not lead to salvation but are more likely to put us in error and call us away from God. People who get involved in arguments about such things do not pay much attention to their souls. But is not true wisdom to recognize what is beneficial and ignore what is a hindrance? Whatever stops the soul from taking care of itself is a hindrance. It is therefore quite right to say that whoever has acknowledged Christ has found the treasury of wisdom and knowledge, because he has recognized what is useful to him.

***4I say this in order that no one may delude you with beguiling speech. 5For though I am absent in body, yet I am with you in spirit, rejoicing to see your good order and the firmness of your faith in Christ.***

Paul warns them not to let their minds be led astray by the arguments of wicked people and the cleverness of iniquity, because the wise of this world do their best to ensnare the souls of simple people by their trickery and by the subtleties of their arguments, so that by the logic of worldly things they may take them away from the hope that is in Christ. This is why the apostle says that he is there in the Spirit, so that they will keep their respect for him before their eyes and avoid such people.

If the spirit of Elisha the prophet saw the deception of Gehazi when he went to Naaman the Syrian in order to get things from him in Elisha's name which the prophet had not asked for, and when he arrived Naaman readily gave him more than he asked, how much more could the apostle see in the Spirit what he was saying?[12] There was more grace in the apostles than there was in the prophets. In order to make them more eager for the gospel tradition, Paul says that he rejoices in their way of life, for knowing how to please God has made them firmer in that having become worthy to see their usefulness grow, they have learned the meaning of their faith.

***6As therefore you received Christ Jesus the Lord, so live in him, 7rooted and built up in him and established in the faith, just as you were taught, abounding in thanksgiving.***

Paul warns and encourages them like this so that their devotion will not decrease or retreat from the faith which they had adopted and so that they will not be led astray by evil fables and accept Christ in a way different from what they had learned. There were many people going around trying to corrupt the faith and seduce the simple by preaching Christ with trickery and pretense. Paul warns them to avoid such people with great caution so that they may remain stable and firm on the foundation of the Trinity, giving abundant thanks for the mercy of God in the hope of their future rewards.

[11]Dan 2:47. [12]Cf. 2 Kings 5:26.

***[8]See to it that no one makes a prey of you by philosophy and empty deceit, according to human tradition, according to the elemental spirits of the universe, and not according to Christ. [9]For in him the whole fulness of deity dwells bodily,***

Paul speaks here of earthly philosophy, which those who want to be thought of as wise in this world are habitually seduced by. It is composed of arguments and the subtlety of hair-splitting arguments. It pretends to be investigating physical causes but has other things added to this, which are exhortations about leading a good life or documents put together to explain measures and numbers perhaps, or else the qualities and quantities of the elements. Whoever gets caught up in such disputations rarely manages to extricate himself from them. He is absorbed in probable causes and possible explanations, believing that there is nothing as true as what is observed and understood in the elements. Because what we have in front of us and see with our eyes seems attractive and desirable, it seduces those who think that spiritual reasoning is to be despised and ridiculed because they have no hope for the future. Bound to carnal logic, they attribute all power to the stars and do not think that anything heavy can possibly be taken up to heaven, or that anything light can come to earth. Rejecting the power and providence of God, they deny that any corporeal thing can be brought into being without some admixture of different things.

They know that it is possible to read in the ancient divine tomes of the Hebrews that many things were done by Moses which the human mind does not accept, and similarly in the new books there are things done by the Lord or through the apostles which human thought finds incredible. Paul calls this tradition or philosophy fallacious and inept, because it is not worked out according to the power of God but according to the weakness of the human mind, which restricts the power of God to the limits of its own knowledge, so that no one will ever believe that it is possible to do anything other than what carnal reason accepts. In this way they can employ individual parts of divinity in different ways of worship, so as to tie down the minds of the unskilled and prevent them from reaching up to the true God. This is why Paul tells them to beware of that tradition, because it worships the world and not the one God. It does not lead to Christ but away from him in whom the perfection of divinity is found. Everything which the Father has he gave to the Son, when he bore him in the fullness of divinity bodily. So because he is the head, his creation is the body. Whatever the heavenly creation may be thought to be, it must be believed that it is all fully in Christ, so that no one will decide to worship anyone else. If someone thinks there is anything great in something else, more will be found in Christ, because everything derives from him as members from the head. He, however, is always complete in himself.

***[10]and you have come to fulness of life in him, who is the head of all rule and authority.***

Paul indicates that more can be given to believers than can be found in the elements, because whoever is in Christ is full of the abundance of divinity which the elements do not have. Then too, the Holy Spirit dwells in believers, something which cannot be said of the elements, because to them it is unworthy and incongruous for the invisible to dwell in a visible substance or the incorporeal to dwell in what can be perceived. Therefore let those who worship such things hear and come to believe in Christ, so that they may become greater than those whom they now worship.

***[11]In him also you were circumcised with a circumcision made without hands, by putting off the body of flesh in the circumcision of Christ;***

***[12]and you were buried with him in baptism, in which you were also raised with him through faith in the working of God, who raised him from the dead.***

Those who renounce the worship of all human tradition and unite themselves to Christ in their heart are the ones who are circumcised in Christ. They are not circumcised in the flesh but in the Spirit, because they do not serve him in the flesh. That way they are converted from earthly to heavenly things, from the human to the divine, from error to truth, to their head and Author, to whom they are joined in love. Because they have been buried in baptism, they have also risen again through faith in God, whom they believed would raise them from the dead following the example of Christ. The old man is put off and the new one put on. He dies to sin so that he might live to righteousness; he renounces the elements so that he might be joined to Christ, holding the promise of his future resurrection by the example of the Savior who rose from the dead. Paul therefore warns them to persevere in renouncing the pomp and prestige of Satan, who tries to persuade people to worship the elements in order to take them away from God, wanting to make them partakers of his apostasy. But because he cannot persuade them by using his own name (since his name horrifies people), he tries to accomplish his will by using some other name.

***[13]And you, who were dead in trespasses and the uncircumcision of your flesh, God made alive together with him, having forgiven us all our trespasses, [14]having canceled the bond which stood against us with its legal demands; this he set aside, nailing it to the cross. [15]He disarmed the principalities and powers and made a public example of them, triumphing over them in him.***

[Paul reminds them of the blessing of God which he gave to the human race, so that those of the Gentiles who are grateful for this might give humble thanks to his majesty, who for his own sake bore the burden without their asking, so that they might remain devoted to him, knowing that once they were without the law of God, that is, in the uncircumcision of the flesh without hope. However, by the grace of God they were called by Christ to life, when he forgave the sins of their ancient error in baptism.][13]

[Having defeated the princes and powers by the death of Christ, God annulled the sentence which had been decreed against us by the sin of Adam, for just as the names of those who act well are in the book of life, so also the names of sinners are in the book of death. Therefore God annulled the sentence by which we were guilty of death both by our own sin and by that of our ancestor, having conquered death in Christ and triumphed over the devil and his puppets in his own flesh.][14]

[Since Christ was not only innocent but also righteous, although he was killed as if he were a sinner, God triumphed over them in the cross of Christ, for they were found to be godless and cruel toward someone who had

[13]An alternative version of this paragraph reads: "Paul says that the Gentiles were dead, first because they were unwilling to accept the law which was given in order to bear witness to the Creator and to condemn vices, and then because they were unworthy of life because of the ungodliness of their sins. He therefore separated them from the one God as being enemies of that God. The Jews continued to believe in the one God, and when Christ came they found out what the mystery of God was, which they had been waiting for in order to secure their justification, so that they might receive forgiveness by that which was taken away from them, since it is impossible to be sinless."

[14]An alternative version of this paragraph reads: "This is why, after talking about the Gentiles, Paul includes the Jews also, saying: *Forgiving all our sins*, thereby adding the universal to the particular, because he forgave everyone's sins. But because, as the Lord said: *The one who has been forgiven more must love more* [cf. Lk 7:42-43], Paul warns the Gentiles that they must consider the causes of their evil deeds and how great was the grace which they received from God in Christ, and give their entire devotion to the service of the one by whom they have been delivered from a very different punishment of death."

not sinned. Thus it came about that those who had become guilty did not dare contradict the Savior or stop him from leading souls out of hell and up to heaven. They insulted him because of the sin of the man Adam, only to find that they had sinned even more seriously by killing Christ. So the bond based on the sentence passed when Adam first sinned was annulled by the Word of God who said: *You are of the earth and will go back to the earth*[15] when he rose again from the dead. The devil had claimed the human race on the basis of that sentence, but when he was conquered and defeated he lost it again.][16]

[It was right to pass sentence on sin, but because Adam sinned when he was tempted by the subtlety of the devil, God ensured by the providence of the just judge that he is, that this devil, who held deceived man captive because of his bad behavior, should become guilty on account of the one he insulted, so that he would have no power to object to having that man taken away from him. God did this through Christ so that the one who began to reign because of sinful man should lose his power through the sinless man when he was openly conquered by God in Christ.][17]

So all sins have been forgiven, allowing them to rise from the dead. Since death comes from sin, the resurrection of the dead occurs when sin is taken away. This could hardly have happened if he had not nailed sin to the cross. Since the Savior by not sinning defeated the sin which held the human race bound, and moreover was killed by it even though he was innocent, he crucified sin. When sin was defeated it was said to have been put to death. The cross is not the death of the Savior but the death of sin. The innocent man who was killed in that way makes those who killed him guilty. By sin we understand the principalities and powers at whose urging the first Adam sinned. This term must be applied to its authors, whose death he indicated by the word "despoiling."[18] Their death occurred because they were defeated by the Savior and put to death when they were despoiled of the souls which they had held in captivity.

They became guilty because although they held the souls which had sinned by the authority given to them, they themselves were found to be even greater sinners because they killed the one who had overcome them by not sinning. Thus they were justly despoiled, as Paul said, publicly, that is, on the cross, which means that they were openly conquered by God in Christ. (If someone is openly defeated and the spoils are made public, he has been conquered!) The one who insulted others was then laid prostrate before everyone. The decree which Paul mentions is not what the pagans call fate, because they say that fate is not unfavorable to everyone, since some come out well and others not. Paul, however, says that this decree was unfavorable to everyone, for the sentence was against all human beings.

***16Therefore let no one pass judgment on you in questions of food and drink or with regard to a festival or a new moon or a sabbath. 17These are only a shadow of what is to come; but the substance belongs to Christ.***

[15]Gen 3:19. [16]An alternative version of this paragraph reads: "How has God pardoned us all our sins? Paul said: *By annulling the bond which was against us.* What this means he explains in what follows: *And he took it from our midst.* Thus he destroyed it by taking it from our midst. He took it from our midst, Paul said: *When he nailed it to the cross.* Paul explained that to nail something to the cross was to despoil the principalities and powers publicly and to triumph over them in Christ. It is obvious that these things are obscure and for that reason they must be expounded with appropriate care." [17]An alternative to this paragraph reads: "The apostle explains by the meaning of the different causes what the protection of God is. He recalls many things: that the human race came to receive pardon, that he not only forgave us our own sins but also took away the sin which came from the transgression of Adam, which he called a bond in the decrees. He also said that God would not allow us to rise from the dead unless he had taken this away from our midst. Otherwise those who came out of hell after receiving forgiveness would have been kept imprisoned there." [18]This is how Ambrosiaster read the word translated here as "making a public example."

Because all hope and confidence is in Christ, Paul told us not to subject ourselves to any superstition or law. Therefore those who proclaim, loudly or softly, anything which is irrelevant to the faith of Christ are to be rejected. The only one to be followed is the one by whom death has been overcome and the resurrection of the dead has been given to us. Some of the Jews are used to judging believers because they eat the things which were forbidden by Moses, although God made everything clean. The Jews are considered unworthy to eat such things which they are forbidden to do by their betters. They are also accustomed to upbraid us because we ignore their holidays or because we do not observe the beginnings of months which they call new moons, and above all because we do not keep the sabbath by passing it in idleness and feasting to excess, which is more likely to cause offence than to be a means of grace. All these things are the body of Christ, because they are the names of the elements by their effects. This is why it says in the Gospel: *The Son of Man is Lord also of the sabbath.*[19] All the things which were given by Moses derive from him and are a shadow or figure of what is to come, so that when the truth appears the shadow will cease. Just as the emperor's image has authority when he is absent but does not have it when he is present, so also these things were meant to be observed in their time, before the coming of Christ, but when he appeared they lost their authority. For which of the Lord's deputies rules when he is present? If the prefects' deputies are deprived [of their authority] when they are present, how much more must the servants of the Lord be subject to him when he is present.

***18Let no one disqualify you, insisting on self-abasement and worship of angels, taking his stand on visions, puffed up without reason by his sensuous mind, 19and not holding fast to the Head, from whom the whole body, nourished and knit together through its joints and ligaments, grows with a growth that is from God.***

What Paul warned the Colossians earlier on to beware of under the name of philosophy, he now teaches more clearly should be watched by those who pursue earthly wisdom and assert that whatever lies open and visible for investigation ought to be worshiped, thereby ensuring that souls will be held down under the firmament by the worship of these things and not allowed to climb up above it to the upper heavens and worship the God of all. What the enemy does is to hold down humbled souls on the earth when he knows all along that he has been cast out of heaven and will face the just judgment of God because he fakes religion, which is the greatest sacrilege. Those who observe the motion of the stars, which they call angels, not by divine authority but by human superstition, are puffed up. Their superstition leads to the loss of everything, because they do not want to hold the faith of Christ who is the Creator and Lord of all. All things derive from him, which is why they are called his body if they acknowledge him. When they are converted they are built up again. Integrated by his faith, with the help of the gospel, they are all united like members of a body in the love of Christ, so as to give God the increase. When those who have turned away from him in their error and diminished the supply of his riches by denying that they were his go back to God, they give God an increase, because after having been lost they are won back for him. Paul says all this about the Jews because they too labor under the elements, though not the way the pagans do.

***20If with Christ you died to the elemental spirits of the universe, why do you live as if you***

[19]Mt 12:8.

***still belonged to the world? Why do you submit to regulations,***

Everyone who is baptized in Christ dies to the world. He renounces all the errors of superstition and follows the faith of Christ alone. Taking away what belongs to natural justice, the discipline given by God is left, by which we live to God through the hope which is in Christ. He dies to the things to which he had been subject by error, because he denies that those whom they had presumed existed are really there. So it is that because of the hatred of the one who renounces these things, the person and the worship of the elements are said to be dead to one another. When Paul mentions the world he means the error of the flesh, for every visible thing is included in the term "flesh." This is why the apostle John says: *Do not love this world or the things which are in this world,*[20] that is, we should love neither the elements by which the world is formed, nor the errors which human tradition has invented, but only Christ who died for us in order to unite us who were lost to his body. Therefore those who are buried together with Christ have died to the elements and no longer pay any attention to them because they have learned to cling to things above, which can give them eternal life. These elements give no life in the present and stand in the way of receiving future blessings. If anyone has doubts about some things after being baptized and thinks that some of the ancient ways ought to be venerated, he shows that he is living for the elements which he thinks ought to be worshiped or is not sure ought to be condemned. He will remain within the bounds of this world, cut off from God, because someone who is still clothed in the old man will not be able to pass carnal things by.

21***"Do not handle, Do not taste, Do not touch"***
22***(referring to things which all perish as they are used), according to human precepts and doctrines?***

Paul forbids them from worshiping, agreeing to or thinking about anything out of a hope of earthly rewards, because what they promise is corruptible. The habit of worshiping them leads to death, because their precepts and doctrines are not of God but of human beings, in whom all hope is vain. Human error has invented these things in opposition to the Creator. It prohibits the faith of the one God and introduces the superstition of many gods instead.

23***These have indeed an appearance of wisdom in promoting rigor of devotion and self-abasement and severity to the body, but they are of no value in checking the indulgence of the flesh.***

These people think they have an understanding of wisdom because they give the name of religion to human tradition and call it religion when it is sacrilege, because whatever goes against the Author has been invented by a sacrilegious mind. Therefore he invents a name so that he can claim that false things are true and bring down human minds to earth so that they cannot rise to higher things. By worshiping earthly things they turn away from the heavenly things above and stand in the way of the body whose head is Christ according to the design of primeval reason. Weighed down like this, they will not be able to go up and be united to their head, so that being restored to him they might become honored, after having been cut off from the body at the beginning and giving themselves over completely to the world, so as to fulfill the desire of the flesh. Human tradition is the bewitcher of the carnal mind, because it says that what the wisdom of the

[20]1 Jn 2:15.

flesh has handed down is all that is necessary. It appears to have the understanding of wisdom according to the flesh because all corporal birth is from the elements. Therefore they say that it is not inappropriate to bow down to them because it is by them that the human race is governed. It ought therefore to submit to them because it sees that they are the brightest things in this world, nor should it go in search of spiritual things, because, as they say, it has been permitted to make use of these guides alone, and for that reason they ignore their Author.

## Colossians 3

***1If then you have been raised with Christ, seek the things that are above, where Christ is, seated at the right hand of God.***

Paul asserts that those who think about the heavenly places where Christ is seated, where God the Father has given his right hand to the Son so that he may reign and judge (for no judge sits on the left), have risen with Christ in baptism. The resurrection occurs in two stages. First the mind rises from the earth to the heavens and then when it is captured by Christ it rises from the dead with its [new] body.

***2Set your minds on things that are above, not on things that are on earth.***

Paul encourages us to seek the habitations of the heavenly powers which are eternal by separating ourselves from everything which is in the firmament or under the firmament. Whoever has busied himself with these superstitions has burdened himself with an impediment, because he will not be able to get beyond the things to which he bows himself as if they were his lords.

***3For you have died, and your life is hid with Christ in God.***

In worldly terms, Christ appears to be dead and so do his disciples, even though it is clear that he is alive and with them all. The life of Christ and of those who belong to him in God is hidden from the carnal and worldly beyond the world in his heavenly kingdom, where they all live.

***4When Christ who is our life appears, then you also will appear with him in glory.***

Christ is our life, for we read in the Acts of the Apostles that he is the author of life,[21] whom unbelievers do not believe will be their future judge. When he comes in the power of heaven and is seen to be what nobody believed him to be, then those who did believe in him will appear with him and it will be shown to all unbelief[22] that he lives with them in glory. This consolation produces confidence in the hope that if we lay everything else aside and follow Christ we have the assurance of future life.

***5Put to death therefore what is earthly in you: fornication, impurity, passion, evil desire, and covetousness, which is idolatry.***

In the epistle to the Romans Paul compares all sins taken together to a body,[23] which is why now he describes particular transgressions as members of that body, so that after they have received and kept the gospel message about the fullness of the Savior they may devote their efforts to leading a good life by abstaining from every wickedness and evil desire, so as not to lose the fruit of their experience of God. It is no good at all if you know the truth but then fail to live it out in your subsequent actions. This is why the Lord said elsewhere: *Whoever knows the will of his Lord and does not obey it*

[21]Acts 3:15. [22]I.e., *unbelievers*. [23]Cf. Rom 6:6.

*shall be severely beaten.*[24] He compared greed to idolatry, in order to show that there was nothing worse. By using one word he described two terrible and godless things which he warned them to avoid at all costs. The first and most serious of these is the crime of idolatry. What could be more pernicious or destructive than to attribute the name of God's honor to wood, stones or other metals to the injury of God the Creator, when they themselves would never allow a servant to be called by the name of his master, even though it is not his nature but only his social condition which has subjected him to servitude? The other crime is greed, which is equal in wickedness but different in name.

This is why Paul said to Timothy: *Greed is the root of all evil.*[25] It is capable of every sin, being always hungry and always thirsty because it is impossible to satisfy the desire of its lust. Paul therefore understandably lumps both evils together under one name. They amount to the same thing because idolatry tries to take glory away from the one God and deprive him of what is peculiar to him, that is, having the name of deity which is worthy of him alone. So also greed reaches into the things of God, and one person tries as hard as he can to appropriate the creation for himself when God has made it for everyone. This is why God said through the prophet: *The gold is mine and the silver is mine.*[26] Both things are hostile to God, for both deny God what belongs to him.

***6On account of these the wrath of God is coming.***

Paul says that the judgment of God will come because of the above-mentioned evils, and that he will be vindicated in those who prefer to follow what is forbidden because of their contempt for God and the law.

***7In these you once walked, when you lived in them.***

Paul is not silent about what a great benefit the grace of God through Christ has brought to them. They ought to rejoice at having escaped his wrath, which will soon come on unbelievers the world over, and they should show themselves to be the kind of people who are equal to the precepts of the one by whom they have been delivered from the second death.

***8But now put them all away: anger, wrath, malice, slander, and foul talk from your mouth. 9Do not lie to one another, seeing that you have put off the old nature with its practices 10and have put on the new nature, which is being renewed in knowledge after the image of its creator. 11Here there cannot be Greek and Jew, circumcised and uncircumcised, barbarian, Scythian, slave, free man, but Christ is all, and in all.***

Now Paul warns them against things which appear to be minor sins, in case, after having just ordered them to put to death sins which might appear to be more serious, they might think that they can commit these or at least not avoid them because of any danger. Having put off the old man, that is, avoiding both words and deeds which are wicked and corrupt, they have been made new in Christ by acknowledging the truth which was once hidden but which has now been revealed to believers by the new law, so that they might become like the image of him who created them.

This image is to be understood as leading a good life, as Paul says in 1 Corinthians: *Just as we have borne the image of the man of earth, so we shall bear the image of him who is from heaven.*[27] He is himself the Creator of the human race, whose image he orders us to bear in holiness and good works, which derive from a

[24]Lk 12:47. [25]1 Tim 6:10. [26]Hag 2:8. [27]1 Cor 15:49.

knowledge of the Son of God. No one can have a good and clean life unless he has something he can show to the one from whom he can expect, if not a reward, then certainly at least praise.

With God we can hope for both praise and a reward, because God's righteousness, which has conquered the sins of the flesh, does not allow a person merely to be crowned. No one is excluded from this knowledge as being unworthy, as if he did not deserve to come to the faith of Christ. All who come are made one. What they were is wiped out, and what they have started to become is written down, so that because they are all of one faith they will also be of one merit. Those whom faith unites cannot be separated merely because they are different by nature, race or status. Christ is all and in all of them. Since they are all members of him, Christ is all, and since their common confession is of their hope in him, Christ is in all. In this way all are his body, so that their confession and their nature will coincide. This image, which Paul says is created by knowing the Savior, is one thing, and the image according to which the first man was made is another. This image is also in women who acknowledge the one who created them and who conform to his will by abstaining from a wicked life and from evil behavior. The other image is found in the man alone, as Paul says in 1 Corinthians: *The man should not cover his head because he is the image and glory of God.*[28] If the woman was not supposed to cover her head either, then she would also be the image of God. It says in Genesis: *And God made man, in the image of God made he him.*[29] Just as God is one, so the man made from him was one, so that just as all things come from the one God, so the entire human race throughout the world comes from the one man. Thus the One made one to have the image of his unity, and in man and woman there is a likeness of the mystery of the Father and the Son.

Nevertheless, Paul distinguished the barbarian from the Scythian, just as he distinguished the slave from the free man, not in Christ, in whom all are one, but in savageness of behavior and barbarity of nation. He wanted it to be understood that the Scythians were worse than barbarians before their conversion, although there are Greek books which testify to their righteousness when they followed the guidance of nature, because they regarded theft as a very serious sin. Paul says that the Greeks had to discover the paths of righteousness with great effort and teaching, but praises the Scythians for having picked it up naturally. However, since everything degenerates, later on they became more blameworthy than they had been praiseworthy before. Their women started to behave like men, and in ancient times they were called Amazons, who subdued the whole of Asia in a way which defied nature. For this reason, the men became rabid in the way that dogs are, inhuman, bestial and uncouth more than the barbarians were, so changed that they were plunged into eating human flesh. How can we be surprised, since even the Romans were once very different from what they are now. For the sake of their chastity, the use of wine was unknown to their women, just as the use of water is unknown to them now. The authority of discipline was so effective that the vessel subject to it could not do what it wanted to.

***[12]Put on then, as God's chosen ones, holy and beloved, compassion, kindness, lowliness, meekness, and patience, [13]forbearing one another and, if one has a complaint against another, forgiving each other; as the Lord has forgiven you, so you also must forgive.***

Paul encourages them to do what will gain them merit with God if they want to gain

[28]1 Cor 11:7. [29]Gen 1:27.

something. Fear makes us abstain from sin, for a person is afraid that if he does wrong he will be subjected to punishment. What Paul now tells them to do are things which pertain to the advancement of merit, because they are done freely and not under compulsion. Therefore, whoever abstains from unlawful things has praise, but the one who moderates his use of lawful things has both praise and reward.

***14And above all these put on love, which binds everything together in perfect harmony. 15And let the peace of Christ rule in your hearts, to which indeed you were called in the one body. And be thankful.***

Paul encourages the Colossians to pursue love above all because it is greater than anything else. If they do that then everything which he has just ordered them to observe will bring them closer to their reward, if they walk the way of the law under the guidance of love. Whoever does something out of love acts with his whole mind. There is no hypocrisy or pretense in love. This is why the apostle John said: *There is no fear in love.*[30] The person who is afraid is not perfect. *Perfect love casts out fear.* This is why the Lord said that he would rather be loved than feared. It is this which binds us together, this which makes us all one body, this which has true peace which it keeps with a pure heart. It is possible to speak peace and not have love, but love always brings peace with it.

***16Let the word of Christ dwell in you richly, teach and admonish one another in all wisdom, and sing psalms and hymns and spiritual songs with thankfulness in your hearts to God.***

Paul tells them always to meditate on what speaks of Christ, always to have in their heart what returns thanks to God the Father, so that the voice of singing may worship him, the psalm praise him, and the hymn extol him. And since he is the only one who sees the secrets of the mind and a reward is hoped for from him, Paul ordered them to sing to him in their hearts so that they would not be influenced by the favor of men and lose their gains.

***17And whatever you do, in word or deed, do everything in the name of the Lord Jesus, giving thanks to God the Father through him.***

Paul has already ordered us to praise God in our hearts and return thanks to him, and so now he encourages us to praise and exalt the name of the Lord Jesus both in word and in deed in every aspect of our lives, because when our words lack bitterness and our deeds are good, the Lord Jesus is magnified, and with him in control his disciples are blameless. Thus we give true thanks to God through him if we keep the way of his commandments.

***18Wives, be subject to your husbands, as is fitting in the Lord.***

Paul tells women to be subject to their husbands in the same way that God told the woman elsewhere: *Your desire shall be for your husband and he will rule over you,*[31] and by this rule and discipline she is to fear her husband as the Lord from whom she derives her being.

***19Husbands, love your wives, and do not be harsh with them.***

Paul softens the rigor of the law for men, so that no one will overdo the power which he exercises over his wife. The husband must respect and love her, because the woman is his flesh. If he humiliates her too much he will bring out the exact opposite in her.

[30]1 Jn 4:18. [31]Gen 3:16.

***[20]Children, obey your parents in everything, for this pleases the Lord.***

It is not possible to please God except by being righteous and godly. Children can attract God's favor if they give due honor to their parents, are ready to obey them and slow to ignore them, knowing that parents never do anything deliberately to harm their children.

***[21]Fathers, do not provoke your children, lest they become discouraged.***

Paul tells fathers to be gentle with their children so that they will not be pressured by them into sinning against them and offending God, when they do not want to. Anger is not a thoughtful thing, and sometimes the person who gets angry does not spare himself. Fathers should remember that they were once sons and sons should consider that they will one day be fathers, so that by the balanced assessment of both parties, sons should be obedient and fathers should be gentle.

***[22]Slaves, obey in everything those who are your earthly masters, not with eye service, as men-pleasers, but in singleness of heart, fearing the Lord.***

Since it is impossible to serve God other than with a pure heart (for God sees the secrets of the heart), Paul tells us that we must serve other people in the same way. Whoever serves superficially does something quite different in secret, but whoever serves with the mind is the same on the outside as he is on the inside. Therefore if someone is faithful in this service he will earn the Lord's favor, because he said: *Whoever is faithful in small things is faithful in large ones also.*[32] If someone is not faithful to the one who vindicates him now, how will he be faithful to him whom he hears will be his judge after death? For this reason, Paul wants slaves to be fair and obedient to their earthly lord, so that they may be faithful and obedient in the things of God also. If a slave is loyal in this life, when he knows that his only rewards will be perishable ones, how much readier will he be in his devotion to God, whom he knows will give immortal rewards to those who are faithful to him.

***[23]Whatever your task, work heartily, as serving the Lord and not men, [24]knowing that from the Lord you will receive the inheritance as your reward; you are serving the Lord Christ. [25]For the wrongdoer will be paid back for the wrong he has done, and there is no partiality.***

In order to make them ready for service and in faith, Paul promises them that they will receive a reward for their good works from God in Christ's kingdom. For this to be tried and accepted, Paul wants them to obey [whomever] as if he were the Lord from whom they are waiting for their reward, or else punishment if they have done wrong. Whoever has done wrong has not only offended man but also God, if he has shown contempt for his earthly master by admitting to having cheated him. But if he has done well, the slave of man will not be looked down upon by God, but will be rewarded as if he were free among men, because he is a slave of Christ, which is a name of honor.

## Colossians 4

***[1]Masters, treat your slaves justly and fairly, knowing that you also have a Master in heaven.***

In order to prevent secular masters from exalting themselves in their pride by pulling

[32]Lk 16:10.

rank, Paul restrains and restricts their minds by telling them to consider what the human race is like and that God did not create slaves and freemen, but made everyone free-born. However, by the wickedness of the world it came about that when one group invaded the territory of another it took free people captive. It was because they were captured by hand that the ancients referred to them as "mancipates." This is how the present state of affairs came into being, for some were redeemed from captivity but others remained slaves. With God, however, a slave is someone who has sinned. Ham became a slave because of his sin.[33] The ancients agreed with this sentence to the extent that they said that all wise men are free and all stupid ones are slaves. This is because the wise man avoids sin and remains free because he does what is right, but a slave subjects himself to sin through the unwise behavior of his foolishness. This is why Ham was called a slave, because he stupidly laughed at his father's nakedness. Paul shows these masters that they are not really masters, but only appear that way, because they are masters of bodies but not of minds. The only Lord and Author of things is the invisible God who controls both bodies and minds. They should think about this and demand from their servants only that just service which they want their common Lord to demand from them. They do not serve God, whom they do not deny has power over everything and whose daily gifts are exhibited for human use by the agency of creation, in the right way, if they demand such heavy service from their fellows—I do not say from their brethren—that they cannot bear it. Such people do not remember that, like it or not, they are servants too, and you can see what they are worth.

***[2]Continue steadfastly in prayer, being watchful in it with thanksgiving; [3]and pray for us also, that God may open to us a door for the word, to declare the mystery of Christ, on account of which I am in prison, [4]that I may make it clear, as I ought to speak.***

Paul shows that those who are wise in the mysteries of the Lord Christ and careful to avoid the evils of sin continue steadfastly in prayer, in order to increase the merits which are lacking because of the temptations of the adversary. He holds these people in such high regard that he thinks that they can help him by their prayers to sow the seeds of the gospel, which he had received a commission to declare.

***[5]Conduct yourselves wisely toward outsiders, making the most of the time. [6]Let your speech always be gracious, seasoned with salt, so that you may know how you ought to answer every one.***

Since we have to live among unbelievers and transact business with them in the course of daily life, Paul warns us to behave wisely so as not to scandalize the Gentiles, so that they will not find occasion to blaspheme because of us and be encouraged to persecute [the church]. What need is there to talk to someone if you know that he is intractable and has an obstinate mind, ready to criticize you? Paul therefore tells us that we should discuss religion at the right time and place and in great humility, and keep quiet if one of these people is shouting at us in public. We should behave one way toward the powerful, another way toward the middle class, another way toward those lower down the social scale, and yet another way to those who are gentle and another way to those who are irritable. Letting them be is redeeming the time, because if you give way to someone who attacks the Lord's words or who rages because he is free to do so, you turn the insults of this unhappy experience into

[33]Cf. Gen 9:25.

gain. If the head, that is the king, agrees with the body, there is freedom to speak the words of God with gentleness, so that people may be challenged to do good. But when it comes to those who argue and object to our beliefs it is always best to let them be, for you win when you give way.

***7Tychicus will tell you all about my affairs; he is a beloved brother and faithful minister and fellow servant in the Lord. 8I have sent him to you for this very purpose, that you may know how we are and that he may encourage your hearts, 9and with him Onesimus, the faithful and beloved brother, who is one of yourselves. They will tell you of everything that has taken place here.***

Paul says that he sent the brethren so that everyone could find out what each other was doing. Although earlier on he had said that he was present with them in spirit and could see what they were doing, he still needed intermediaries. A person pays more attention when he knows that someone is coming to see him in order to find out what is going on in his life. He will be more afraid if he imagines that he is being watched. Although God sees everything and we know that he knows everything, because we do not see that he sees us, we do things which go against his will.

***10Aristarchus my fellow prisoner greets you, and Mark the cousin of Barnabas (concerning whom you have received instructions—if he comes to you, receive him), 11and Jesus who is called Justus. These are the only men of the circumcision among my fellow workers for the kingdom of God, and they have been a comfort to me.***

This Aristarchus appears as a man of good life and merit, who because of his devotion to the Lord is mentioned as the apostle's colleague and fellow worker. In commending Mark, Paul explains who he is by saying that he is to be held in honor as the cousin of Barnabas, who is a praiseworthy man. He also adds Jesus, whom he says goes by the name Justus. He bears testimony only to them because they were assistants drawn from the circumcision who agreed with him and shared his conviction that they should no longer preach that it was necessary to be circumcised. This is why he calls them fellow workers in the kingdom of God. It is not spiritual to preach the need to practice circumcision and to keep the sabbath and new moons, but carnal.

***12Epaphras, who is one of yourselves, a servant of Christ Jesus, greets you, always remembering you earnestly in his prayers, that you may stand mature and fully assured in all the will of God.***

Paul makes his letter more meaningful to the Colossians by mentioning someone who is one of them. Paul testifies that he is always concerned to pray for their welfare and shows that this man, who was a fellow citizen of theirs and held in the highest esteem by everyone, shared in his devotion for their advancement.

***13For I bear him witness that he has worked hard for you and for those in Laodicea and in Hierapolis.***

In order to make them pay more attention to their own salvation, Paul shows them how much other people are concerned for them. A person will be shamed into paying more attention when he realizes that someone else is concerned for his welfare.

***14Luke the beloved physician and Demas greet you.***

Luke was clearly very dear to the apostle because he abandoned everything and always followed him. He is also credited with having written the Gospel and the Acts of the Apostles.

***[15]Give my greetings to the brethren at Laodicea, and to Nympha and the church in her house.***

Since Paul was just as concerned for those who were at Laodicea, in his letter to the Colossians he asked for the Laodiceans to be greeted as well. He had a particular affection for Nympha, whose household he mentions. It seems that she was so devout that her entire household was marked by the sign of the cross.[34]

***[16]And when this letter has been read among you, have it read also in the church of the Laodiceans; and see that you read also the letter from Laodicea.***

Since the apostle's instructions were universally applicable and his letters were written for the benefit of everyone, he directed that this letter should also be read to the Laodiceans so that they might learn from it what they should be doing. He also wanted the Colossians to read their letter, for the same reason.

***[17]And say to Archippus, "See that you fulfil the ministry which you have received in the Lord."***

Paul uses the church members as a means of telling their leader to be concerned about their faith. It was because the letter was directed only to the church members that it was not sent to the pastor but to the church. Archippus took over the government of their church after Epaphras, who had started it.

***[18]I, Paul, write this greeting with my own hand. Remember my fetters. Grace be with you.***

Paul signs the letter in his own hand in order to confirm it and reminds the Colossians to remember the sufferings which he was enduring for the salvation of the Gentiles. He wanted them to behave in a way which would not make it hard for him to suffer injury for their sake.

[34]This was a way of saying that they were all Christians.

# AMBROSIASTER

## *Commentary on 1 Thessalonians*

### Preface

In order to encourage others to grow in their faith by following the example of these people, that is, the Thessalonians, Paul praises them because they have remained faithful to the grace which they have received, and have matured in their quest for their reward by making the better choice. As a result, they were heading toward perfection themselves, and because of their virtues, the dignity which they had aimed for was stirring others up too. The spirit of faith which they had imbibed was so strong that the hope of future reward was enough to make them willing to suffer the persecutions launched against them by their fellow citizens of Macedonia because of the name of Christ. Therefore, in order to demonstrate by letter both their merit and his pleasure at their progress, he writes to them as follows.

### 1 Thessalonians 1

***1Paul, Silvanus, and Timothy,***
***To the church of the Thessalonians in God the Father and the Lord Jesus Christ:***
***Grace to you and peace.***

The letter is sent in the name of three bishops, but the style and content are those of the apostle alone. Because they are all rejoicing together at their progress, they agreed to write the letter to the congregation in praise of God the Father and the Lord Jesus Christ, wishing them grace and peace.

***2We give thanks to God always for you all, constantly mentioning you in our prayers,***
***3remembering before our God and Father your work of faith and labor of love and steadfastness of hope in our Lord Jesus Christ.***

Since all good things come from God, they first offer thanks for their progress, because God has been pleased not only to give his gift to people who were still in bondage to sin, but also to adopt them as his children, at the same time helping them to put up with all suffering so that they might become worthier. For this reason the authors say that they remember the people in their prayers because they have grown in the work of faith more than other churches and by God's grace were perfecting the work which they had eagerly begun. In the presence of God, they were full of love, patience and hope in the coming of the Lord, who was pleased to send his Son to become a man for the salvation of the human race. God is pleased if we are growing in Christ.

***4For we know, brethren beloved by God, that he has chosen you; 5for our gospel came to you not only in word, but also in power and in the Holy Spirit and with full conviction. You know what kind of men we proved to be among you for your sake.***

The authors mean that they were humble when they were among them in order to set them an example of gentleness. It was not that they were lacking in the great miracles which would encourage them to have faith, for the power of signs and wonders furthered the might of gospel teaching, not in some fantasy but in the fullness of truth. Help was available to meet every need, but superabundant grace was revealed in their teaching, in their behavior and in the healing of the sick. As a result, the perfect work of the Holy Spirit appeared in the churches of the Thessalonians, who saw that they were in no way inferior to the churches of the Jews and rejoiced in the gift of God, who had been pleased to grant them a share in the promise of Abraham.

***6And you became imitators of us and of the Lord, for you received the word in much affliction, with joy inspired by the Holy Spirit; 7so that you became an example to all the believers in Macedonia and in Achaia.***

Those who desired the faith suffered rebuke and insults from their fellow citizens, but they put up with them because they were confident of their future reward. This is why they are called imitators of the apostles and of the Lord himself, because the Lord suffered the same things from the Jews, and the apostles who followed the faith of God suffered persecutions, rejoicing that *they were found worthy to suffer dishonor for the name of the Lord,*[1] knowing that there would be great rewards promised to them for that.

A servant proves himself when he offends his Lord's enemies for his sake. Remembering this, they rejoiced in the hope of the promise when they were suffering. This is a great encouragement to go on [in the faith], when Paul says that they have been made like Christ and the apostle so as to set an example to other believers in those parts, among whom their reputation was circulating.

***8For not only has the word of the Lord sounded forth from you in Macedonia and Achaia, but your faith in God has gone forth everywhere, so that we need not say anything.***

This is the same thing that Paul said to the Romans when he wrote: *For your faith is proclaimed in all the world.*[2] But here there is more to it, because it was not just their faith but the work of their faith which was reaching everywhere.

***9For they themselves report concerning us what a welcome we had among you, and how you turned to God from idols, to serve a living and true God, 10and to wait for his Son from heaven, whom he raised from the dead, Jesus who delivers us from the wrath to come.***

The authors say that the report of the welcome they received and of the people's conversion when the gospel was preached had spread so widely that there was no need for them to add anything. It is superfluous to talk about things that are already well known. The word had reached everyone on the network [of churches], so that they were telling others with what devotion the Thessalonians had received the apostles and that they had been more than ready to do everything they had heard from them, abandoning dead gods and waiting for the [coming of] Christ from heaven. They had heard that for the sake of human salvation he had died and risen again, overcoming death, and that he had been taken up into heaven in a ministering cloud, much to the consternation of the wise of this world, who, taking into consideration how heavy the nature of the flesh of earthly beings is, think that there is no way that it can be lifted up into heaven. This was the work of the Holy Spirit who puts the wise of this world to shame.

## 1 Thessalonians 2

***1For you yourselves know, brethren, that our visit to you was not in vain; 2but though we had already suffered and been shamefully***

[1]Acts 5:41. [2]Rom 1:8.

***treated at Philippi, as you know, we had courage in our God to declare to you the gospel of God in the face of great opposition.***

The persecution which Paul now mentions is one which he suffered along with Silas in Philippi on account of the Pythonic spirit which he had cast out of the girl, something which is explained elsewhere.[3] Far from giving in to such pressure, Paul was strengthened in his resolve to preach, and in the hope of his promised reward he was not afraid to say that the Thessalonians should rejoice in the certainty of their future reward too. He says that it is the sign of a devout and faithful preacher not to be afraid to preach the Word of God under pressure, indicating thereby that whoever is afraid to preach because of current fears is useless. The person who is sure of the promised hope will not give in, [but will persevere] so that he may receive the crown.

***3For our appeal does not spring from error or uncleanness, nor is it made with guile; 4but just as we have been approved by God to be entrusted with the gospel, so we speak, not to please men, but to please God who tests our hearts.***

Paul says this on account of the false apostles who were preaching by deceit and fraud, and not because they were sent, in order to lead the Gentiles astray and subject them to the law of works. He himself demonstrates in many different ways that he has been chosen and sent to preach. Under pressure his resolve was strengthened and his behavior was irreproachable. The signs accompanied him so that there would be nothing in him which would appear to be unworthy of God. Some people preached Christ for the sake of gain, seeking the approval of others. However, they were less successful in making their case because they lacked authority and were unable to withstand tribulation, since their works did not come from the heart but were deceitful. Everyone who does anything without hope succumbs to tribulation when it arises.

***5For we never used either words of flattery, as you know, or a cloak for greed, as God is witness;***

Now Paul explains what he mentioned earlier, when he said *Not as a cloak for greed.* He calls God as his witness that he was doing this from the heart and not out of hypocrisy, pretending to reject small things in the hope that more might be offered him. This struck a chord with them because they knew and were convinced that he had not been adulated by anyone. The false apostles, however, chose to present themselves as a model of greed, so that on occasions when they saw the true apostles accepting everything offered to them, they might rob the simpler people without scruple.

***6nor did we seek glory from men, whether from you or from others, though we might have made demands as apostles of Christ. 7But we were gentle among you, like a nurse taking care of her children.***

Paul underlines the case of the false apostles in order to say that he is not at all like them, even though he could have demanded their assistance in suppressing those who had neither ability nor shame, yet who demanded honor for themselves, wanting themselves and not the doctrine of God to be promoted. The apostle, however, was looking for glory not in this world but in the next, and made himself humble so that the preaching of God might be exalted.

***8So, being affectionately desirous of you, we***

[3]Cf. Acts 16:16-24.

***were ready to share with you not only the gospel of God but also our own selves, because you had become very dear to us.***

Paul shows that he has such great love for the Thessalonians that he wants it to be seen not only in words but in deeds, because words can be deceptive and he is honest. Stirred up by these exhortations, the people would love the apostle with their whole mind.

***9For you remember our labor and toil, brethren; we worked night and day, that we might not burden any of you, while we preached to you the gospel of God.***

This is what it says in the Acts of the Apostles: *These hands ministered to my necessities and to those who were with me.*[4] This is also why Paul said in another letter: *He who does not work shall not eat.*[5] He said this against the false apostles, who ate without doing anything and pretended to be preachers. So in order to set an example as to how the Christian life should be lived, and to expose frauds, Paul concentrated on human labor, thereby attacking the false apostles, particularly because those who are busy working have no time for wicked thoughts. They occupy their minds [with other things] and refrain from evil.

***10You are witnesses, and God also, how holy and righteous and blameless was our behavior to you believers; 11for you know how, like a father with his children, we exhorted each one of you and encouraged you and charged you 12to lead a life worthy of God, who calls you into his own kingdom and glory.***

These things are clear. Paul reminds them of how they had believed when he preached to them, what kind of man they knew him to be and what commands he had given them, so that they might be worthy of God who has called them from earth to heaven in order to bring them happiness.

***13And we also thank God constantly for this, that when you received the word of God which you heard from us, you accepted it not as the word of men but as what it really is, the word of God, which is at work in you believers.***

They give thanks to God who has opened the minds of the Thessalonians to receive his gospel. It is the preachers' glory when their hearers believe without difficulty. They received the word with such devotion that they proved that they had understood that it was God's teaching.

***14For you, brethren, became imitators of the churches of God in Christ Jesus which are in Judea; for you suffered the same things from your own countrymen as they did from the Jews, 15who killed both the Lord Jesus and the prophets, and drove us out, and displease God and oppose all men 16by hindering us from speaking to the Gentiles that they may be saved—so as always to fill up the measure of their sins. But God's wrath has come upon them at last!***

The complaint here is about those unbelieving Jews who were hostile not only to their own salvation but also to that of others, because they tried to stop them from believing and being saved. They were parricides from the beginning. Those who did not spare their fellow servants and their masters ought at least to have spared the Lord who is common to us all, but they did not do so, and so their sins had increased to the point where there was no hope that they would ever deserve to receive mercy. Paul says that the Thessalonians have suffered the same things at the hands of their

4Acts 20:34. 5 2 Thess 3:10.

fellow citizens in imitation of the suffering of the saints and of the Lord Jesus Christ, the authors of whose death he claims were the Jews. He also points out what great glory those who suffer for the name of Christ are worthy of, and how vengeance is being prepared for these dreadful unbelievers.

***17But since we were bereft of you, brethren, for a short time, in person not in heart, we endeavored the more eagerly and with great desire to see you face to face; 18because we wanted to come to you—I, Paul, again and again—but Satan hindered us.***

The authors of the letter say that they are cut off from the Thessalonians in body but not in mind, for love is not divided or separated, but they say that they want to see them face to face in order to be able to instruct them better. In the things of God they were missing certain things which they needed in order to understand what could be said. A whole day was not long enough to write down what could be explained to them verbally in an hour, not to speak of the secret mysteries of our religion which cannot easily be published because of the scandal they might cause, since not everything can be said to everyone. Everything must be geared to the capacity of the hearers—one thing for the simple and another for the well grounded. This is why Paul's bodily presence was required, for in that way the truth of love would be perfected. Even though love is not divided, bodily absence makes the heart grow fonder. When they met, the will of their minds would be expressed by hugs and kisses. Paul asserts that Satan has prevented all this from happening. He was putting his restraining hands on the apostles in order to prevent the message of truth from being spread to other people. He was also inflaming the minds of unbelievers so that they might stop the apostles by beating and imprisoning them so that they could not preach the Word of God. As the elders of the Jews had said to the apostles: *Have we not strictly told you not to preach to anyone in this name (of Jesus)?*[6] But because what is not of God cannot last, Satan's hindrances will disappear.

***19For what is our hope or joy or crown of boasting before our Lord Jesus at his coming? Is it not you? 20For you are our glory and joy.***

It is clear that the perfection of the disciples is the master's joy and crown. They are the ones who will bring forth the fruits of their labors; the master's fruit is an obedient disciple, who eats the result of his labor as long as the disciple's good behavior brings credit on his master. The labor of a disciple in good works gives a crown to his master when Christ comes to judge.

## 1 Thessalonians 3

***1Therefore when we could bear it no longer, we were willing to be left behind at Athens alone, 2and we sent Timothy, our brother and God's servant in the gospel of Christ, to establish you in your faith and to exhort you, 3that no one be moved by these afflictions. You yourselves know that this is to be our lot. 4For when we were with you, we told you beforehand that we were to suffer affliction; just as it has come to pass, and as you know.***

Paul has expressed the reasons for his abovementioned desire. They wanted to go to be with them in order to strengthen their minds so that no one there would be scandalized by the sufferings of the apostles. Even those who did such great miracles were sometimes laid low to the point where they were subjected to beatings and imprisonment. He says that

[6]Acts 5:28.

he has already sent Timothy, a most excellent teacher, to explain all this and to show that merits multiply to Christians if they give thanks for having suffered for the name of the Lord, from whom they await a reward for this. At the same time they were to pray to God and ask him to keep them firm [in their faith]. They preached that they would suffer persecution in order to justify those who claimed that if they knew what was coming they could run away and avoid such injuries, but because there was great hope tied up in them, they ought to be willing to suffer whatever was inflicted upon them.

***5For this reason, when I could bear it no longer, I sent that I might know your faith, for fear that somehow the tempter had tempted you and that our labor would be in vain.***

Paul says this for the benefit of those who might be led astray by the wiles of Satan, because in every congregation there is a strong element and a weaker one. It was for the latter group that Paul was concerned, because he did not want to lose the fruit of their faith. And because he could not bear to be ignorant any longer about what exactly they were doing, he sent Timothy, whom he had made a bishop, in order to be informed by him.

***6But now that Timothy has come to us from you, and has brought us the good news of your faith and love and reported that you always remember us kindly and long to see us, as we long to see you—7for this reason, brethren, in all our distress and affliction we have been comforted about you through your faith; 8for now we live, if you stand fast in the Lord.***

Paul explained why he was writing so positively to them. It was because his envoy had come back and recounted the firmness of their devotion in faith and in love for the apostle that he had been made happy and by common agreement [among the three] was writing to them because he was sure of the fruit of their faith and good behavior.

***9For what thanksgiving can we render to God for you, for all the joy which we feel for your sake before our God, 10praying earnestly night and day that we may see you face to face and supply what is lacking in your faith?***

Paul says that there is nothing so valuable that it can be enough to compensate for the salvation which the Gentiles have obtained. Since they had advanced by the perseverance of their faith and the practice of a better life, he wanted to see them all the more in order to be able to teach them what they needed to go on to perfection, the sacraments, as it were, of spiritual things which cannot easily be proclaimed, so that they might discover who and how great was the judge whom they were waiting for. It is one thing to accept the faith and another to accept its exposition. The debate about the nature of the Father and the Son is different from that about their persons. The Father is unbegotten but the Son is begotten. The persons appear to be different but the nature is one and indivisible. The unity is not in person but in substance. The Holy Spirit is not to be regarded as inferior merely because he is placed third. Whatever is clear about the second person applies to the third as well.

***11Now may our God and Father himself, and our Lord Jesus, direct our way to you;***

Paul prays that his journey will be properly organized, by God the Father first of all, because all things come from him. He wants the power and foresight of the Father and the Son to protect his coming, so that he will be accepted by those who hear him, and the hindrances of the devil may be removed so that he can make his way to them.

***[12]and may the Lord make you increase and abound in love to one another and to all men, as we do to you, [13]so that he may establish your hearts unblamable in holiness before our God and Father, at the coming of our Lord Jesus with all his saints.***

In order that the joy with which he rejoices in them may be increased, Paul prays that they may grow in all good things, so that when he comes to them he may find in them even more praiseworthy things than what he had heard from Timothy. He wants them to be found blameless with the saints in the love of God the Father and at the coming of our Lord Jesus Christ, when the cross-examination starts and tests each one before his judgment seat. Paul calls him God because of the terror of his majesty, but Father because of the kindness by which he has been pleased to adopt those who believe in him as his children, something which will be made clear when the Lord returns.

## 1 Thessalonians 4

***[1]Finally, brethren, we beseech and exhort you in the Lord Jesus, that as you learned from us how you ought to live and to please God, just as you are doing, you do so more and more.***

This is what I said above. Paul wants them to grow in good works according to the commands of the apostles, so that his joy may increase.

***[2]For you know what instructions we gave you through the Lord Jesus. [3]For this is the will of God, your sanctification: that you abstain from unchastity; [4]that each one of you know how to take a wife for himself in holiness and honor, [5]not in the passion of lust like heathen who do not know God; [6]that no man transgress, and wrong his brother in this matter, because the Lord is an avenger in all these things, as we solemnly forewarned you.***

Although Paul praises them throughout the letter, he nevertheless warns them not to be led astray into unlawful activities by some form of subtlety, and thereby incur the penalty which they have learned is the recompense for evil. They know that they will please God if they keep their bodies pure, but they must also deal honestly with their brethren so as not to become like the Gentiles and lose their entitlement to adoption.

***[7]For God has not called us for uncleanness, but in holiness. [8]Therefore whoever disregards this, disregards not man but God, who gives his Holy Spirit to you.***

In order to compel them to do what he teaches, Paul calls on the person of God, saying that whoever disregards the commandments *disregards not man but God.* He says that God has given us the Holy Spirit so that we may live in a holy way: *For the Holy Spirit does not dwell in a body subject to sin.*[7]

***[9]But concerning love of the brethren you have no need to have any one write to you, for you yourselves have been taught by God to love one another; [10]and indeed you do love all the brethren throughout Macedonia. But we exhort you, brethren, to do so more and more,***

Paul praises the Thessalonians for what they are doing but urges them to do still more. He says that those who have been taught by God himself ought to be even more eager in demonstrating brotherly love. *Because of his great love*[8] God has taken pity on us, and when we have been made imitators of him we quite rightly show that we have been adopted by God as his children.

[7]Wis 1:4. [8]Eph 2:4.

***[11]to aspire to live quietly, to mind your own affairs, and to work with your hands, as we charged you; [12]so that you may command the respect of outsiders, and be dependent on nobody.***

Paul once more encourages them to exert the effort needed for them to abound in good works. He often does this in order to show that this is what is really pleasing to God. The way of righteousness is to be followed in order to obtain mercy in the right way. Those who have fewer possessions must work with their hands so that by having the same sense of purpose they may be taken away from common worries and wicked thoughts and so that their self-discipline may be praised even by unbelievers and perhaps win them to the faith.

***[13]But we would not have you ignorant, brethren, concerning those who are asleep, that you may not grieve as others do who have no hope. [14]For since we believe that Jesus died and rose again, even so, through Jesus, God will bring with him those who have fallen asleep.***

The logic is clear, because if we believe in a future resurrection of the dead, those who pass away in the sign of the cross are not to be mourned. It is unbelievers who really ought to be grieved for, because they go from here to hell, where they learn that what they did not want to believe is true. Believers, however, will rise to glory, and those who are considered stupid in this world because of their faith will appear to be wise because they have foreseen their glory. These are the people who pass away through Jesus, that is to say, in the hope of their faith in him, and who will be brought back with him when he returns so that they may be seen by other people. Although Paul forbids us to mourn the passing of a dead person, elsewhere he says: *Lest I should have sorrow.*[9] But we have already discussed that in its proper place.

***[15]For this we declare to you by the word of the Lord, that we who are alive, who are left until the coming of the Lord, shall not precede those who have fallen asleep. [16]For the Lord himself will descend from heaven with a cry of command, with the archangel's call, and with the sound of the trumpet of God. And the dead in Christ will rise first; [17]then we who are alive, who are left, shall be caught up together with them in the clouds to meet the Lord in the air; and so we shall always be with the Lord. [18]Therefore comfort one another with these words.***

Paul claims to be speaking with the mind of God when he says: *This we declare to you by the word of the Lord.* In order to demonstrate that the hope of the resurrection promised to the saints is sure and that its glory is confirmed, Paul explains how it will happen by the grace of Christ the judge and the revelation of the Holy Spirit, so that with that hope, those who have sent their loved ones on before them will not grieve, knowing that those who have died in Christ will be the first to rise again when Christ returns.

Christ the Lord will himself come down by the will of the Father, rather like the chief angel of God with the heavenly host, as is written in the revelation of John,[10] and will wage war in God's name against the antichrist. After he has been wiped out, the dead will rise again at his command. To come down with the sound of God's trumpet means to wage war in the name of God. It is what Christ himself, the commander and chief of God's army, said to Joshua the son of Nun, for which reason he was called an archangel.[11] When he comes down with the trumpet of

[9]Phil 2:27. [10]Rev 12:7.

God he is God, for the Scriptures speak of angels when they mean the Son of God, as in Exodus, where we read that an angel appeared to Moses in a flame only to realize immediately from what follows that this is God, that is, the Son of God, as the same Scripture says: *And going near Moses turned aside because he could not look at the face of God.*[12] So he is God, because he is the true Son of God. He is also the commander and chief, because he is the head of all things, since everything comes from him. Those who have died in Christ will rise first, and then we who are still alive will be caught up together with those processional clouds to meet Christ in the air. Thus everyone will come with Christ to the battle, and those who had killed them will see them alive, because just as the clouds accompany the Lord, so also will those whom he has been pleased to call his brethren.

*So we shall always be with the Lord.* In this rapture, death will come as it were through sleep, and the soul which has departed will be given back in a moment. When they are taken away they die, and when they reach the Lord they receive their souls back again in his presence, because they cannot be dead if they are with Christ. Paul orders them to console one another with this hope, because they still thought they ought to mourn the passing of their loved ones as the Gentiles did.

## 1 Thessalonians 5

***1But as to the times and the seasons, brethren, you have no need to have anything written to you. 2For you yourselves know well that the day of the Lord will come like a thief in the night. 3When people say, "There is peace and security," then sudden destruction will come upon them as travail comes upon a woman with child, and there will be no escape.***

This is just what the Lord said in the Gospel: *Watch, for you do not know the time when your Lord will come.*[13] And again: *If someone says to you, Here is Christ or there he is, do not believe them.*[14] He will appear suddenly and without warning, as the first ray of dawn appears from the east to the west, having with him the host of the army of God the Father for the destruction of antichrist and his minions. It will be just when the unbelievers from the kingdom of the devil feel safe because they have killed the saints (like Enoch and Elijah) and are rejoicing in the victory by giving presents to one another, as Revelation says,[15] that sudden death will come upon them. Christ will destroy them all when he comes, and when the saints see what they have escaped from they will rejoice.

***4But you are not in darkness, brethren, for that day to surprise you like a thief. 5For you are all sons of light and sons of the day; we are not of the night or of darkness.***

The words "in darkness" mean ignorance and falsehood, while the day refers to knowledge and truth. Paul says that Christians are not in darkness, but that the Gentiles and unbelieving Jews were children of the dark because they worshiped a lie. He indicates that believers are safe because they are not unaware of the Lord's future return but are eagerly awaiting his coming. As for those who are ignorant because they do not believe in him, he will quickly round them up in their unpreparedness and kill them.

***6So then let us not sleep, as others do, but let us keep awake and be sober. 7For those who sleep sleep at night, and those who get drunk are drunk at night. 8But, since we belong to the day, let us be sober, and put on the breastplate of faith and love, and for a helmet the hope of salvation. 9For God has not destined us for wrath, but to obtain salvation through our***

[11]Cf. Josh 5:14. [12]Ex 3:2-6. [13]Mk 13:35. [14]Mt 24:23. [15]Cf. Rev 11:7-13.

***Lord Jesus Christ, [10]who died for us so that whether we wake or sleep we might live with him. [11]Therefore encourage one another and build one another up, just as you are doing.***

It is clear what Paul is saying. He warns us not to act incautiously because we trust in the name of the Savior, and tells us that we must be armed with three weapons—faith, hope and love. Where there is faith it gives rise to hope. Hope is necessarily concerned with the promise and does not sleep. Love offers worship to God and does not tolerate anything contrary to him. The Lord Jesus died for us and rose again, so that whether we watch (that is, live) or whether we sleep (that is, die), we shall enjoy eternal life with him. This is what Paul said above, because at the coming of the Lord all believers, alive or dead, will be caught up to meet with the Lord and will live with him for ever. He teaches them to ponder this so that they may build one another up in this understanding.

***[12]But we beseech you, brethren, to respect those who labor among you and are over you in the Lord and admonish you, [13]and to esteem them very highly in love because of their work. Be at peace among yourselves.***

This is what Paul says in another letter, that presbyters are to be doubly honored because they labor in the word and in teaching.[16] What benefit is there in having honor if it brings no return? Why should it be so hard to give someone material things when he is handing out spiritual ones? It might easily put off someone who is suffering want if he has to make a special effort to keep his hearers happy. Just as riches go hand in hand with a neglect of salvation, so poverty falls away from righteousness when it tries to get rich. This is why Solomon asked not to be too rich or too poor.[17] This should, however, be done in love, so that the honor given to the priest will not be based on fear but on love, so as to benefit the person who gives it as well. Something which is not done voluntarily will not have any effect. Even if it benefits the receiver for the time being, it will not do anything for the giver in the future. Because a lot of quarreling generates evil, he urges them to be at peace with one another.

***[14]And we exhort you, brethren, admonish the idlers, encourage the fainthearted, help the weak, be patient with them all. [15]See that none of you repays evil for evil, but always seek to do good to one another and to all. [16]Rejoice always, [17]pray constantly, [18]give thanks in all circumstances; for this is the will of God in Christ Jesus for you.***

Since there will always be some people in the congregation who are out of order, some who are fainthearted (that is, fearful) and some who are weak in their faith, Paul prays and urges those who are mature, courageous and well-grounded in their faith to help the others so that they may grow by carrying them along with themselves. Otherwise, if they suffer retribution for their faults, they will only become worse. Paul encourages them to seek only the good, not only when dealing with their brethren, but in their dealings with everyone. It is possible that unbelievers will be drawn by their good works to the faith, at which there is always rejoicing in the Lord, that is to say, in what is good. They are to pray without ceasing because constant prayer provokes the mind of the judge to show mercy. In every good deed thanks are to be given to God, who has given us this teaching in Christ Jesus our Lord.

***[19]Do not quench the Spirit, [20]do not despise prophesying, [21]but test everything; hold fast what is good, [22]abstain from every form of evil.***

[16]Cf. 1 Tim 5:17. [17]Cf. Prov 30:8.

Paul says this because it is not easy to stop someone who is speaking by the Spirit. The Spirit is quenched if the fervor of whoever is starting to speak is dampened by being contradicted. He was afraid that those who did not understand that he was talking about spiritual things might do injury to the Holy Spirit and sin through ignorance. Someone who is expounding the Scriptures ought to be heard out patiently, but everything he says must be examined and judged in such a way that they do not reject the author by refusing to accept that grace has been given to a brother. Paul warns them to test everything that is said and to keep it soberly and well. Whatever agrees with the words of the apostles and the Lord himself is to be regarded as correct and must be retained. On the other hand, whatever appears to be inimical to the faith must be avoided. Unclean spirits have a habit of deceiving people by saying good things (which they copy from others) and interspersing them with evil thoughts, so that by the acceptance of what is good evil will also enter in. This is because what is said will appear to come from one Spirit and no distinction will be made, with the result that what is unlawful will be recommended by what is lawful, using the authority of its name and not the logic of its power.

Some people manage to teach wicked and contrary doctrines in the name of the apostles and of the Lord himself, and so Paul warns us to test everything, because God's words cannot be self-contradictory. This is why it says in another letter of the apostle John's: *Do not believe every spirit, but test the spirits, to see whether they are of God.*[18] If someone says many good things but then falls into something which goes against the faith, it is clear that this is not of the Holy Spirit. No error can be found in the Holy Spirit, but it is possible to learn how to say some spiritual things and some carnal ones (for all error is attributed to the flesh), or at least to invent some good things by a certain manner of cleverness and then insert bad things alongside them, as I mentioned above. This is what the spirit of this world simulated in Montanus, Priscilla and Maximilla, the Montanist prophets, by imitating what was good to some extent, so that he could pass himself off as the Holy Spirit by saying many things which were plausible and even true.

***23May the God of peace himself sanctify you wholly; and may your spirit and soul and body be kept sound and blameless at the coming of our Lord Jesus Christ.***

Since everything the Father has belongs to the Son, the apostle chooses him to sanctify us by enlightening us with the godliness of his mercy and directing our every action in perfection, so that the spirit given to us may be sound. This will be the case if we pursue a good life, keep our minds clean and our bodies out of trouble, so that the whole man may be perfect. (It is possible for the body to be clean and the soul to be corrupted by evil thoughts. This is why he says that the spirit of a man must be clean.) If a bad life (or bad thoughts) get in the way, the spirit will not be sound, because it abandons the person who is bound by sin. When it turns away from God, the soul and the body (even though it lacks a mind) are cut off from it, and when it loses them, the spirit is no longer sound. It is given to people in order to dwell in them and act as their head. Therefore it will not be sound in a person who turns away from it by doing things that the Holy Spirit forbids.[19]

***24He who calls you is faithful, and he will do it.***

***25Brethren, pray for us.***

[18]1 Jn 4:1. [19]An alternative version of this sentence reads: "Therefore it will not be sound because it loses members when a person turns away from it by doing things which the Holy Spirit hates."

Paul says that God is faithful to his promises, so they must live properly because they are certain of a reward. Because those who live a good life according to the gospel will easily obtain what they ask for, he encourages them to pray for him, since when many pray, it is easy for them to get what they all want.

**[26]*Greet all the brethren with a holy kiss.***

The kisses in a Christian greeting are holy, but others are carnal, because whatever is done without Christ is carnal and for that reason mortal. Whoever despises the author of life is dead.

**[27]*I adjure you by the Lord that this letter be read to all the brethren.***

Paul enjoins them to make sure that they read his letter to all the brethren so that they might understand both his praises and his warnings, by which they will be made perfect.

**[28]*The grace of our Lord Jesus Christ be with you.***

Paul wants them to grow in good works so that the grace of our Lord Jesus Christ will remain in them forever.

# AMBROSIASTER
## *Commentary on 2 Thessalonians*

### Preface

In his first letter to the Thessalonians Paul had written something about the return of Christ and the resurrection of the saints, among other things, and so now he sends them another letter in which he outlines, albeit obscurely—for he could not write this openly—the destruction of the Roman Empire, the appearance of the antichrist, the condemnation and the tribulation of some of the brethren.

### 2 Thessalonians 1

***1Paul, Silvanus, and Timothy,***
***To the church of the Thessalonians in God our Father and the Lord Jesus Christ:***
***2Grace to you and peace from God the Father and the Lord Jesus Christ.***

Paul writes to them with solemn words. The beginning of the letter starts with the usual form of words, and the three men in whose name it is written are the same as in the first letter [to the Thessalonians].

***3We are bound to give thanks to God always for you, brethren, as is fitting, because your faith is growing abundantly, and the love of every one of you for one another is increasing.***

The authors say that they are bound to give thanks to God for their progress, and in order to show that this is no ordinary obligation, Paul adds *as is fitting,* so that they testify that great thanks must be given to God for such an infinite gift. Since receiving the first letter, the Thessalonians had become better than they were, to the point where they appeared to be abundant and overflowing in the command which we have after that of devotion to our Lord and God, which is that we should love one another.

***4Therefore we ourselves boast of you in the churches of God for your steadfastness and faith in all your persecutions and in the afflictions which you are enduring.***
***5This is evidence of the righteous judgment of God, that you may be made worthy of the kingdom of God, for which you are suffering—***

The authors testify that their glory is found in the behavior of the Thessalonians and the persecution which they have endured, so much so that they talk about their example in other churches. By imitating the Thessalonians they too might grow in the devotion of their sufferings for Christ and deserve to obtain what has been promised to the saints in the day of God's righteous judgment, for the love of which they were convinced that they should reject the world. Such pressures are indications of future merit in those who suffer for their glory, as well as of future perdition in those who persecute them.

***6since indeed God deems it just to repay with affliction those who afflict you, 7and to grant rest with us to you who are afflicted, when the Lord Jesus is revealed from heaven with his mighty angels in flaming fire, 8inflicting vengeance upon those who do not know God and upon those who do not obey the gospel of***

***our Lord Jesus.*** [9]***They shall suffer the punishment of eternal destruction and exclusion from the presence of the Lord and from the glory of his might,***

Since Paul says that evidence of God's righteous judgment appears both in the good and the bad, he goes on to add: *Since indeed God deems it just to render to everyone according to his works.* What could be more just than that those who oppress good people in this world and frighten them with persecutions should in the future suffer what they inflict on others? Meanwhile, those good people will be in peace with the other saints who will come out of great tribulation and receive the eternal kingdom when Christ comes again from heaven with his heavenly host and ministering fire, to take revenge on the pagans who do not know that God is the Father of Jesus Christ and on the Jews who say that they know God but do not believe the gospel of Christ which God the Father gave him to pass on to his servants. In the presence of the Lord and the glory of his majesty, fire will burn them all up, and they will pay the due penalty of eternal death. They will always be conscious and not completely unaware, for in some way the penalty itself will keep them in being until it too is consumed.

[10]***when he comes on that day to be glorified in his saints, and to be marveled at in all who have believed, because our testimony to you was believed.***

This has a double meaning. Christ will come to punish the bad and glorify the good. He himself will appear bright and wonderful in those who believe in the example and faith of the apostles when they were crowned. The gospel will bear witness to them in the day of the Lord, for he will appear to be harsh toward unbelievers when they start to be afflicted by eternal punishments. The disciples' crown is their master's glory, and his truth is the punishment of unbelievers because they did not believe what was preached.

[11]***To this end we always pray for you, that our God may make you worthy of his call, and may fulfil every good resolve and work of faith by his power,*** [12]***so that the name of our Lord Jesus may be glorified in you, and you in him, according to the grace of our God and the Lord Jesus Christ.***

Paul adds his prayers with joy. Because they are devout, God has been pleased to help them bring the work they have begun to completion for the glory of our Lord Jesus Christ, so that the perseverance of the disciples bears witness to the master for his glory. The master's authority is in the confidence of the disciples that they are making themselves worthier by the grace which they have received.

## 2 Thessalonians 2

[1]***Now concerning the coming of our Lord Jesus Christ and our assembling to meet him, we beg you, brethren,*** [2]***not to be quickly shaken in mind or excited, either by spirit or by word, or by letter purporting to be from us, to the effect that the day of the Lord has come.*** [3]***Let no one deceive you in any way; for that day will not come, unless the rebellion comes first, and the man of lawlessness is revealed, the son of perdition,*** [4]***who opposes and exalts himself against every so-called god or object of worship, so that he takes his seat in the temple of God, proclaiming himself to be God.***

Paul enjoins the Thessalonians not to be lightly or easily persuaded that the return of the Lord is imminent and gives the command that even if someone like a prophet were to speak to them in the spirit they should not believe him, nor should they agree to any book or letter even if it is written in the name of the apostles. Deceivers have a way of counterfeiting letters under the name of some well-known person in order to mislead, so that the authority of the name may recommend something which would never be accepted on its own. He says this so that they will not be upset by their own lack of caution and be led astray into the worship of the devil, who will act in such a way as to appear in the name of the Savior and try to trick the saints into worshiping him, in order to ensnare those who believe in Christ. But so that that most shameless Satan should not have the space or opportunity which he thinks he has to deceive others, Paul pointed out the time and the signs of Christ's return. The Lord would not come back until the Roman Empire fell and the antichrist appeared, who would kill the saints and give the Romans back their freedom, but under his name. Knowing that the Lord would come to suppress him, Satan would usurp his name, both in order to make it appear that his rule is genuine and in order to take with him those who would perish along with him. He would even sit in Christ's seat in the house of God and declare that he, and not the Son of God, is God himself.

This is why the Lord says to the Jews in the Gospel: *I have come in the name of my Father and you have not received me; if someone else comes in his own name, you will receive him.*[1] Thus it appears that this person whom they are expecting to come will be either of the circumcision or at least circumcised himself, so that the Jews will have the confidence to believe in him. Therefore when writing to the Thessalonians, Paul teaches them to be cautious about this matter.

***5Do you not remember that when I was still with you I told you this? 6And you know what is restraining him now so that he may be revealed in his time.***

Paul says that it only remains for the one who is to come before the [return of the] Lord to be revealed, because he is already expected and the Lord is coming. He already said this in a guarded way when he wrote: *Unless the rebellion comes first*, which I mentioned must be understood as the destruction of the Roman Empire. When it collapses and the antichrist comes, then we will believe that the return of the Lord is near.

***7For the mystery of lawlessness is already at work; only he who now restrains it will do so until he is out of the way.***

The mystery of iniquity began with Nero,[2] who in his zeal for idolatry killed the apostles at the instigation of his father the devil, and went on to Diocletian,[3] and most recently Julian.[4] They started persecution with some cleverness and trickery but could not bring it to fruition because they were not permitted to do so. Satan uses these servants so that meanwhile in a crowd of gods he can feign a revelation of the one God and lead people astray as long as the Roman Empire survives. This is what Paul said: *until it is out of the way*.[5]

***8And then the lawless one will be revealed, and the Lord Jesus will slay him with the breath of his mouth and destroy him by his appearing and his coming. 9The coming of the lawless one by the activity of Satan will be with all power and with pretended signs and wonders,***

[1]Jn 5:43. [2]Emperor from 54 to 68 and the first persecutor of the Christians, after the great fire of Rome in 64. [3]Emperor from 284 to 305 and the author of the great persecution of 303–305, when many churches were torn down and copies of the Bible were seized in a futile attempt to stamp out Christianity. [4]Emperor from 361 to 363. Brought up as a Christian, he reverted to paganism and is known to history as "the Apostate." He tried to prevent Christians from teaching the pagan classics in schools. [5]This is how Ambrosiaster interpreted the last clause of this verse.

Paul says that antichrist will appear after the collapse of the Roman Empire, as has been stated. Most recently, the devil, knowing that his end is nigh (for the Roman Empire is crumbling and he will be cast down out of heaven and thrown to earth, as it says in the Revelation of the Apostle John)[6] will commandeer to himself certain signs of power as and when he can, doing this with the permission of the righteous God, and will offer himself for worship as if he were God. He will copy the Son of God, who after he was born and made a man, demonstrated his divinity in signs and wonders. Satan will also appear as a man and present himself as God by the powers of the lie, as was said above.

This is the revelation of the mystery of iniquity. When antichrist appears, he will be recognized as the god of those whom the common people once worshiped as gods with his permission. He himself is the first or chief of them all, because by the powers of his signs he will do something which is believable. Paul called these the portents of the lie, because Satan wants himself to be believed in by these signs, which is not the same thing as deceiving those whom he has led astray. All this is revealed to the saints in advance so they will know what to beware of.

***10and with all wicked deception for those who are to perish, because they refused to love the truth and so be saved.***

Paul says that the deception of the iniquity of his miracles is of advantage to those who will perish. Because they have rejected the love of the truth by which they could have been saved through the preaching of the apostles, they have been handed over to the devil. They did not want to be saved and so they have been abandoned by God.

***11Therefore God sends upon them a strong delusion, to make them believe what is false, 12so that all may be condemned who did not believe the truth but had pleasure in unrighteousness.***

The working of error is to put faith in what is false. Those who did not want to admit that the brightness of the light is day think that darkness ought to be called daylight instead. That way they become guilty of even greater sin and are damned without contradiction as enemies of the truth and accomplices of iniquity.

***13But we are bound to give thanks to God always for you, brethren beloved by the Lord, because God chose you from the beginning to be saved, through sanctification by the Spirit and belief in the truth. 14To this he called you through our gospel, so that you may obtain the glory of our Lord Jesus Christ.***

In this passage the foreknowledge of God comes through clearly. He knows the minds of all before they are born, nor is it a secret to him who will believe. He has known from the beginning who would become believers and which of them will increase in faith and not decrease. They have been sanctified by faith in the truth of the gospel of the Son of God and received what is needed for the increase of the glory of the body of Christ, just as Paul says in another letter: *That everything may grow in the increase of God.*[7] Those who abandon the devil and take refuge in the faith of Christ bring an increase to God in the body of Christ, when previously they had detracted from it.

***15So then, brethren, stand firm and hold to the traditions which you were taught by us, either by word of mouth or by letter.***

In order for God's foreknowledge to remain favorable to their salvation, Paul warns them

[6]Cf. Rev 12:9. [7]Col 2:19.

to stand and to persevere in the tradition of the gospel. They must take care not to grow weary through idleness or sloth and so fail to complete the work of God which they have begun. God foresees that they will believe and can remain [in the faith] if they are motivated by abundant warning.

***16Now may our Lord Jesus Christ himself, and God our Father, who loved us and gave us eternal comfort and good hope through grace, 17comfort your hearts and establish them in every good work and word.***

Since the Father and the Son are one power, one divinity and one substance, Paul did not hesitate to name our Lord Jesus Christ first of all, and then God our Father, not by the truth of his nature but in his rank, because he loved us so much that he gave his Son for us, God for the human race, the Lord for his servants, the true Son for the adopted children, so that his death might be our life and his resurrection our justification. His second coming will be rest for our life and glory in eternity. That hope is our comfort in present troubles, and based on it the Thessalonians might grow in good works and doctrine.

## 2 Thessalonians 3

***1Finally, brethren, pray for us, that the word of the Lord may speed on and triumph, as it did among you, 2and that we may be delivered from wicked and evil men; for not all have faith.***

Paul encourages them to go on praying so that God may be pleased to direct his teaching along a steady course and transmit it by the mouth of his apostle to the ears of his hearers, so that they may restrain and put down the rebellions of wicked men who do not believe in the truth, and that the apostle may have greater confidence in speaking, so that his fruit will increase and many will be converted.

***3But the Lord is faithful; he will strengthen you and guard you from evil.***

Since God has promised to believers and people of good will that his help will not be wanting in their necessity for their strengthening, the Thessalonians have been imitators in both their faith and their works of such good men. Therefore Paul says that God will be faithful to his promises, because his providence will be with them.

***4And we have confidence in the Lord about you, that you are doing and will do the things which we command.***

Because they had deserved it, Paul was confident that they would be kept safe by the protection of God, and so he did not doubt that they would do the things which he prescribed for them in the name of the Lord.

***5May the Lord direct your hearts to the love of God and to the steadfastness of Christ.***

Paul asks this for them from God because he has no doubt that they can thrive and that in the love of God their hearts may stand fast until the expected coming of the Lord. They would turn away from the world and eagerly await the coming of the one who has conquered.

***6Now we command you, brethren, in the name of our Lord Jesus Christ, that you keep away from any brother who is living in idleness and not in accord with the tradition that you received from us.***

Since in every congregation not everyone is obedient to the word of doctrine and some prefer their own pleasure and determination, not that of the law, Paul directs the Thessalonians to turn away from them so that they will realize their error.

***[7]For you yourselves know how you ought to imitate us; we were not idle when we were with you, [8]we did not eat any one's bread without paying, but with toil and labor we worked night and day, that we might not burden any of you. [9]It was not because we have not that right, but to give you in our conduct an example to imitate.***

Paul says that the Thessalonians are not ignorant of his work and the labor which he undertook with determined consistency. He would not live off someone else's food in order to set an example for others to follow in imitating him. There would have been nothing wrong if he had accepted food from them for the health of his body, because he gave them spiritual food for their souls, which also obtained for them an immortal body with glory. But there is complete freedom when someone is content with his own food and does not depend on anyone else for nourishment or money. The thing which is most praiseworthy of all is that although he had every right to take these things, he refused to do so. A person like that may be of great benefit to those who hear him. They will respect his self-discipline and will not be able to ignore what he commands them to do.

***[10]For even when we were with you, we gave you this command: If any one will not work, let him not eat.***

Paul not only taught with words but encouraged others by his deeds. It is the sign of a perfect teacher when he backs up his teaching with deeds. Those who learn know that what they are hearing is true if they see that these things are not neglected by their teacher. Even if they know that what they are being taught is obviously true, if they see that it is ignored by their teacher, it will make little impression on his hearers, because actions speak louder than words. For this reason those who progress in both deeds and understanding on the basis of the words alone (their teachers neglecting to follow them themselves), are worthy of great reward. Therefore Paul was a model to those of modest or small means in the congregation, so that they would learn not to lose their liberty. This is why Solomon said: *Let your foot be seldom in your friend's house, lest he become weary of you and hate you.*[8] Whoever dines often at someone else's house is given over to idleness and must flatter the person who is feeding him, but our religion calls people to freedom. So Paul says that if someone refuses to eat then he does not have to work, but because nobody can live without food, everyone should strive to live independently and in that way please God.

***[11]For we hear that some of you are living in idleness, mere busybodies, not doing any work.***

Those who want to be idle do this as often as they can and thereby make themselves welcome in the houses of the rich. They go about quietly collecting stories and opinions, knowing who wants to hear what about whom, so that they will be freely invited to dinner. The discipline of the Lord abhors that kind of thing. Their belly is the god of those who get what they need by disreputable means.

***[12]Now such persons we command and exhort in the Lord Jesus Christ to do their work in quietness and to earn their own living.***

In order to convince them more easily, Paul interjects the name of our Lord Jesus Christ and encourages them to obey what is useful for them.

[8]Prov 25:17.

[13]***Brethren, do not be weary in well-doing.***

[14]***If any one refuses to obey what we say in this letter, note that man, and have nothing to do with him, that he may be ashamed.*** [15]***Do not look on him as an enemy, but warn him as a brother.***

Because Paul has just taught that everyone ought to eat his own food, he immediately adds this, in case some of them might seize the opportunity to display meanness and inhumanity. He says: *You brethren, do not be weary in well-doing.* It is not the person who is generous and liberal who will come under attack but the one who wants to live a life of idleness when he is well able to work. If the authority of this letter does not put that kind of person right, then Paul teaches that he must be marked out and avoided. If he is confused by the fact that he is being shunned by everyone else, he may submit himself to the teachings of the apostle. Paul wants this to be done without anger or reproach. People should walk away from him quietly, so that if an opportunity arises to speak with him he can be warned that he is allowing himself to be corrupted and that he should not go on rejecting the apostle's commands. At the same time it is wrong to be on familiar terms with him as long as he is obdurate. If he is assailed with abuse to the point of anger, he will only get worse. He will be driven to argument and start to defend his error, after which he will be ashamed to change his ways because he will not want to appear to be confessing things which earlier on he had been explaining away.

[16]***Now may the Lord of peace himself give you peace at all times in all ways. The Lord be with you all.***

In his usual way, Paul encourages them with good wishes as his dearest children, praying that peace will always be with them, which is the guide to eternal life. The Lord has promised to be with those who are peaceful.

[17]***I, Paul, write this greeting with my own hand. This is the mark in every letter of mine; it is the way I write.***

Because of interpolators and corrupters of Scripture, Paul always bears witness in every letter that he has added his greeting with his own hand, so that the letter cannot be accepted as coming from someone when it has not been signed by his own hand.

[18]***The grace of our Lord Jesus Christ be with you all.***

This greeting was written by the hand of the apostle. In it he prays that the grace of our Lord Jesus Christ will be with them. Amen.

# AMBROSIASTER
## *Commentary on 1 Timothy*

### Preface
Timothy was the son of a Jewish mother and a Greek father, which is why he could not be circumcised as a baby. His mother ensured that he learned the Scriptures, and by diligently following them, he led a good life. When the apostle wanted to take him on, knowing that Timothy would be an ideal evangelist, he was forced to circumcise him at the insistence of the Jews, and for their sake.[1] This was because his mother was Jewish and it seemed improper to take him on in a teaching role when he was still uncircumcised. This was because he had to be a witness to his own people. In this letter Paul instructs him, after he had become a bishop, how to run a church.

### 1 Timothy 1

***[1]Paul, an apostle of Christ Jesus by command of God our Savior and of Christ Jesus our hope,***

***[2]To Timothy, my true child in the faith:***
***Grace, mercy, and peace from God the Father and Christ Jesus our Lord.***

Paul shows that he has become an apostle at the command of the Father and the Son, in order to preach salvation in God the Father and hope in Christ his Son, so that no one may deny that there is salvation in God or doubt that there is hope in Christ Jesus, whom they must recognize that God has raised from the dead and given as an example of this hope. He writes to Timothy in this vein so that he will have more assurance of his ordination, because he has been chosen by the command of the Father and the Son to be a teacher. Paul calls him his true son, but in faith, as he says to the Corinthians: *I have begotten you by the gospel in Christ Jesus.*[2] This is the true and certain generation which knows no death, sickness or diseases, which is a stranger to hunger and thirst. Paul taught that in the kingdom of God no one would go without, because by the gift of God there will be a glorious immortality in the kingdom of God and Christ, whose grace, mercy and peace he prays will remain with Timothy.

***[3]As I urged you when I was going to Macedonia, remain at Ephesus that you may charge certain persons not to teach any different doctrine, [4]nor to occupy themselves with myths and endless genealogies which promote speculations rather than the divine training that is in faith;***

The son did not have to be asked by his father, but because of the feeling of love and in order to show him a model of humility, Paul the bishop asked Timothy his fellow bishop not to allow the Jews to teach the people anything other than what had been imparted to them by the apostle. This was so that they would not be beguiled by fables which the Jews habitually told about the origin of their genealogies, about Abraham, Isaac and the other patriarchs, about circumcision and the things which were later handed down by Moses. They were

---

[1]Acts 16:1-3. [2]1 Cor 4:15.

not to be led astray into worshiping these things, which had been given for carnal reasons. What is the purpose of mentioning genealogies, when it is clear that they have grown endless in the telling? Why recount what was done by each of the people mentioned, and how, rather than summarize the whole thing by saying that they were all seeking salvation by faith? Questions arise whenever mention is made of what was done, and when, and how and why. Things like that just get in the way of salvation.

***5whereas the aim of our charge is love that issues from a pure heart and a good conscience and sincere faith. 6Certain persons by swerving from these have wandered away into vain discussion, 7desiring to be teachers of the law, without understanding either what they are saying or the things about which they make assertions.***

Since love is greater than anything else, Paul said that it was the end, that is, the perfection and fulfillment of all the commandments, as long as it was from a pure heart and a good conscience. True love cannot have a wicked life or a fictitious faith, because it is in life and faith that all the law and the prophets are fulfilled.[3] Some of the Jews are ignorant of the mystery of the law and the prophets. They were handed down and meant to be kept until the coming of Christ, but the Jews were wrong to think that after Christ was preached it was still necessary to keep the law of works in new moons, circumcision and food laws. Therefore Paul says that they have wandered away into vanity, because they wanted to teach what they did not understand.

***8Now we know that the law is good, if any one uses it lawfully, 9understanding this, that the law is not laid down for the just but for the lawless and disobedient, for the ungodly and sinners, for the unholy and profane, for murderers of fathers and murderers of mothers, for manslayers, 10immoral persons, sodomites, kidnapers, liars, perjurers, and whatever else is contrary to sound doctrine, 11in accordance with the glorious gospel of the blessed God with which I have been entrusted.***

Paul does not deny that the law given by Moses was good, but he wants its meaning to be understood and the purpose for which it was given to be accepted. The person who understands the law and why it was given is the one who, once Christ has been preached, will abandon that part of it known as the law of works. Nevertheless, out of love for God, he will make use of it by proclaiming and confirming those things which are said of the savior in the law and the prophets. The person who uses the law correctly is the one who can distinguish the things which were given for a time from those which are eternal. As for the things which concern the sacrament of Christ, it is not necessary for them to be kept in the future as if it were still thought that he was coming when he has already arrived. Therefore if everything is understood in its proper context all is well, but if not, the same things will be bad for the person who keeps them wrongly, for to take things out of context is to sin.

Moreover the righteous, that is to say, those who have been justified by accepting the forgiveness of sins, have no need of the law. They no longer live under it but have been delivered from it by the gift of God through faith in Christ, so that from now on they will keep the law of nature, which admits to a knowledge of the Creator and encourages people not to sin, and wait for the day of judgment when the righteous will be rewarded for keeping the natural law. If the human race had a leader, the law written down by Moses would never have

[3]The meaning of this sentence is obscure.

been given. But because the natural law was brought into contempt, as if it had no authority, it was confirmed in writing, so that it would be understood both that it must be kept right now and that the one who ratified it will one day examine what has been neglected and what has been kept, and by whom. Therefore Paul says that the law has been given not only because of evil deeds and the sins of the flesh, but also because of unbelief, by which they have rejected the Creator, [and which prevents them from] learning how to live properly and give thanks to him.

***12I thank him who has given me strength for this, Christ Jesus our Lord, because he judged me faithful by appointing me to his service, 13though I formerly blasphemed and persecuted and insulted him; but I received mercy because I had acted ignorantly in unbelief, 14and the grace of our Lord overflowed for me with the faith and love that are in Christ Jesus.***

Because every unbeliever suffers from a weakness of mind which prevents his human reason from understanding spiritual things, Paul says that he has to thank Christ because the appearance of his majesty strengthened the weakness of his mind. Previously, he had thought that what was preached about the Lord's power, about his double birth, about his resurrection and about hope was impossible. Being strengthened in this way he was regarded as worthy and able to become a dispenser of the Lord's sacrament, so that he might confirm by the law that those things were true which earlier, out of love for the law, he had judged to be incredible. He could also rejoice in persecutions whereas previously he had inflicted them on "godless" believers because he thought it was the right thing to do. He was sorry for what he had done but happy that he had suffered. He had discovered that his hope in Christ, whom he had previously persecuted, was so great that now he was happier to suffer than he had been to persecute. He had not done that out of malice but in error, which is easy to admit and repent of. Someone who knows that what he denies is true is not acting from error but out of malice, and his wound is incurable because he is forced by jealousy to say that what he knows to be true is actually false.

***15The saying is sure and worthy of full acceptance, that Christ Jesus came into the world to save sinners. And I am the foremost of sinners; 16but I received mercy for this reason, that in me, as the foremost, Jesus Christ might display his perfect patience for an example to those who were to believe in him for eternal life.***

What could be more pleasant and satisfying than to preach forgiveness to sinners? Who is without sin and would not take this gift with all thanks, exalting God its author and praising him in Christ? Who was it who came down from heaven to earth and took on sinful flesh in order to cleanse human beings from their sins? Who mingled with earthly things so that he could make people heavenly? Who was it who allowed himself to die in order to rescue us from death and make us immortal in paradise? Who would not extol these blessings which God has given to man, the Lord to his servant, the Creator to his creature, ad infinitum, so that there should be more blessings for the human race now than there were after he made what did not exist? Moreover, though he was rejected, despised and attacked with insults, he added to these blessings without being obliged to do so. He thus became more pleasing and more attractive when he put things right than when he originally made them, and showed that he who can do all these things is one and the same person. Therefore Christ took our place in a way which did not violate his purity or diminish his power. He decided to be born as a man, knowing for certain that he was not violating himself by contact with the flesh. He mingled with other people on earth, knowing that he could not be corrupted by sin. He allowed himself to be killed, knowing that death could not control him, but that he would overcome it by his power.

Christ did this in order to teach that he could do all things. This humility did not lead to any lessening of his being, but rather to glory, and not only to his but also to that of those who believe in him. It is an honor to be the servant of someone who is powerful. Although there were many Jews from among those who killed the Lord who believed in him before the apostle did, the apostle still grieves over his unbelief and, in order to humble himself, calls himself the chief of all sinners.

Since above all else, Paul has clothed himself in the sacrament of the Savior, he wants to get closer to understanding his greatness and accuses himself all the more for having taken so long to acknowledge such a good thing. He would have gone on, but was prevented by God's mercy, and so he too became a witness of the divinity of the man whom he had previously thought was dead. The guilt was his, but the praise belongs to the Savior, who called the one who had persecuted him to grace in order to be an example for other believers. By his patience and his generosity toward Paul, Christ could then show others that he was as merciful to his enemy as he would be in the future to those who came running to him.

***17To the King of ages, immortal, invisible, the only God, be honor and glory for ever and ever. Amen.***

These attributes belong to the person of God the Father, whom Paul calls the only immortal and invisible one. All immortality comes from him and in truth exists in relation to him alone. Whoever is immortal is not immortal in his own right but derives it from him. Likewise we read in the Gospel that the Lord said: *There is no one good except God.*[4] He also said: *The good man out of the treasure of his heart produces good.*[5] Yet there is no one who is good except God alone because he is the fount of goodness from which others drink in order to become good. He is the one and only invisible God who has never been seen by anyone at any time. He does everything through the Son, whom we say has been seen and recognize that he too has appeared [in the Son], albeit in a way different from his true being. Paul therefore proclaims honor and glory to God the Father in truth, by whose faithfulness and foresight Christ has delivered sinners from death.

***18This charge I commit to you, Timothy, my son, in accordance with the prophetic utterances which pointed to you, that inspired by them you may wage the good warfare, 19holding faith and a good conscience. By rejecting conscience, certain persons have made shipwreck of their faith, 20among them Hymenaeus and Alexander, whom I have delivered to Satan that they may learn not to blaspheme.***

After listing how many and how great the blessings of God the Father and Christ his Son are toward sinful human beings, whom he not only forgave but also justified and adopted as his children when they should have been punished, Paul goes on to show how church discipline affects the people, exhorting the holy Timothy to remember his election and fulfill the task for which he was predestined. Timothy was predestined from the moment he was chosen by the apostle for this task, so that he might be ordained and judged worthy to become a future bishop and thus fulfill his gospel service in faith and with

[4]Mk 10:18. [5]Lk 6:45.

a pure conscience. The person who is faithful in his teaching cannot have a bad conscience. He would demonstrate his faith by his preaching if he avoided everything contrary to it, so that by the example of his good works he would provoke many to believe by trusting in the hope of his preaching. Whoever rejects the faith undoubtedly has a bad conscience. Such a preacher is either a hypocrite or an open blasphemer, as were Hymenaeus and Alexander, who abandoned the faith and were shipwrecked, that is to say, they were stripped of the truth and deprived of life. After all, what is truth if it is not life? Paul says that he has handed them over to Satan so that they may be cured of their blasphemy. This handing over means that the apostle was moved by their blasphemies to pronounce sentence against them. The devil, who is ready to take those who have turned away from God into his power, rebuked them when he heard their sentence, so that they would understand that they were being subjected to punishment because they blasphemed. This is why the Gospel says elsewhere: *Sin no more, that nothing worse may befall you,*[6] showing by this that sometimes weaknesses are inflicted on our bodies because of sin. Because it is the devil who produces these things, the Lord declared among many other things: *Ought not this woman, a daughter of Abraham whom Satan bound for eighteen years, be loosed from this bond on the sabbath day?*[7]

## 1 Timothy 2

***[1]First of all, then, I urge that supplications, prayers, intercessions, and thanksgivings be made for all men, [2]for kings and all who are in high positions, that we may lead a quiet and peaceable life, godly and respectful in every way. [3]This is good, and it is acceptable in the sight of God our Savior, [4]who desires all men to be saved and to come to the knowledge of the truth.***

This church rule, which all our priests make use of, was handed down by the teacher of the Gentiles—that they should make supplication for everyone. They are to pray for the rulers of this world, that they would be able to keep their people subject to them, so that left in peace, we might serve our God in tranquility of mind and quiet. They are also to pray for those to whom supreme power has been entrusted, that they might govern the state in righteousness and truth and supply all things in abundance, so that the disruption of rebellion might be taken away and happiness put in its place. Since bread strengthens the heart and wine gladdens the mind,[8] they are to pray for those who are in different kinds of need, so that once rescued and delivered from that, they may praise God the author of their security and give thanks to him for the things which by his providence are given to us every day for our life. In all these things God the Father is to be praised, from whom all things come, and his Son, through whom all things come, so that once everything which is hostile and inimical to his rule has been destroyed, we may serve God in a spirit of godliness and chastity, for disturbance and captivity protect neither of these things.

How can someone be godly if he is naked? How can someone be chaste when he is not free to be so? For these things to be preserved peace is necessary, so that service pleasing to God may be given to him who wants everyone to be saved and to acknowledge the truth. As he says: *This is eternal life, that they know you, the only true God, and Jesus Christ whom you have sent.*[9]

If God, who is called Almighty, wants everyone to be saved, why is his will not fulfilled? Every saying has a hidden meaning and condi-

[6]Jn 5:14. [7]Lk 13:16. [8]Cf. Ps 104:15. [9]Jn 17:3.

tion attached to it, as the apostle Peter says: *All Scripture requires interpretation.*[10] God wants everyone to be saved, but only if they come to him. He does not want this if it means that people are saved when they do not want to be. He only wants them to be saved if they also want this. Just as he gave the law to everyone, so he excludes no one from salvation. Compare this with a doctor who states publicly that he is ready to heal everyone, as long as he is asked to do so by those who are sick. It is not true salvation if it is given to someone who does not want it, nor can someone rejoice in the salvation he has received if he gets it unwillingly. If by chance he takes the medicine, I must say that it will have no effect on him unless he, the sick man, adapts himself to it, because this medicine is not physical but spiritual, and so does nothing for those who doubt it or who do not want it. It is faith which gives salvation, and unless the mind accepts it with total willingness, it will not only do him no good, it will also harm him. The grace of faith has the power to infuse divine healing into those who believe, but to those who do not believe it brings sickness, from which the whole man will die.

***5For there is one God, and there is one mediator between God and men, the man Christ Jesus,***

Paul indicates that the will of God and the will of Christ are united in the salvation of the human race. This is why he says that there is one God and Father, because all authority comes from him, and one mediator between God and human beings, Jesus Christ. He was sent by the Father to become the arbiter who would reconcile God and men by reforming them so that they would acknowledge him. Because the Father and the Son are one, not in person but in their undifferentiated nature, the Son of God took on flesh and was born as a man, in order to be the arbiter between God and men. In order to become the mediator between God and men, Christ Jesus was a man, that is to say, he first of all made himself a man, but not without his divinity, because the man was in God and God was in the man, in order to be the mediator between both and reconcile them to each other. If he had stayed within the unity of God he could not have been called the mediator between God and men, because as God only he would have been an alien being calling people who had turned away from him back to grace. But as a man who had not sinned against the law which had been given, he became the arbiter between the one who had sinned and the one who knew no sin, so that he could forgive the sinner and human beings might then remain in the faith of God.

***6who gave himself as a ransom for all, the testimony to which was borne at the proper time. 7For this I was appointed a preacher and apostle (I am telling the truth, I am not lying), a teacher of the Gentiles in faith and truth.***

Since even the man reconciled to God was still subject to physical death and could not go up to the God to whom he had been reconciled without passing through it, the Savior allowed himself to die even though this was unjust, in order to bring his decision into effect. By descending to hell he condemned the death of ungodliness which he had imposed on the devil and removed those whom he had held captive, so that in the future anyone who bore his sign could no longer be held captive by it. He bore witness to this at the time of his resurrection. The resurrection of the dead is the destruction of death. The apostle was sent to preach this hope to the Gentiles, so that they might learn from him what hope there was in Christ. He was given as their master, to teach them faith and truth.

[10] 2 Pet 1:20.

***[8]I desire then that in every place the men should pray, lifting holy hands without anger or quarreling;***

The mind must be peaceful in prayer if it is to have any effect, for the hands are holy when the heart is clean. When Paul commands us to pray in every place, this is to be understood as every suitable place. He did not mean in some inappropriate or sordid place. The Lord forbade his disciples to pray in public,[11] but Paul says this so that people will not think that they can only pray in church.

***[9]also that women should adorn themselves modestly and sensibly in seemly apparel, not with braided hair or gold or pearls or costly attire [10]but by good deeds, as befits women who profess religion.***

Women ought to pray wearing modest clothing, and not all dressed up. Whoever wants to be heard [by God] must humble himself and put away all pomp in order to call on the mercy of God. Fancy clothing does not achieve anything and gives the wrong impression. What wise man does not steer clear of fancily dressed women? How much more will this be true of God who made the body free but now sees it weighed down with metal? Humble dress suits a good profession of faith, because then it will not be thought to be anything other than what it is. The woman who wants to be seen all dressed up in the house of God is not doing this for God's sake, but for that of other people. She gets what she wants from them, to whom she looks glorious, but she will not get anything from God except a stain. The more splendid she appears to men, the more she will be despised by God.

***[11]Let a woman learn in silence with all submissiveness. [12]I permit no woman to teach or to have authority over men; she is to keep silent.***

Paul not only says that a woman must dress modestly but also that authority is denied to her and she must be subjected to her husband, so that both in dress and in service she is to be under the power of her husband, from whom she derives her origin.

***[13]For Adam was formed first, then Eve; [14]and Adam was not deceived, but the woman was deceived and became a transgressor. [15]Yet woman will be saved through bearing children, if she continues in faith and love and holiness, with modesty.***

Paul puts the man ahead of the woman because he was created first and therefore the woman is inferior, since she was created after the man and out of him. He also adds something else, which is that the devil did not seduce the man but the woman, and the man was deceived through her. For this reason no independence is to be allowed to her, but she must be humble, because it was through her that death came into the world. Paul says that she *will be saved through bearing children,* as long as she maintains faith, love and a pure life. Paul says that those who are born again by faith in Christ are these children, because if they persevere in their regeneration she will be delivered along with them and rise from the dead. It is not that she will be delivered by them, but by their [new] birth. When those who are destined for eternal life believe, it amounts to a resurrection from the dead, and she will be saved if they believe and lead a pure life. The resurrection is being held up until all those who are predestined to salvation come to faith.

## 1 Timothy 3

***[1]The saying is sure: If any one aspires to the office of bishop, he desires a noble task.***

[11]Cf. Mt 6:5-6.

Since a bishop must be a person of good life, whoever wants to become one desires a good work. Such a person will be seen to desire a good life as long as he does not fall away from the standards which Paul goes on to list, since then it might look as if he had done this from ambition or out of a desire for money.

***2Now a bishop must be above reproach, the husband of one wife, temperate, sensible, dignified, hospitable, an apt teacher,***

Paul describes what a bishop ought to be like, so that nobody will desire a bishopric unless he is trustworthy and can abstain from everything which tends in the opposite direction, so that he will not be unworthy of his office. Although it is not forbidden for him to have a second wife, if he wants to be worthy of the office he ought to refuse even things which are lawful because of the greatness of the rank, since someone who is desirous of this position ought to be better than others.

***3no drunkard, not violent but gentle, not quarrelsome, and no lover of money. 4He must manage his own household well, keeping his children submissive and respectful in every way;***

Paul says that it is the man who keeps these things which he lists as being good who should be made a bishop. These are the marks of the episcopal dignity. If someone has chosen the harder way and dedicated his body and his mind to God so as not to be joined in marriage, he will be all the worthier. Paul mentions only the weaker man here, because there was no doubt about the other kind.

***5for if a man does not know how to manage his own household, how can he care for God's church?***

It is clear that the suitability of a future pastor can be tested by seeing whether he can control his own household properly first. *He who is faithful in small things is faithful in large ones also.*[12]

***6He must not be a recent convert, or he may be puffed up with conceit and fall into the condemnation of the devil;***

It is true that someone who is immature in his faith is likely to exalt himself in pride, particularly if he is ordained. He will be puffed up by the novelty and power of it all and think that he is worthier than other people. If he is raised up to some honor in the first year of his conversion he will think that he is no longer called to grow himself but only to help others improve, as if it were some blessing to give to religion more than one receives from it. Someone who is puffed up like that is being trapped by the devil. As soon as he gets the chance to play on his pride, Satan will cause him to fall. This is why we read in Solomon: *God resists the proud.*[13] It is also why the same apostle says in another letter: *Whoever thinks he is something deceives himself.*[14] And the Lord says: *Whoever exalts himself will be humbled.*[15]

***7moreover he must be well thought of by outsiders, or he may fall into reproach and the snare of the devil.***

Paul follows the Lord's intention when he says that a future bishop must have a good reputation among those outside the church, because *Whoever is faithful in small things will also be faithful in large ones*, as the Lord says.[16] And he goes on: *If you have not been faithful with someone else's mammon, who will give you any of your own?*[17] It is clear that someone who is found to be unfaithful in worldly matters and

[12]Lk 16:10. [13]Prov 3:34. [14]Gal 6:3. [15]Lk 14:11. [16]Lk 16:10. [17]Lk 16:11. Ambrosiaster's interpretation is different from the one commonly accepted today.

ordinary human behavior will undoubtedly be unsuitable for handling the things of God. If you keep faith with other people, how much more should you do so with God.

If a bishop does not have the fear of God before his eyes but appeals more to the spirit of the age, God will abandon him as an unbeliever and a false prophet. Whoever preaches one thing and does another will look deformed and spotted to everyone. He will accuse himself with his own words, because he has been consigned to the flock of Satan. The person who tries to practice what he preaches is the one who will be shown to be speaking the truth. Great care must therefore be taken in electing someone to rule over the house of God. If suitable administrators are required for earthly things, how much more are they needed for heavenly ones!

***8Deacons likewise must be serious, not double-tongued, not addicted to much wine, not greedy for gain; 9they must hold the mystery of the faith with a clear conscience. 10And let them also be tested first; then if they prove themselves blameless let them serve as deacons.***

Paul gives instructions that deacons are to be chosen with great care because it is clear that they are the servants of the priests. He wants them to be just like bishops, as he himself says, men who are irreproachable and conduct their affairs in public, with no shady dealings. He knows that there are some people who are only after money and there is no more to it than that. Paul calls it shady dealing when somebody appears to be godly but is only after money. Such a person pretends to be pure but is discovered to be wicked. After dealing with bishops, Paul goes on to talk about the ordination of deacons. Why does he do this, except that bishops and presbyters are the same thing? Both are priests, but the bishop comes first, so that while every bishop is a presbyter, not every presbyter is a bishop.[18] The bishop is the one who is first among the presbyters. Paul indicates that Timothy was ordained a presbyter, but as he had no one over him, he was a bishop. This is why he shows him how to ordain a bishop, for it is neither right nor permissible for an inferior to ordain a superior. No one can give what he has not received.

***11The women likewise must be serious, no slanderers, but temperate, faithful in all things.***

Because he has instructed that only a holy person can be made a bishop, and the same holds for a deacon, Paul does not want the congregation to be any different from them, particularly as the Lord said: *Be holy even as I am holy.*[19] Thus he wants even the women (who appear to be inferior) to be blameless, so that the church of God may be pure. The Montanists seize on this verse to fall into error on the ground that because Paul mentions women immediately after deacons, they too ought to be ordained as deaconesses. They defend their position with vain presumption, even though they know that the apostles chose seven deacons. How could it be that no suitable woman was found, when we read that there were holy women among the eleven apostles? But since heretics like to fill their minds with the words and not with the meaning of the law, they use the apostle's words to contradict the apostle's meaning, so that where he orders a woman to keep silence in church, they say the opposite and even claim the authority of ministry [for women].

***12Let deacons be the husband of one wife, and let them manage their children and their households well; 13for those who serve well as deacons gain a good standing for themselves***

[18]The English word "priest" is a corruption of "presbyter," but is used here to translate the Latin *sacerdos*. [19]Lev 19:2.

***and also great confidence in the faith which is in Christ Jesus.***

Paul now adds things which he had not said about the ordination of deacons, showing that they too ought to be husbands of one wife, so that only those who have not transgressed the law of God should be chosen for the service of God. God decreed that a man should have only one wife with whom he would be blessed. No one who has a second wife is blessed. Those who control their children well and their households, that is to say, their helpers or servants, will be worthy of the priesthood and have confidence with God, because they know that they can ask whatever they want as long as they stay away from sexual intercourse with women.

The ancient Levites and priests were allowed to have wives because they spent a lot of time in idleness away from their ministry or priesthood. There were a lot of priests and a large number of Levites, each one of whom took part in the divine ceremonies for a certain time, according to the rule of David. He created twenty-four classes of priests who took their turn to serve.[20] Thus Abijah belonged to the eighth class and it was during their turn that Zacharias was serving as a priest.[21] As it says in 1 Chronicles, during the time when they were not serving at the altar, they managed their households.[22] When the time was coming for them to serve, they would take a few days to purify themselves and then go up to the temple to offer sacrifices to God. Now, however, there must be seven deacons and as many presbyters, so that each church can have two and every city have one bishop. For this reason they must all abstain from the company of women, because they have to be present every day in the church and there is no time for them to be purified according to the law, as the ancients were after they had slept with women. Even if they do not have to offer daily sacrifice, they have to do so on a weekly basis and in some special places, twice a week. They cannot afford to go away since sick people are baptized almost every day. The ancients were allowed not to appear in the temple for a long time, but they were deprived. If Paul orders ordinary people to abstain for a time in order to pray, so that they can make room for prayer,[23] how much more should the Levites or priests do so, in order to pray day and night for the people entrusted to them! They should be cleaner than others because they are agents of God.

***[14]I hope to come to you soon, but I am writing these instructions to you so that, [15]if I am delayed, you may know how one ought to behave in the household of God, which is the church of the living God, the pillar and bulwark of the truth.***

As far as Paul knew, it would not be long before Timothy would see him, but since God often wished otherwise, and his providence is known to him alone, Paul says: "I am writing to you in case I am delayed, so that you will know how to order the church, which is the house of God." Even though the whole world belongs to God, the church is still called the house of God, whose pastor nowadays is Damasus.[24] The world is in transgression because it is convulsed with different kinds of error. Therefore it is necessary for a house of God to be set apart where the truth will be respected according to his will. His servants confess what he himself has been pleased to teach them, and so that his words will not be nullified, he has confirmed them with miracles which cannot be done by anyone else, so that the unbelief of which they are accused is inexcusable and perishes. These signs and wonders are the pillar and ground of truth.

[20]Cf. 1 Chron 6:31-48. [21]Lk 1:5. [22]1 Chron 24:1-19. [23]Cf. 1 Cor 7:5. [24]Damasus I was bishop of Rome from 366 to 384.

***[16]Great indeed, we confess, is the mystery of our religion:***
***He was manifested in the flesh,***
***vindicated in the Spirit,***
***seen by angels,***
***preached among the nations,***
***believed on in the world,***
***taken up in glory.***

God does not deny that any believer can look on the sacrament of the truth preached in the church, which he calls godliness. In his generosity and mercy he has given divine gifts to those who recognize him, apart from the forgiveness of sins, which he is now bestowing.

Paul says that the sacrament of the mystery of God, which is Christ in the flesh and was once hidden in the Spirit, has now been made known. The Son of God who was once hidden with God has been born as a man and has proclaimed himself by word and deed to the creation. To be justified in the Spirit means to have revealed in works and power who this man in the flesh actually was. Later he appeared to the angels, not in the form of humility but of power. He appeared in the form of humility in the flesh only until he conquered death and rose again from the dead, when his majesty was revealed. The one who was born as a man was not just a man, as the angels who recognized that the mystery which had previously lain hidden was now declared in the flesh, bowed the knee to him and gave him thanks as if he were God, because they had learned the truth which was preached to the Gentiles in order to set them free from the error in which the world lives, so that they would not be condemned. Thus the sacrament of God was believed on in the world so that unbelief could not claim the excuse of error, as the Lord said to the Jews: *If I had not come and spoken to them, they would have no sin, but now they will have no excuse for their sin.*[25] What they despised as weak and deformed was taken up into glory. After the cross, where his person and power were manifested, the Savior publicly ascended to heaven with clouds surrounding him.

## 1 Timothy 4

***[1]Now the Spirit expressly says that in later times some will depart from the faith by giving heed to deceitful spirits and doctrines of demons, [2]through the pretensions of liars whose consciences are seared, [3]who forbid marriage and enjoin abstinence from foods which God created to be received with thanksgiving by those who believe and know the truth. [4]For everything created by God is good, and nothing is to be rejected if it is received with thanksgiving; [5]for then it is consecrated by the word of God and prayer.***

Paul does not conceal what the Holy Spirit has revealed of the future for the instruction of the churches and for a warning that the churches which have been so forewarned must take care not to be deceived by such people. How could Paul forewarn them so clearly and openly, in an unmistakable voice, to avoid, or better condemn, men of this pestiferous teaching, to the point where he called it the deceptive and false doctrine of demons, so that when they heard talk of it, they would know that it was a doctrine invented by the devil? The Holy Spirit had predicted that they would say false things about the incarnation of the Savior, something which is now to be observed among the Marcionites, though they have almost disappeared now, the Patricians and above all the Manichaeans? They deny that Christ was born, forbid marriage and tell people they must abstain from certain foods. Paul says that their consciences are seared, which means that they are damned. [From the way in which

[25]Jn 15:22.

he expresses himself it is clear that his words carry the implication of condemnation. This is the sign.][26]

In order to misrepresent the maker of mankind (for they do not regret having been born), they forbid marriage and take Christ's flesh away from him, and in order to do him even more harm, they teach that the things which he gave us for our use ought to be renounced, so that what they despise as evil will look as if it came from an evil creator. This is why the apostle says that everything which God has made is good as long as it is used with thanksgiving. These things are unclean to the person who does not praise his creator for them. They cannot be of any benefit to someone who uses them in such a way as to misrepresent their Creator.

***6If you put these instructions before the brethren, you will be a good minister of Christ Jesus, nourished on the words of the faith and of the good doctrine which you have followed.***

What is so true, so clear and so sensible as that Christian doctrine should be handed on uncorrupted, so that its fruit may be praised as fertile and productive in the Lord's field, in other words, that on the day of judgment it should not be condemned and thrown into the fire? A good teacher and faithful minister of the Lord Jesus Christ is one who he says has been nourished by the words of faith and good doctrine, which he asserts he has followed from his childhood. Whoever had memorized all the books of the Hebrews made a perfect teacher once he accepted the faith.

***7Have nothing to do with godless and silly myths. Train yourself in godliness; 8for while bodily training is of some value, godliness is of value in every way, as it holds promise for the present life and also for the life to come.***

Profane words are those which are anti-Christian, and silly myths are forms of madness. These things have a habit of leading to dissension when people start arguing about them, and the result is a debate about some silly thing which does nothing except waste people's time. Paul therefore warns Timothy to stay away from things which are contrary, and likewise from things which are silly, because they have been invented by some kind of vanity. There are always some people hotheaded enough to launch into such disputations.

Paul urges Timothy to pay attention to godliness because it has great benefit. Those who practice mercy doubtless bring honor to their parents. God's help will not desert them in this life, and in the world to come they will have immortality with glory. Paul says that physical exercise is of some use, but to fast and to abstain from certain foods is of little benefit as long as the Creator remains in control, unless they are accompanied by godliness, whose effort to gain the Lord is helped by the prayers of many. Finally, the gospel message bears witness that those who are generous to the brethren and obedient in various ways will obtain eternal life, whereas those who turn away from this work will go into eternal fire.

The exercise of the body is nothing other than the restraint of the flesh. Mercy is a great thing, but if someone goes on allowing the lust of the flesh to rule him, what will happen? No doubt he will be beaten, because he should have shown mercy and not bothered about the exercise. If he has done nothing but exercise his body, the eternal fire will punish him as

[26]An alternative version of these two sentences reads: "Paul says that their conscience is seared, which means corrupted by hypocrisy. Just as a brand-iron sears a hide and leaves a mark on it, so deception, which knows one thing but in the cleverness of its malice says another, marks the conscience for destruction. Paul says that such people cannot change and be saved because just as the brand cannot be altered, so their mind cannot be changed either, for there is nothing worse than hypocrisy. These people are like those Jews who knew that Christ worked by the power of God but said that what he did came from Beelzebub [Mt 12:24]."

the Lord promised in the Gospel,[27] because the essence of our discipline lies in mercy and godliness.

Carnal people exercise their bodies in one way and spiritual people do it in another. Carnal people feed their bodies by wining and dining, and so hasten to their damnation, but spiritual people control their bodies by fasting and abstinence, so that the pledges they make about their desires may be worthy of the coming resurrection. The spiritual person beats his body for the sake of his future hope, whereas the carnal one has no hope of the future and so pampers it for the time being, thereby encouraging it to sin.

***9The saying is sure and worthy of full acceptance. 10For to this end we toil and strive, because we have our hope set on the living God, who is the Savior of all men, especially of those who believe.***

To suffer persecution for the hope which is in God is something which is perfectly worthy and must be endured, because in the present life hope leads nowhere, but in the promise of God it is firm and certain. God is the salvation of everyone who lives from him and by him. This is true of everyone as far as the present life is concerned, but it is true of believers with respect to the salvation which is promised to us. God has promised that after this life, which ends in death, he will give another one, which lasts for ever, to those who know him. This is why Paul says *especially of those who believe.*

***11Command and teach these things. 12Let no one despise your youth, but set the believers an example in speech and conduct, in love, in faith, in purity.***

Timothy was a young man in terms of his age, but in terms of his morals and behavior he was old and mature. Paul therefore urges him to grow so that he will be an example of all good works. That way a wonderful and very mature discipline would appear in a young man, so that his acts would belie his age and he would be regarded not as a young man but as an elder. People older than he was would then be ashamed if they did not behave like him, mature in their behavior and morals, whereas young people would have a teacher who was the same age as they were. The most holy Timothy was a wonderful young man, by whose example the indisciplined extravagances of youth were to be restrained and the irreverence of older people was to be punished.

***13Till I come, attend to the public reading of scripture, to preaching, to teaching. 14Do not neglect the gift you have, which was given you by prophetic utterance when the council of elders laid their hands upon you.***

Paul wants Timothy to be intent on and dedicated to the exercise of reading, so that by every exertion and diligence he might strive to encourage and teach others. We encourage others when we use a kind word to spur them to do good works, and we teach them when we communicate to the minds of those who hear us what is hidden from them. If the head of the congregation hides such things from them, he is neglecting the grace which has been given to him. It is for this reason that a leader has been given to the congregation, so that he can take care of their salvation by warning and teaching. That way ordination serves the purpose for which God instituted it, which is to further the salvation of his people. Therefore whoever is placed in this position and does not do his job will be regarded as someone who despises God and is called least in the kingdom of God, nor will he be able to do what he is

[27]Cf. Lk 11:42.

not fit to teach. Yet Paul indicates that grace is given to those who are ordained by prophecy and the laying on of hands. Prophecy is the way in which a future teacher is chosen as suitable, whereas the hands of imposition are secret words by which the person chosen is confirmed for this work and receives authority, his conscience bearing witness, that he may dare to offer sacrifice to God as the Lord's representative.

***[15]Practice these duties, devote yourself to them, so that all may see your progress. [16]Take heed to yourself and to your teaching; hold to that, for by so doing you will save both yourself and your hearers.***

Paul urges Timothy to be a model to everyone, not only in good works but also in the practice of teaching. He indicates that progress in his duty must appear both in his teaching and in his deeds. A good tree produces good fruit. Likewise, good teaching cannot produce bad works, and so when good works are seen it may be understood that they are the fruit of divine teaching authority, and the hearers can benefit from them. They will understand that what is said to them is true and ought to be heeded when they are seen to be observed with great veneration by the person who teaches them. The pastor of the congregation benefits in two ways. He will receive a reward both from his own good works and also from those of his hearers, but if he neglects his duty, then he will have to give account not only for himself but for them as well.

## 1 Timothy 5

***[1]Do not rebuke an older man but exhort him as you would a father; treat younger men like brothers, [2]older women like mothers, younger women like sisters, in all purity.***

Out of respect for his age, an older person is to be gently prodded into doing good works so that he will accept the instruction more easily. Once he gets the message he may be afraid of being caught out later on, which is shameful to an older person. Old age is honored in every society, which is why the synagogue, and later on the church, had elders, without whose advice nothing was done in the church. I do not know why the custom has faded out. Perhaps it is because of the laziness of the teachers, or more likely because of their pride, since they want to be seen as the only ones who do anything. Paul thinks that the younger people are to be encouraged like brothers, in a friendly way, so that when they realize that they are being admonished out of love they will correct themselves more readily, especially if they see that Timothy's own behavior corresponds with his preaching. Old ladies should be treated like mothers, and when they see that they are being handled with kindly words they will accept it without grumbling, because it is hard for old people to be caught out by younger ones. Paul wants things to be controlled with an even temper, so that both the speaker and the hearer will benefit. He orders the young girls to be treated like sisters, so that they will be quick to adopt the discipline of good behavior. When somebody sees that he is being persuaded to accept things that contribute to a good life without arrogance, he will agree to be humble and defer to the person advising him. Things are often obtained by persuasion which cannot be had by laying down the law. When the baser instincts are stirred up, they usually succumb to gentle treatment.

***[3]Honor widows who are real widows.***

Paul says that widows who are genuine widows must be honored. Although they can remarry, if they choose to be better and worthy of God they will reject second marriages in the knowledge that marriage is blessed only once and emulate the most holy Anna, who served God night and day by fasting and prayer after she had lost her one and only husband.[28]

***[4]If a widow has children or grandchildren, let them first learn their religious duty to their own family and make some return to their parents; for this is acceptable in the sight of God.***

Paul says that a widow must first be tested to see whether she suits that kind of life and behavior, and only then should she be enrolled as a church widow, because she must not submit to church discipline for financial reasons as opposed to devotional ones. Her merits should precede her, so that due honor may be paid to her when she arrives. Those who have dealt with their relatives in a godly way and who have run their households well have kept God's law and made themselves worthy to receive the church's support.

***[5]She who is a real widow, and is left all alone, has set her hope on God and continues in supplications and prayers night and day;***

A widow who has children or grandchildren must not be enrolled on the church's charity list automatically, because if she has run her household in a godly and conscientious manner, her family is bound to repay her in the same way as she has repaid those close to her. But if, as sometimes happens, ungodliness has been at work and the old woman is rejected by her family when she has treated them well, then it is right for her to be taken on by the church, because she has acted faithfully according to the law of the Lord. A widow who is all alone, or who has been rejected by her family, puts her hope in God. Seeing that she has no help from anywhere else, she is devoted to God with her whole mind, and expects help for her life and salvation from him alone.

***[6]whereas she who is self-indulgent is dead even while she lives.***

For a widow to be called a true widow, Paul indicates that she must be the kind who spends all her time in prayer to God so as to draw closer to the Lord. She must serve him night and day and show that she has refused a second marriage in order to apply herself to the Lord's teaching. If she claims to be a widow but spends her time in amusements or in self-indulgence, she is to be considered dead even though she is still alive, because to say one thing and do another is a form of hypocrisy. These women do not want service and devotion to God but only the respect due to widowhood, whereas the profession of this name ought to indicate that after her husband's death, the widow has chosen to serve God with her whole mind for the sake of the life promised to her.

***[7]Command this, so that they may be without reproach.***

Paul wants a widow to be so careful about her behavior and morals that she cannot be reproached. Removed from any hope of a worldly life and from the need to take care of her body, she has turned wholly to God in order to lead an irreproachable life. Once the opportunities which generally provide openings for sin are taken away, good behavior can remain uncorrupted.

***[8]If any one does not provide for his relatives, and especially for his own family, he has disowned the faith and is worse than an unbeliever.***

A widow who has failed to educate her relatives in the teaching and discipline of the Lord is not to be honored, because like unbelievers

[28]Lk 2:36-37.

she has not obeyed the law of the Lord. Someone who lives under the law and in the fear of God but who ignores this is necessarily worse than someone who is not subject to the law. The latter is ignorant, but the former knows what he should do and ignores it.

***9Let a widow be enrolled if she is not less than sixty years of age, having been the wife of one husband; 10and she must be well attested for her good deeds, as one who has brought up children, shown hospitality, washed the feet of the saints, relieved the afflicted, and devoted herself to doing good in every way.***

If a widow is commended on the basis of her previous works, Paul teaches that she should be enrolled. Her name is to be added to the church lists by God's judgment, since her previous life declares her to be worthy of this. Fully engaged in the service of God and directing her life by it, she is to be taken into the bosom of the church to which she long ago vowed herself by legitimate forms of service.

***11But refuse to enrol younger widows; for when they grow wanton against Christ they desire to marry,***

Paul prohibits younger widows from being formally enrolled. No confidence should be placed in women of such a fickle age. There have been examples of some who, after making their profession, have been led astray by a desire for the pleasures of this life. They have the name of widows but not the deeds, and turn away in search of marriage. Whoever tries to live a life of pleasure in Christ will not escape unscathed. Extravagance will draw her away to her own kind and she will fall into sin, for pleasure is the gateway to sin. The person who loves a loose life is not unaware of where it is headed.

***12and so they incur condemnation for having violated their first pledge.***

Paul shows what awaits such people so that they will not easily attempt things which are difficult to carry out. If the mind is pledged to this [form of] devotion, let it keep this to itself, because it is dangerous to claim something which ought not to be imposed on someone who is still young. A person who fails to keep something which he had correctly done binds himself to damnation. Much as it is praiseworthy if he manages to do something which is believed to be beyond his powers, he is all the more subject to punishment if he tries to impose such a thing on himself by audacious daring when he cannot do it, nor will he be able to excuse himself, because he was unfaithful from the beginning.

***13Besides that, they learn to be idlers, gadding about from house to house, and not only idlers but gossips and busybodies, saying what they should not.***

Some virgins and widows rely on their formal profession (what a glorious name this state of life has!) to ingratiate themselves in the houses of the rich. They do this in order to comply with their desires, going about and asking what they can do for them and what they like. They become idle and fond of gifts, falling into the bad habit of being more interested in gossip than in hard work. Puffed up and arrogant, they go about acting against their profession. Behavior of this kind is usually detrimental to them in this life, because what they think can be kept hidden is inevitably revealed. What difference does it make if they say things that should not be said? They become entertainers at weddings, they know a lot of secrets, they are flatterers, and they stir up the servants.

***14So I would have younger widows marry, bear children, rule their households, and give the enemy no occasion to revile us. 15For some have already strayed after Satan.***

This means that they should control their families and not give the adversary any cause to speak evil of them. Paul has said that the things listed above are contrary and unlawful, and they will lead these women to their death. He therefore advises and enjoins them to do things which are lawful. It is better to run one's own household well than to be fawned upon in someone else's house. It is much better to marry than to raise eyebrows under the cover of a good and godly profession. It is better to work for a living and keep one's self-respect than to do nothing and wait shamelessly for handouts. In that way Satan finds an opportunity to undermine ill-advised souls who claim to be godly but act unjustly, for nothing is more dangerous than if one's deeds belie one's profession. Satan does not go after open evil in order to rejoice in it. It is when he sees somebody trying to practice deception that he acts to show that such a person is his child, and not God's, and God does not intervene to prevent this.

***16If any believing woman has relatives who are widows, let her assist them; let the church not be burdened, so that it may assist those who are real widows.***

Why should it be surprising that the power given to the apostles was able to predict future events? What Paul said has now occurred, because [these days] there are many widows of believers who burden the church. There are those who are rich in this world who retire women from clothmaking because of their old age but then take away their food and clothing (if not completely then at least in part), so that they turn to the church in their need in order to be able to survive. These rich people should not only have been generous to their own dependents, but they should also have taken care of other needs as well. There is a lot of trouble here. Although something is given to one group of widows, others are left with little or nothing when they should have been given priority because they are worthy of being supported by church funds. A church is burdened if it is forced to provide for many when it ought to be looking after only a few. A congregation which can only minister to a few adequately is forced to turn many others away, or else it grumbles and drags its feet in taking care of them. Where Paul ordered that only a widow who had been the wife of one husband was to be enrolled, now we find not only wives of two or three husbands, but even those who have been prostitutes. Sometimes this happens through negligence, but sometimes it occurs because those who want help are very persuasive.

***17Let the elders who rule well be considered worthy of double honor, especially those who labor in preaching and teaching;***

Good and faithful administrators are not only to be judged worthy of heavenly honor; they are to be given earthly reward as well so that they will not complain about their low wages but rather rejoice in their faith and teaching. A person is more willing to do things if he is not weighed down by poverty, and his self-confidence grows when he sees that he is earning the reward of his labor in this life, not to get rich but to have enough to live on.

***18for the scripture says, "You shall not muzzle an ox when it is treading out the grain," and, "The laborer deserves his wages."***[29]

The preacher of the kingdom of God ought to receive a salary which he can neither complain nor boast about.

***19Never admit any charge against an elder ex-***

[29]Deut 25:4.

***cept on the evidence of two or three witnesses.***

Since this is the highest honor (for presbyters are the vicars of Christ), accusations against a presbyter should not be readily entertained. It should be just as impossible to believe that someone who is God's representative could be a hardened criminal as it is possible to believe that an actor leads a wicked life.

***20 As for those who persist in sin, rebuke them in the presence of all, so that the rest may stand in fear.***

Although it must not be easy to believe that a presbyter has committed a crime, if one is proved or if it is clear that he has behaved in a way unsuited to his office, Paul says that he must be publicly rebuked so that the others will be frightened. This is good not only for the ordained but also for the laity, for when they see a prominent man disciplined because of his error, they will certainly be more cautious themselves.

***21 In the presence of God and of Christ Jesus and of the elect angels I charge you to keep these rules without favor, doing nothing from partiality. 22 Do not be hasty in the laying on of hands, nor participate in another man's sins; keep yourself pure.***

Paul deposits his testimony with God the Father, Christ his Son and the elect angels, whom the Lord calls the holy ones in the Gospel.[30] These angels are elect because the others are reprobate. They are not angels of God but of the devil, because they concur in his apostasy. Paul then testifies under oath that what he commands for the good order of the church must be kept. He orders that nothing should be done without prior investigation, so that no one may easily acquire a church position unless there has been some discussion of his life and morals beforehand so that he may be worthy to be approved as a minister or ordained as a priest. That way, if he later turns out to be unworthy, the head of the church will not have to feel responsible for not having clearly foreseen what someone whom he ordained without proper examination turned out to deserve. Neither should someone whose sins have come under suspicion be ordained, lest the person ordaining him should be contaminated by his sins and transgressions. If the person's crimes are totally unknown, the bishop will be free of guilt, because his conscience is clear. It is suspicion which produces hesitation, and a bishop sins if he ordains such a person without examining him first. Someone who is to be ordained must be shown to be better than others. It is not enough for him to be simply crime-free; the merits of his good works must stand out so that he will be regarded as worthy of ordination. The bishop who follows these rules will demonstrate that he is pure in religion and will be rewarded for this in the future.

***23 No longer drink only water, but use a little wine for the sake of your stomach and your frequent ailments.***

Paul now gives Timothy some private advice, telling him to take care of his health. God wants to be served wisely. He does not want his servants to weaken themselves by extreme behavior and end up requiring medical treatment. Moderation must be the rule, and if possible, the ministry embarked upon should be gradually developed and not diminished by thoughtlessness. Extreme behavior upsets the soul, and if it has to cope with illness it will be less dedicated to the service of God. Lack of foresight brings trouble, but the soul which is put at rest lifts its whole heart to God and prays for what is needed with its entire mind.

30 Cf. Mk 8:38.

*[24]The sins of some men are conspicuous, pointing to judgment, but the sins of others appear later. [25]So also good deeds are conspicuous; and even when they are not, they cannot remain hidden.*

Paul wants it to be understood that people who follow those whose sins are open and obvious will not be excused, so that if they avoid them they will have greater honor. He therefore indicates that the man of God should stay away from such people, particularly if he is a clergyman who may even have the power to discipline them. Those who promise to reform themselves are to be retained. Paul shows, however, that others follow the evil deeds of those who are thought to be good people during their lifetime but are exposed when they die, so that those who previously presented themselves as respectable are later declared to have been hypocrites.

By the same logic, good deeds are manifested in the same way that bad ones are, because a good life and humble acts cannot be hidden. If they are done in a godly manner they make people perfect. Just as there are some bad things which are presently hidden, so also there are some good things [which are hidden] too. No one can know everything about other people, but each of us decides and judges on the basis of what we see and hear. It all depends on whether the things which are said, good or bad, fit the person about whom they are said or not. What is hidden from human beings will be revealed on the day of judgment. It is for this reason that these things are said, that they may realize that some people are worse off than others. It is worse if a bad person pretends to be good than if he is just openly bad.

## 1 Timothy 6

*[1]Let all who are under the yoke of slavery regard their masters as worthy of all honor, so that the name of God and the teaching may not be defamed.*

Paul wants masters to give thanks to God because of the obedience of their slaves. If slaves show faithful service to their masters by following the doctrine of God, perhaps those masters will also submit themselves to that teaching.

*[2]Those who have believing masters must not be disrespectful on the ground that they are brethren; rather they must serve all the better since those who benefit by their service are believers and beloved.*

*Teach and urge these duties.*

If Paul orders us to serve non-Christian masters with total dedication, how much more should we serve believing ones! The slave proves that he is subject to the fear of God if he is totally obedient to his temporal lord. Nor should the slave think that he can disobey his master on the ground that the latter is a brother in the faith which they both share, for someone who despises a believing master will be punished all the more. Paul wants God's teaching to be manifested so that those who despise it will be confounded, since what they reproach is not part of the teaching at all. They will also have to remember that there are secret evils in their own sacred rites and be ashamed of what they cannot be pardoned for.

*[3]If any one teaches otherwise and does not agree with the sound words of our Lord Jesus Christ and the teaching which accords with godliness, [4]he is puffed up with conceit, he knows nothing; he has a morbid craving for controversy and for disputes about words, which produce envy, dissension, slander, base suspicions, [5]and wrangling among men who are depraved in mind and bereft of the truth, imagining that godliness is a means of gain.*

Paul says that those who deviate from catholic teaching are to be avoided, particularly the ones who are convicted and disciplined but do not want to submit because of the disquiet of their corrupt minds, and are pleased by and nourished on arguments. An arrogant person will not allow himself to be defeated but will prefer to break into conflict in search of approval, something which must be avoided by meek and good men. There is never any disagreement without a dispute, which would not be too bad if that were all there was to it, but blasphemies and hatreds must also be factored in. These things are foreign to God's servants, but they are a useful indicator of who is corrupted in his mind and deprived of the truth. They think that the worship of God and godliness are means of gain because they have no hope of anything in the future. All they are concerned about is how to manage in the present, just like those worldly sects which have clearly been invented for financial reward in this life. They know perfectly well that some people will lend a willing ear to whatever brings them gain in this life, and therefore such people are to be avoided.

***6There is great gain in godliness with contentment;***

Paul says that there are great riches and gain when a believer is content with what he has. A godly person is one who appears to himself and to others as one who by God's mercy has been won for the future life. For this reason, he thinks that what he has is plenty for the present and does not doubt that it has all been bestowed by God himself. Every greedy person is ungodly and harmful both to himself and to others.

***7for we brought nothing into the world, and we cannot take anything out of the world; 8but if we have food and clothing, with these we shall be content.***

Paul openly declares that mortal men who want to amass fortunes and become rich do so in vain, because they know that nothing they have in this world really belongs to them. What is the point of human greed other than to be its own worst enemy? The greedy person brought nothing into the world and will take nothing out of it. Why does he worry about it then and try to hoard things? He will pass away just as he came into the world. This is what the most holy Job wrote during his suffering: *Naked I came from my mother's womb and naked I shall return to the earth.*[31] If greedy people did not persist in their perversity, a few people could store up enough to bring benefit to many to their own advantage.

***9But those who desire to be rich fall into temptation, into a snare, into many senseless and hurtful desires that plunge men into ruin and destruction. 10For the love of money is the root of all evils; it is through this craving that some have wandered away from the faith and pierced their hearts with many pangs.***

There is nothing more bitter or more dangerous than if a churchman, and especially one in a high position, is concerned with the riches of this world, because then he is a hindrance not only to himself but to others as well. He sets a bad example for other people, for there will certainly be many who will copy him to their own destruction. So the higher a man's rank is, the more he will persuade others to copy him, especially in matters which are detrimental in this life, and greed is the gateway to all kinds of evil. It is for this reason that it is the root of all evil, because it commits crimes, murders, obscenities and all sorts of wickedness in order to fulfill its desires, which is impossible. It is

[31]Job 1:21.

never satisfied in this life because it always wants more, and in the future [life] it stands condemned.

***11But as for you, man of God, shun all this; aim at righteousness, godliness, faith, love, steadfastness, gentleness.***

Paul encourages and orders the man of God to cut himself off from greed, so that he will be safe and rewarded with divine gifts in the future. The person who rejects something that appeals to so many will be worthy to receive the crown.

***12Fight the good fight of the faith; take hold of the eternal life to which you were called when you made the good confession in the presence of many witnesses.***

Because greed is a wicked thing, Paul orders the man of God to reject it and to follow righteousness, godliness and the other things which he lists. He will not be able to avoid it unless he clings to these things which are hostile to greed. How is it possible for a greedy man to be a believer, when his deeds deny what he professes with his words? Where is the lover of the brotherhood whose hands are empty? How can someone be patient if he is always going after things which do not belong to him? How can someone have peace of mind if he burns day and night with a lust for greed? Because such iniquity is foreign to Timothy, the man of God, he is ordered to fight the good fight of faith. Faith has the victory, because all sins and crimes will be suppressed so that the one who has it may come to the rewards of eternal life. When the witnesses are asked and give their reply, his confession will be found among those basics of the faith which are recorded on the rolls of the church.

***13In the presence of God who gives life to all things, and of Christ Jesus who in his testimony before Pontius Pilate made the good confession, 14I charge you to keep the commandment unstained and free from reproach until the appearing of our Lord Jesus Christ; 15and this will be made manifest at the proper time by the blessed and only Sovereign, the King of kings and Lord of lords, 16who alone has immortality and dwells in unapproachable light, whom no man has ever seen or can see. To him be honor and eternal dominion. Amen.***

It is with great vigilance and foresight that Paul gives these commandments to the pastor of the church, because the salvation of the entire congregation is bound up in his person. It is not because of any particular concern for Timothy that Paul is so careful. He is more worried about Timothy's successors, hoping that they will follow Timothy's example in maintaining the discipline of the church and that they too will be a model for future generations. This is why he says: *I charge you to keep the commandment unstained and free from reproach until the appearing of our Lord Jesus Christ,* making it clear that he is commanding this in the presence of God and Christ.

In order to put fear into them, Paul recalls the suffering of Christ, saying that whoever rejects what Christ suffered for will be guilty and have to suffer it himself. Nor does he refrain from speaking about the day of judgment, which will come at a time predetermined by the will of God, whom he declares is the only blessed and powerful, King of kings and Lord of lords. He is the only one who has his own blessedness and power, dominion, rule and immortality, which he did not get from anyone else. The Father has all these things and so does the Son, from the Father. The inaccessible light belongs to the Father alone, because he has never appeared to anyone. Finally Paul adds: *Whom no man has ever seen or can see.* It is not that the Son has some other light, because it is written in Psalm 36: *In your light shall we see light.*[32] This means that the light of the Father is in the Son, but because nobody has seen the Father, he dwells in inaccessible light. There is no way to see God other than through Christ. The one who is of God sees God. Because the Son does everything, he is the one who is said to appear and be seen. What is peculiar to the Father is what is said above. *To him be honor and eternal dominion. Amen.*

***17As for the rich in this world, charge them not***
***to be haughty, nor to set their hopes on uncer-***
***tain riches but on God who richly furnishes***
***us with everything to enjoy. 18They are to do***
***good, to be rich in good deeds, liberal and gen-***
***erous, 19thus laying up for themselves a good***
***foundation for the future, so that they may***
***take hold of the life which is life indeed.***

The true life is the one which we look for in the future, which does not die or come to an end in time. It is eternal, which is why it is properly called "true." What we have now is an image of life, not the truth. And because the image is not totally empty, the life to come is acquired in this life. And in order to hasten toward that life, the truth is learned through the image which declares it, because it is not tainted by pride or by the hope of riches, but is marked by humility and hope in God, who has promised it. We must hope in him because he gives us what we need, not in the supplies themselves but in the author of them. What hope is there in things which are perishable and uncertain, particularly when so many of them are fading away? Those who cling to such things gain no benefit from them for the future. They only lose out, unless they suffer along with those in need, nor are they eternal in a way which offers a foretaste of the future life. These things make people proud, as if they had been promised immortality.

We have a model of the resurrection in Christ, but many people do not love Christ nearly as much as they love wealth, of which they have no example which can deliver anyone from death. It is Christ who has redeemed us, not wealth. He shows himself as the pattern of our future life, so that we may reject everything else and follow him until we come to the immortal and heavenly riches. We must therefore strive to be rich in good deeds and gain spiritual riches by using our earthly resources wisely. Let us sow on earth so that we may reap in heaven, where the eternal treasure is located.

***20O Timothy, guard what has been entrusted***
***to you. Avoid the godless chatter and contra-***
***dictions of what is falsely called knowledge,***
***21for by professing it some have missed the***
***mark as regards the faith.***
***Grace be with you.***

Paul repeats his warnings, so that what he has said above may be kept. Things which are contrary to true religion, which usurp only the name of knowledge, are to be avoided, as are those who make a false profession of faith in order to deceive the simple. They pretend to have a faith which they have abandoned, in order to bring in unbelief instead. He signs off in his own hand, saying: *Grace be with you. Amen.*

[32]Ps 36:9.

# AMBROSIASTER
## *Commentary on 2 Timothy*

### Preface

Paul writes another letter to Timothy who was now well instructed in church discipline and in the hope of the promise, in order to encourage him to face martyrdom, following his own example. He also wanted to say that a time was coming when some people would be lured away from sound doctrine, because it seemed too hard for them to accept, and be converted to myths, which are only human opinions.

### 2 Timothy 1

***1 Paul, an apostle of Christ Jesus by the will of God according to the promise of the life which is in Christ Jesus,***

***2 To Timothy, my beloved child:***

***Grace, mercy, and peace from God the Father and Christ Jesus our Lord.***

This is how Paul indicates that he has been called to be an apostle of Christ Jesus by the will of God, in order to teach what and how great the future promise of faith in Christ is, so that by his preaching there may be an increase in those who are to be saved by the Lord's teaching. The best servants are those who by their own faith and initiative increase the possessions of their masters. Paul writes to Timothy as to his most beloved son, so that he may be an imitator of these things and hand them on to others, so that through his agency Timothy may be a good and faithful teacher, who will preach the truth and win many to the promised life.

In his concern for Timothy, Paul prays that the grace of God the Father may be with him, as well as that of Christ Jesus our Lord. God bestows his grace through Christ, because there is one grace common to both of them.

***3 I thank God whom I serve with a clear conscience, as did my fathers, when I remember you constantly in my prayers. 4 As I remember your tears, I long night and day to see you, that I may be filled with joy. 5 I am reminded of your sincere faith, a faith that dwelt first in your grandmother Lois and your mother Eunice and now, I am sure, dwells in you.***

Since it is right to remember good people, Paul gives thanks because he remembers that Timothy was a wonderful man, which was in itself a gift from God. Someone who thinks about good people is right to do so. Since the God of the Christians is the same as the God of the Jews, Paul testifies that he gives thanks to him as the God whose service he had inherited from his forefathers. Since his ancestors were waiting for the coming of the one whom Paul began to proclaim, they shared the same faith. And because he continued in the service of his parents and still belonged to them because they served the same God, he rightly says: *Whom I serve, as did my fathers.* And how do I serve him? *With a clear conscience,* he says. Once upon a time he had persecuted the church, but he did that out of love for God and not out of malice. Similarly, it is written in the epistle to the Hebrews that Levi, who received tithes, also gave tithes to Melchizedek, because he was in the loins of Abraham when Abraham paid tithes to Melchizedek.[1] So Levi is also said to have served God in his forefathers, because he paid tithes through his great-grandfather. (Levi's father was Jacob, his grandfather was Isaac and his great-grandfather was Abraham.) Paul says that he remembers Timothy often and is eager to see him because of the recollection of the tears which he had shed out of love for the apostle, when he went away from him (as it is understood he did). Paul quite rightly wants to see the man who loves him, and so be filled with the joy which comes from a common happiness born of a sincere faith, which he indicates had also been present in his grandmother and his mother, as it most certainly was also in him. All these family connections were rooted in the faith which they had maintained uncorrupted.

***6Hence I remind you to rekindle the gift of God that is within you through the laying on of my hands; 7for God did not give us a spirit of timidity but a spirit of power and love and self-control.***

Paul indicates that he has recalled the sincerity of the faith of his parents in order to strengthen Timothy. Who could hear the praise of those people in whom he also has a share and not grow by adding his own determination to their strength? This is how he rekindles in himself the grace of God which he received by the ordination of the presbytery. He nourishes his spirit by rejoicing in himself with great joy of mind, just as he rejoices in the newness of his ordination. Paul then adds: *God did not give us a spirit of timidity but of power.* The renewed man leaves fear behind and receives a spirit of rejoicing on account of his justification. Everyone who is unjust is in fear, not strong but weak, not in love but in hatred, not in self-control but wounded by error. But if anyone desires these things, he can be strong, loved and sober through faith.

***8Do not be ashamed then of testifying to our Lord, nor of me his prisoner, but share in suffering for the gospel in the power of God,***

Paul teaches that Timothy must remain firm and not be shaken in his profession of faith. There is no reason to be ashamed of it, because although Christ appeared as a man, God was seen in his actions, and although he was crucified, he nevertheless rose again from the dead and ascended into heaven on a cloud, after many people had seen him. This is not a cause of weakness but of power, because wherever there is thought to be some feebleness power will appear. It is therefore silly to say that someone has been weakened when it is clear that he has conquered. For this reason there was nothing in the apostle which might cause him to be ashamed, because if he is said to have been humiliated by persecutions and blows, he confounds his attackers insofar as he appears to be a miracle-worker because of the signs and wonders which he performs by God's will. The reason for this is so that it might be understood that he is not being humiliated because of his weakness, but willingly in order to gain more merit. God allows his servants to be humiliated by wicked people so that it will not look as though he is giving them rewards unjustly.

***9who saved us and called us with a holy calling, not in virtue of our works but in virtue of his own purpose and the grace which he gave us in Christ Jesus ages ago,***

Since death has been conquered by the power of God so that we may be saved, we ought therefore to give something back to our Redeemer. Because we cannot repay him for all his benefits, let us do the task which he has assigned to us faithfully and promptly.

A *holy calling* is when people are chosen

[1] Cf. Heb 7:9-10.

to govern the holy people of God. There is no doubt that someone who is chosen to be a leader of sanctity is called to a holy calling. It is true, if you really want to know, that there is no human being worthy enough to be called the vicar of Christ, because everyone whom he has chosen had previously been a sinner. These people have been found worthy in comparison with others, but as far as the thing itself is concerned, they are all unworthy.

Because God, of his own good pleasure, long ago decreed that he would save sinners (for God knew in advance what human beings would be like, even before he created them and they sinned), he foreordained how they would be brought back, at what time, through whom and in what way they might be saved, so that they are not saved by their own merits, nor by the merits of those through whom they have been called, but this gift is seen to be offered by God's grace through faith in Christ.

***10and now has manifested through the appearing of our Savior Christ Jesus, who abolished death and brought life and immortality to light through the gospel. 11For this gospel I was appointed a preacher and apostle and teacher,***

Paul declares that the gift of God which had been hidden in mystery before all ages has been declared in the incarnation and coming of Christ, when people began to receive forgiveness of their sins. Paul shows how Christ saved his people by destroying death, which was man's enemy and prevented him from coming back from hell. He then illuminated this life with eternity, so that whoever came back from the dead would not be able to die again. The life which is limited by time is called dark because it sleeps in ignorance. Paul shows how it is illuminated by life, because eternity is given to those who believe the gospel which has been preached by the teacher of the Gentiles.

***12and therefore I suffer as I do. But I am not ashamed, for I know whom I have believed, and I am sure that he is able to guard until that Day what has been entrusted to me.***

Whoever preaches the gift of God suffers the devil as his enemy. The devil brings persecution on the preacher because he has snatched the people from his jaws. Paul is sure that there is a great reward promised for sufferings and is not confounded by them. Instead, he glories in the pressures put upon him. What Paul is saying is that he is secure in the hope and confidence of the Savior's greatness and that what he has entrusted to him is being kept safe. What has he entrusted to him other than his salvation? Thus, by suffering for him he will find salvation in him when he comes to judge, for when he punishes the unbelievers he will find Paul worthy of eternal life.

***13Follow the pattern of the sound words which you have heard from me, in the faith and love which are in Christ Jesus; 14guard the truth that has been entrusted to you by the Holy Spirit who dwells within us.***

Paul calls his commandments with their accompanying actions the model of saving doctrine, which he orders Timothy to follow and maintain under the guidance of the Holy Spirit.

***15You are aware that all who are in Asia turned away from me, and among them Phygelus and Hermogenes.***

Those whom Paul mentions were full of deceit. They pretended to be the apostle's friends, following him in order to learn, only to attack him or undermine him through others. After they saw that they were unmasked, they went away from him.

***16May the Lord grant mercy to the household***

***of Onesiphorus, for he often refreshed me; he was not ashamed of my chains,***

The refreshment must be understood as being of two kinds. Onesiphorus refreshed him by looking after his needs when he was in detention, and he also supplied whatever needs he or others had. Because of the hope of the things which were promised, he was not ashamed to go and ask for a man who was being held in prison. On the other hand, those whom he mentions above deserted the apostle in his need, because they were ashamed of the cross of Christ.

***17but when he arrived in Rome he searched for me eagerly and found me—18may the Lord grant him to find mercy from the Lord on that Day—and you well know all the service he rendered at Ephesus.***

Paul went to Rome because he had appealed to Caesar and was being held prisoner by soldiers.[2] It was there that Onesiphorus found the man he was looking for after searching diligently for him because of his love and obedience to his master. The apostle was so pleased with his visits that he commended him to God, praying that he would receive mercy from God on the day of judgment. Just as the apostle found mercy when he asked for it, so someone else who sought mercy would obtain it from the Judge. Paul therefore prays that God the Father of heaven and earth would show favor to Onesiphorus and that he would obtain grace from the Lord of the human race, that is to say, from the Son. This is just the same as what we find in Genesis: *And the Lord rained sulfur and fire on Sodom and Gomorrah from the Lord out of heaven.*[3]

*You well know all the service he rendered at Ephesus.* Since some people prefer to serve particular individuals rather than causes, because they want to look good to their superiors, Paul shows that Onesiphorus was good to everybody. In that way, it would not appear that by ministering to the apostle he was ingratiating himself with a particular person when it was clear that he had been generous to everyone.

## 2 Timothy 2

***1You then, my son, be strong in the grace that is in Christ Jesus, 2and what you have heard from me before many witnesses entrust to faithful men who will be able to teach others also.***

Paul urges Timothy to be constant and firm in teaching in the grace of God which is in Christ Jesus, and not only in the grace but also in the mysteries which are in Christ. He wants these secret things to be taught to those who are faithful and worthy, so that they in turn can teach others. He did not want these things to be generally shared with the vulgar and neglectful, and said that a teacher must be chosen with great care.

***3Share in suffering as a good soldier of Christ Jesus. 4No soldier on service gets entangled in civilian pursuits, since his aim is to satisfy the one who enlisted him.***

It is clear that what he is saying is that *no man can serve two masters.*[4] Secular affairs are invariably driven by greed, and people involved with them cannot come to terms with this unless they are liars. They do so, but that is a minor sin. A clergyman, however, proves himself before God by being devoted to him and fulfilling the task which he has entrusted to him. He must be concerned with the things of God and have no involvement with secular affairs. It is not good for one man to have two jobs.

[2]Cf. Acts 28:16. [3]Gen 19:24. [4]Mt 6:24.

***[5]An athlete is not crowned unless he competes according to the rules.***

Paul wants the soldier of God to be so practiced in the works of God and in the task delegated to him that he may attain the merit of glory by caring for the service of God with his whole mind, by rejecting things of this world and by loving heavenly things instead. He has proved himself in this way so as to be rewarded in heaven for his labor.

***[6]It is the hard-working farmer who ought to have the first share of the crops. [7]Think over what I say, for the Lord will grant you understanding in everything.***

The holy Timothy was so abstemious that he even stayed off lawful things. Paul wants this to be understood, because he took nothing from the church treasury, since the Lord had decreed that *those who preach the gospel shall live off the gospel.*[5] Paul therefore tells Timothy that he ought to be paid first because he is the head of the church, and then pay others according to their rank.

***[8]Remember Jesus Christ, risen from the dead, descended from David, as preached in my gospel, [9]the gospel for which I am suffering and wearing fetters like a criminal. But the word of God is not fettered.***

Since in the future there would be many sons of the devil who would deny that the Son of God had been incarnated, Paul reminded Timothy of this, and because they would try to proclaim this deceitfully in the guise of apostles, he added: *according to my gospel,* so as to exclude the false deliberations of an evil mind. No one should believe what they have to say about the apostles and ignore what the apostles have to say about themselves, especially since Paul protested that his own preaching was a struggle. He was afflicted by persecutions and imprisonments because he offended both Jews and Gentiles by preaching things which seemed incredible to them. He made Jews angry because he taught that the law had come to an end. He made enemies of the Gentiles because he preached that there was only one God in Christ. That is why they treated him like a criminal, binding him and locking him up in the hope of keeping him quiet, not realizing that they could not imprison the Word of God. Then again, Paul did not lose anything from his frequent imprisonments but profited from them. There were people to whom he could preach in prison, so that although he was not free to invite them to accept the faith, he could feed them on the Word of God from his prison cell.

***[10]Therefore I endure everything for the sake of the elect, that they also may obtain salvation in Christ Jesus goes with its eternal glory.***

Paul was subjected to trials so that by his preaching he might save people who were predestined to life, knowing that he would benefit from the salvation which he sought for them.

***[11]The saying is sure:***
***If we have died with him, we shall also live with him;***
***[12]if we endure, we shall also reign with him;***
***if we deny him, he also will deny us;***

Paul says that it is possible to come to the immortality and glory of Christ if we remain true to our baptism in which all transgressions die, so that being renewed we may flee all our old sins and crimes and by following in the footsteps of the Author be seen to have died to our sins. If there is anything to add to this, it would be that we should suffer tribulations

[5]1 Cor 9:14.

and persecutions for the name of the Lord without bitterness, because if we endure them we shall reign together with him. It is right that whoever has suffered abuse and afflictions for his sake should appear covered with glory in his kingdom. It is also true that if we have not confessed him before other people, he will say to us in that necessity of future judgment: *I do not know you.*[6] This is the meaning of punishment.

***13if we are faithless, he remains faithful— for he cannot deny himself.***

Nobody can take away from God what belongs to him. Who is stronger than the one through whom all things have come into existence? Nothing can be added to what is perfect, nor can one who believes in him offer him anything, just as someone who does not believe in him cannot take anything away from him. Thus whatever happens works to our benefit so that we may not remain in ignorance. God is not strengthened by us, because he is already strong in and of himself.

***14Remind them of this, and charge them before the Lord to avoid disputing about words, which does no good, but only ruins the hearers.***

Paul warns Timothy to avoid disputes, and says that his commands ought to be given in the fear and terror of the Lord, because argument may produce hesitation among those who are less well-grounded in the faith. They are often landed in such argumentation by the well-honed spirit of malice, and in this way the minds of new believers are unsettled.

***15Do your best to present yourself to God as one approved, a workman who has no need to be ashamed, rightly handling the word of truth.***

Since there are some who say that argument benefits the hearers, the apostle, who knows that it is more likely to stand in their way, orders that each person should make himself approved by avoiding disputes, and calls those who get involved in arguments shameless. Argument inevitably twists matters, especially when many things are said which go against conscience, so that the person who appears to win on the outside actually loses spiritually on the inside. Nobody lets himself be defeated, even if he knows that what he hears [from his opponent] is true. The person who acts well and with a good conscience is the one who talks to those who are willing and peaceful. There should be agreement among God's servants and not disputes.

***16Avoid such godless chatter, for it will lead people into more and more ungodliness, 17and their talk will eat its way like gangrene. Among them are Hymenaeus and Philetus, 18who have swerved from the truth by holding that the resurrection is past already. They are upsetting the faith of some.***

Paul continues with the theme that disputes are to be avoided. It is not fitting for people who share a common faith to have arguments. They ought to bear with one another in discussion and agree with what is good. If something seems to be wrong, then it should be rejected peacefully. Adversaries and dissidents have a habit of provoking one another, particularly if one of them is catholic and the other pagan. Timothy is a catholic, and the apostle warns him to reject and turn away from silly fables. He should be peaceful and always speak conscientiously, so as not to allow himself to be provoked into uttering ungodly words. Such things give some people an excuse to become worse, for there is no lack of people who think evil thoughts when they hear such

[6]Mt 25:12.

profane talk. That is why disputes are a stumbling block.

Paul goes on to produce the names of those for whose sake arguments are to be avoided. He calls them profane and ungodly because they have wandered away from the truth. They have denied that it is the Christian's great glory to believe that they will rise again from the dead in the future. These people, as we are taught by another text,[7] said that the children of God would rise from the dead, but they did not mean the same thing by this. Instead, they twisted the meaning in a way which goes against the faith which they had received in the beginning.

**[19]*But God's firm foundation stands, bearing this seal: "The Lord knows those who are his,"[8] and, "Let every one who names the name of the Lord depart from iniquity."[9]***

God's foundation is the faith which contains what God has promised. This faith cannot be contaminated by the comments of unbelievers and heretics. Although they deny what we believe will happen in the future, God will still give what we believe he will give, as his promise bears witness. Therefore the sign of God's promise is our faith, which confirms the words of God. On the day of judgment, God will recognize those who have his sign and who turn away from the wickedness of unbelievers and heretics, who think they can weaken the promise of God. There is nothing more wicked than to go against the faith of God. This is what was said by Moses to Dathan, Abiram and Korah when they presumed to offer sacrifices against the commandment of God: *The Lord knows who are his*. By saying this, he shows how wickedness controls those who pervert the words of God.

**[20]*In a great house there are not only vessels of gold and silver but also of wood and earthenware, and some for noble use, some for ignoble.***

In saying this, Paul indicated that there are different kinds of people in the church. Some are good and top-notch types, and Paul understands them as the gold vessels. Others are simply good, and these he labels silver vessels. Others, however, are not good, and these he calls vessels of wood and clay, which I think is clear enough. The apostle often has occasion to rebuke this kind of person in the Corinthian church. The situation in our own church is the same, and it is clear from many passages that it was also the case in the temple at Jerusalem, which was the type of the church. There were Sadducees there, from whom sprang Hymenaeus and Philetus. Paul no sooner talked about their perverse opinions than he added that it was not surprising that there were people in the church who disagreed with its teaching. Even in the Corinthian church, of which I have just spoken, there were those who disagreed and denied the resurrection.[10]

Yet that crazy Novatian taught that this verse should be understood differently, because he was trying to popularize his own error. He said that the "great house" should be understood to mean the entire world, because it contains a variety of people, although it is clear that the apostle was using the example of the house of a rich and wealthy person, which although it is well furnished, still has wooden and clay pots in it as well. The church likewise, although it is said to be holy, contains sinners and people who think wicked thoughts, as I mentioned above, whom Paul says are worthy of ignominy. However, he also says that they will not perish, but will be purged by fire, because they are in some ways necessary for the house.[11] But Novatian in his arrogance wanted

[7]This was probably the *Acts of Paul and Thecla*, c. 14. [8]Num 16:5. [9]Cf. Num 16:26. [10]1 Cor 15:12. [11]1 Cor 3:15.

to defend the perfect truth and sanctity of his own church. He decreed that this phrase should be understood to mean that his church was the only true one and contained all those who had been purified, and for that reason he accused us who are innocent [of being corrupt]. But why did he have to talk about the world here? What was he trying to prove by saying that the great house meant the world? The Lord said to the apostles: *You are not of the world, for I have chosen you out of the world.*[12] How then can those who are said not to be of the world be included with the world? The same apostle also said: *What have I to do with judging outsiders?*[13] Those who live in the same house share the same name; they are all known by the name of their master. The world, however, contains people of different beliefs, who proclaim that they have different gods and lords. Therefore Paul did not say that the great house was the world, but rather the church, in which everyone shares the name of their common Lord.

***21If any one purifies himself from what is ignoble, then he will be a vessel for noble use, consecrated and useful to the master of the house, ready for any good work.***

Now another heresy is revealed by its own deception. This is the one which asserts that some souls are evil by nature and cannot be persuaded to do what is good, whereas Paul says that bad people can be changed into good and unclean people can be purified. Even Hymenaeus and Philetus could have changed their ways if they had wanted to and become holy vessels, fit for honor.

***22So shun youthful passions and aim at righteousness, faith, love, and peace, along with those who call upon the Lord from a pure heart.***

Youthful desires are contrary [to faith] because they are worldly lusts which are tied up with all sorts of temptations. For that reason, they must be avoided by the servant of God. Paul orders Timothy to aim for things which seem odd and hard to someone who is young. Whoever has chosen righteousness will do nothing wrong, and whoever loves his faith will keep the commandments. Whoever follows love will be humble toward everyone, for a peacekeeper will not drive anyone to quarreling.

***23Have nothing to do with stupid, senseless controversies; you know that they breed quarrels.***

Stupid questions come partly from unbelievers and partly from heretics, and there are other things which unbelievers bring up which drive even gentle people to quarrel. They may be stirred up by the overwhelming contradiction of their ungodliness and in anger say things which go beyond what they intended. There are some heretics who feign patience (as if they could never hear anything harsh from a catholic) in order to gain a hearing for their own perverse opinions. Therefore they are to be avoided.

***24And the Lord's servant must not be quarrelsome but kindly to every one, an apt teacher, forbearing, 25correcting his opponents with gentleness. God may perhaps grant that they will repent and come to know the truth, 26and they may escape from the snare of the devil, after being captured by him to do his will.***

These things need no interpretation because they are clear. Paul pointed out to what extent gentleness could be beneficial. If there is something in these heretics which seems attractive because they appear to be humble, how much more praiseworthy and fruitful will it be in

[12]Jn 15:19. [13]1 Cor 5:12.

a catholic, whose views will be perceived as sound and whose seriousness will be regarded as something to imitate, if he comes across as meek.

## 2 Timothy 3

***1But understand this, that in the last days there will come times of stress. 2For men will be lovers of self, lovers of money, proud, arrogant, abusive, disobedient to their parents, ungrateful, unholy, 3inhuman, implacable, slanderers, profligates, fierce, haters of good, 4treacherous, reckless, swollen with conceit, lovers of pleasure rather than lovers of God, 5holding the form of religion but denying the power of it. Avoid such people.***

This is the prophecy of the holy apostle, who foresees what great evils will come from both heretics and Jews alike. In them all these things which are inimical to the faith can be detected. The apostle himself said: *What have I to do with judging outsiders?*[14] How can those who think wrongly about God and are not afraid to say things that will do him injury possibly be well-meaning in everyday life? This is why Paul said: *They have the form of godliness but deny its power.* They claim to be Christians when in fact they are anything but, and both their work and their teaching is corrupt. The praise and power of God is not to be found in words more than in deeds.

***6For among them are those who make their way into households and capture weak women, burdened with sins and swayed by various impulses, 7who will listen to anybody and can never arrive at a knowledge of the truth.***

Although all sorts of heretics make their way into houses and capture women by tricks and clever words in order to deceive their husbands through them, in the manner of their father the devil, who seduced Adam by going through Eve, nevertheless, the description fits the Manichaeans more than others. Nobody else is as troublesome, as deceptive or as harmful as they are, for it is clear that they worship one thing but profess another, and that they act one way inside but preach something quite different outside. They defend holiness yet live wicked lives, something which their law supports. They praise mercy even though they act unjustly toward one another. They claim that the world must be rejected but always go about well dressed. They preach publicly that they insist on fasting, although they are all bloated, even if they wear make-up (which makes them look sickly) in order to deceive people. Therefore the apostle was prophesying about them more than anyone else. We know that they did not exist in his time, just as the Arians did not exist then either. The Emperor Diocletian referred to the Manichaeans in one of his laws, calling them a sordid and impure heresy which had recently emerged from Persia. They seek out women who for vanity's sake want to hear something new, and by telling them some attractive things, they persuade them to accept wicked and unlawful ones. Such women are eager to learn but unable to discern what they hear. This always happens when people want to learn but have no understanding of the truth.

***8As Jannes and Jambres opposed Moses, so these men also oppose the truth, men of corrupt mind and counterfeit faith; 9but they will not get very far, for their folly will be plain to all, as was that of those two men.***

The example comes from apocryphal literature. Jannes and Jambres were magi or Egyptian magicians, who thought that they could defeat the power of God working through

[14] 1 Cor 5:12.

Moses by their own lying imitation of it. But whereas in Moses the power of his works kept growing, the others were humbled and confessed with the pain of being wounded that God had worked through Moses. Similarly, Paul says that these people will not get away with the ungodliness of their assertions, because their incompetence will be made clear along with their deception. Whether they want to or not, they will finally be forced to confess their own ignorance.

***10Now you have observed my teaching, my conduct, my aim in life, my faith, my patience, my love, my steadfastness, 11my persecutions, my sufferings, what befell me at Antioch, at Iconium, and at Lystra, what persecutions I endured; yet from them all the Lord rescued me. 12Indeed all who desire to live a godly life in Christ Jesus will be persecuted, 13while evil men and impostors will go on from bad to worse, deceivers and deceived.***

Paul wants Timothy to emulate the things which he lists. In the final analysis, these things lead not to regret but to happiness. For this reason he recalls what and how much he has suffered, in order to proclaim the help of God by which he defends and protects his servants from the impudence of Satan, in order to make them safe and create a situation in which they will not be afraid of what they might be afflicted with by unbelievers, but be happy in persecution, certain that all who have been rightly converted in Christ will be hated, even by other members of his body. Bad people merely get worse when they see others agreeing with them, and so they lead them into error too. When they know that, although they are wicked deceivers, they still flourish and prosper in the world, they attract others to imitate them, with the result that they will be punished not merely for their own errors but also for the errors of those whom they lead astray by their example.

***14But as for you, continue in what you have learned and have firmly believed, knowing from whom you learned it 15and how from childhood you have been acquainted with the sacred writings which are able to instruct you for salvation through faith in Christ Jesus.***

Paul indicates that it is very advantageous to have a knowledge of the Old Testament. He says that its books are sacred writings which proclaim Christ and declare that he will become incarnate for the redemption of the human race. He encourages Timothy to go on studying them. Their antiquity is the backbone of the New. Timothy knows that the authority of the one from whom he has learned is sound because he has seen signs and wonders performed by him, and all his talk is meaningless compared to the signs.

***16All scripture is inspired by God and profitable for teaching, for reproof, for correction, and for training in righteousness, 17that the man of God may be complete, equipped for every good work.***

It is clear that all Scripture, whose author is shown to be God, is useful. It was given in order to help the unskilled and restore the fallen. It also turns the wicked to righteousness, so that the man of God may be perfect in everything he does. By working gradually in the new man, it turns him into a man of God.

## 2 Timothy 4

***1I charge you in the presence of God and of Christ Jesus who is to judge the living and the dead, and by his appearing and his kingdom: 2preach the word, be urgent in season and out of season, convince, rebuke, and exhort, be unfailing in patience and in teaching.***

Paul is so concerned to ensure that the gift of God will be preached without alteration that he summons God the Father and Christ his Son as witnesses when he warns Timothy to take care and persist in this task, so that by faithful preaching and frequent exhortation he may encourage people to improve themselves whenever he gets the chance. Paul advises him to do this without bitterness, so that the people will more easily accept the one who is rebuking them.

***[3]For the time is coming when people will not endure sound teaching, but having itching ears they will accumulate for themselves teachers to suit their own likings, [4]and will turn away from listening to the truth and wander into myths.***

This is likewise a prophecy of the holy apostle in which he foresees future events and instructs Timothy to make sure that he persists in his teaching, so that believers will remain firm, well trained in faith and good works and learned in sound doctrine, so that in the last days, when other people start to turn away from the truth into error, they will remain unaffected. He says that in the future there will be those who will want to be taught in ways which suit their own tastes and that they will turn away from faithful and true masters in order to go after those who teach them those things. They will hear them willingly because the truth will seem harsh to them, and they will leave sound doctrine behind in order to run after myths. They do not want their wicked deeds to be criticized; rather they prefer to have teachers who will adjust to their ways of behavior. Their ears will itch to hear empty fables composed under the name of doctrine, by which they will be tickled. All this fits nobody as well as the Manichaeans, who have I do not know how many different opinions which are given highfalutin names, when in fact they are trivial things and some of them are quite crazy.

***[5]As for you, always be steady, endure suffering, do the work of an evangelist, fulfil your ministry.***

***[6]For I am already on the point of being sacrificed; the time of my departure has come.***

Paul warns and encourages Timothy to keep his eye on church discipline, to act courageously, to expound the Scriptures and to avoid empty myths as wise and learned people do. The apostle knows that his death is near and wants to leave an example of godly living and sound doctrine in holy Timothy, so that by handing things on through him, there will never be a lack of faithful teachers. He calls his final suffering a sacrifice because he is being offered up to the God who suffered for his justification.

***[7]I have fought the good fight, I have finished the race, I have kept the faith. [8]Henceforth there is laid up for me the crown of righteousness, which the Lord, the righteous judge, will award to me on that Day, and not only to me but also to all who have loved his appearing.***

Paul recalls that he has done everything which is useful and beneficial to himself and to others. He has offered himself as an example to his hearers, not only in words but also in deeds, so that by the truth of his preaching he might be a faithful servant of his Author. Having fought against the princes and powers of the world with all the skill and expertise he possesses, he wants to leave behind an example of how those enemies can be overcome. By keeping their doctrine pure and fighting the good fight, God will make his people worthy of receiving the crown, because he is a just judge and will give the most ample rewards to those who love him and wait for his Son to come down from heaven.

***[9]Do your best to come to me soon. [10]For Demas, in love with this present world, has***

***deserted me and gone to Thessalonica; Crescens has gone to Galatia, Titus to Dalmatia. 11Luke alone is with me. Get Mark and bring him with you; for he is very useful in serving me. 12Tychicus I have sent to Ephesus.***

Although it is clear that every detail of church law is contained in the letter, Paul wants Timothy to come to him because of his great love for him. He gives Mark a good report because he remembers his earlier efforts.

***13When you come, bring the cloak that I left with Carpus at Troas, also the books, and above all the parchments.***

The apostle was a Jew by birth and never had anything which did not accord with that. So why did he have a cloak?[15] It was because he came from Tarsus, whose citizens had been accepted into the Roman fold so that in the future they would be called Roman citizens, and for that reason they had to have a courthouse in which they came together robed up in the Roman manner. At that time there were some people who approached the Romans with gifts and were granted perpetual immunity, being called Roman citizens and their brethren, as the apostle himself testifies.[16]

***14Alexander the coppersmith did me great harm; the Lord will requite him for his deeds. 15Beware of him yourself, for he strongly opposed our message.***

This Alexander and the above-mentioned Demas were colleagues. They had once been with the apostle and pretended to be his friends, but because they were both exposed in time as deceivers, they left him. This one, who was a coppersmith, was more daring in his wickedness and went away from Paul in a way which showed him to be a strong opponent of his words. Therefore the apostle rightly advises Timothy to stay away from someone who has dared to oppose him, and he turns him over to the judgment of God.

***16At my first defense no one took my part; all deserted me. May it not be charged against them!***

Paul calls the pressure and tribulations inflicted on him his defense. For Christians, suffering is life and persecution is defense. The pressure brought to bear on him for the sake of righteousness will protect him on the day of judgment and make unbelievers guilty. Paul complains that when these pressures began he was abandoned, and because he knows that this is the custom, he does not want it to be held against them, since the disciples abandoned the Lord when he was arrested by the Jews,[17] just as it is written in the prophet: *I shall strike the shepherd and the sheep of the flock will be scattered.*[18]

***17But the Lord stood by me and gave me strength to proclaim the message fully, that all the Gentiles might hear it. So I was rescued from the lion's mouth.***

Paul says that he was fortified and increased in power by the help of Christ the Lord in order to complete his preaching among all the Gentiles, and so he asks that those who abandoned him in his time of need might be forgiven because since he was well accepted by God he did not seek revenge. In this case he believes that he has received more help from God because he was abandoned by other people.

His fellow apostle Peter says much the same thing: *For our adversary the devil goes about like a roaring lion, seeking whom it may*

[15]Ambrosiaster understood the cloak as the toga of a Roman citizen which was required for formal court appearances. [16]Cf. Acts 22:25, 28. [17]Mt 26:56. [18]Zech 13:7.

*devour.*[19] But because he found no opportunity to deceive Paul, he stirred up pressure on him through his children, so that his life would be taken away not because he was a sinner but because he was a righteous man, so that he would be unable to exhort many to accept the faith.

***18The Lord will rescue me from every evil and save me for his heavenly kingdom. To him be the glory for ever and ever. Amen.***

By the providence of God the apostle was delivered from the devil when the latter had almost overwhelmed him. Now he insults him, saying that he is weak, because he has been snatched from his mouth so that he was unable to accomplish what he wanted to. Paul therefore testifies that he was rescued from death by the help of God. He is sure of the providence of the Lord, and believes that he will be delivered from future temptations—and not only delivered in this life, but also saved for the future on the day of judgment, and that he will reign with the Lord Christ in eternity.

***19Greet Prisca and Aquila, and the household of Onesiphorus. 20Erastus remained at Corinth; Trophimus I left ill at Miletus. 21Do your best to come before winter. Eubulus sends greetings to you, as do Pudens and Linus and Claudia and all the brethren.***

Aquila and Priscilla are the people he stayed with and with whom he worked.[20] Onesiphorus is the same man whom he spoke about in his first letter to Timothy.[21] How can it be that Trophimus was ill when the apostle, who raised the dead, was with him? Signs are done for unbelievers, and because there are different ways in which merit is earned with God, a person should give thanks to God whether he is in trouble or in sickness, nor should he seek help from any hostile quarter if he wants to grow in merit with God. Paul added that Timothy should come to him in the autumn because of the rain and the cold [of winter]. The letter concludes in the usual way with a greeting to the brethren.

***22The Lord [Jesus Christ] be with your spirit. Grace be with you.***[22]

This appendix is the apostle's own, which he says is his sign in every letter. Because the Son of God is also the Son of Man and he is called both Jesus and Christ, so as to indicate that he is both God and man, he is called by both names here. A particular attribute is indicated by each name, which is why both are given here.

[19]1 Pet 5:8. [20]Acts 18:3. [21]2 Tim 1:16. Ambrosiaster is wrong about this, of course. Perhaps the text should be amended to read: "at the beginning of this letter." [22]Ambrosiaster's text had the words "Jesus Christ" interpolated in it, and most of his commentary deals with them.

# AMBROSIASTER
## *Commentary on Titus*

### Preface

The apostle made Titus a bishop, and so now he warns him to be careful about whom he ordains, because there were those who would pretend to be worthy of holding high office when in reality they were heretics, corrupted by the circumcision.[1]

### Titus 1

***[1]Paul, a servant of God and an apostle of Jesus Christ, to further the faith of God's elect and their knowledge of the truth which accords with godliness, [2]in hope of eternal life which God, who never lies, promised ages ago [3]and at the proper time manifested in his word through the preaching with which I have been entrusted by command of God our Savior;***

***[4]To Titus, my true child in a common faith: Grace and peace from God the Father and Christ Jesus our Savior.***

Paul declares that the gift decreed by God, which he had promised before all ages, had been manifested in the time of the Savior in the preaching of the apostles. This is what he had promised.

He also says that it has been entrusted to him to proclaim the mercy of God which was predestined for the Gentiles, so that Titus also, his true son (that is, according to the gospel, for it is what is eternal that is true), should accept God's will with care and devotion, and preach God's grace and peace, so that when the gift was received they might be at peace with God the Father, because everything comes from him, and with Christ Jesus our Savior, because he has delivered us from death.

***[5]This is why I left you in Crete, that you might amend what was defective, and appoint elders in every town as I directed you, [6]if any man is blameless, the husband of one wife, and his children are believers and not open to the charge of being profligate or insubordinate. [7]For a bishop, as God's steward, must be blameless; he must not be arrogant or quick-tempered or a drunkard or violent or greedy for gain, [8]but hospitable, a lover of goodness, master of himself, upright, holy, and self-controlled; [9]he must hold firm to the sure word as taught, so that he may be able to give instruction in sound doctrine and also to confute those who contradict it. [10]For there are many insubordinate men, empty talkers and deceivers, especially the circumcision party; [11]they must be silenced, since they are upsetting whole families by teaching for base gain what they have no right to teach.***

What we read here is clear. Paul wants someone who is holy in his deeds and wise in his words to be ordained bishop, so that he can encourage the brethren and persuade opponents, especially those from among the Jews, who under cover of the name of Christ were teaching Judaism and whom he elsewhere calls false brethren. Though they had been born again in Christ they were not pure Christians, because they wanted to worship the law on

[1]That is to say, by the Judaizing party in the church.

one side and Christ on the other. He refers to them in this way because they were undermining households with their corrupt teaching. They were doubly eager for base gain because they did these things mainly to please the Jews, from whom they expected to receive financial support, so that they could make money off the uncircumcised [by telling them that they had to become Jews].[2] These were their aims, just as the Lord said to the Jews: *You go over sea and dry land to make a single convert.*[3] Paul calls both these things base gain, because those who taught in God's name did not do so out of devotion but in order to get money and had become takers of dirty cash, not unlike those who wanted to gain converts through circumcision. This is why he said elsewhere: *Their glory is in their private parts.*[4]

***12One of themselves, a prophet of their own, said, "Cretans are always liars, evil beasts, lazy gluttons." 13This testimony is true. Therefore rebuke them sharply, that they may be sound in the faith,***

Some Cretan who had become a better person through the Lord's teaching said what ought to be thought about uneducated Cretans, which is that they are wicked, lazy and gluttonous. Because they want to feed on their own wickedness, they are evil beasts who are no good and act only to harm others. The evil here is twofold. The Cretans really were like this, which is why Paul calls this [unknown] Cretan a prophet, but they behaved this way in the interests of other Cretans. Paul asserts that these things are so true that the man who said them was a prophet, because no prophet can be deceived.

***14instead of giving heed to Jewish myths or to commands of men who reject the truth.***

Paul orders Titus to persist in disciplining the Cretans so that they may change their ways and choose behavior which is righteous and appropriate to the law of God. They must turn away from Jewish fables, because if no one is justified before God in the law, how much less will they be justified by the commandments of men!

Anything which is opposed to the truth is an invention of human beings who do not know the power of the Scriptures or their inner meaning. They follow the color of the law and not its flavor.[5] For this reason they are said to tell tales, not the truth. They think that no one should ever abandon what Moses taught, for example, about food, matrimony, new moons, the blood of a weasel or a house which is unclean for seven days, even though they know that their ancestors Abraham, Isaac and Jacob were justified without such things and called friends of God. The prophet Ezekiel also testifies that because they had profaned the law of God and its righteousness, they had accepted precepts and commandments which were not good, by which they could not be justified.[6] This is why the Lord said to the Jews that *Moses wrote these things because of the hardness of your hearts.*[7] It is also why the apostle Peter says: *Why do you put a yoke on the necks of our brethren which neither our fathers nor we were able to bear?*[8] If these things had been useful, they would have been given at the same time as the law [written] on the tables (i.e., the Ten Commandments) was given. But because even after so many signs and wonders and the giving of the law they were still irreverent, faithless and stiff-necked, they received all these laws in which they had no room to breathe. Thus it turned out that even good people had to labor along with bad ones in order to receive the reward. These things were given as proofs, so that at the time

[2]The Latin is somewhat obscure here. [3]Mt 23:15. [4]Phil 3:19. Ambrosiaster's interpretation is different from that usually accepted today. [5]The color refers to the superficial aspect, the flavor to the inner meaning. [6]Ezek 20:25. [7]Mk 10:5. [8]Acts 15:10.

when the promised gift of God should come, the mercy of God would permit everything which it had previously forbidden. The Jews did not understand this, so they remained under the yoke and wanted to tie up the liberty of others with the same chains. Therefore Paul urges Titus to rebuke them so that they would turn away from those people.

***15To the pure all things are pure, but to the corrupt and unbelieving nothing is pure; their very minds and consciences are corrupted.***

Paul indicates that people who have no idea why these things were forbidden and why they were later permitted are clean. If it is written in Genesis that everything which God made is good, there is no doubt that it must also be clean. It is those who do not understand this who are unclean because they are the accusers of Scripture. If it says that all things have been made good, why are some things forbidden as if they were evil? If they are not evil because they are good, these people should recognize that they were forbidden because of the hardness of their hearts, because they were held to be unworthy of making use of the whole of God's creation. The mind and conscience of those who are prohibited from making use of the better things are corrupted, because they accuse God's creation in order to excuse themselves.

***16They profess to know God, but they deny him by their deeds; they are detestable, disobedient, unfit for any good deed.***

Although this saying applies to all heretics, Paul is understood to be speaking about the Jews who say that they alone know the God of Abraham but deny him by their deeds, just as the Lord says: *If you were the children of Abraham, you would do the works of Abraham.*[9] How can they know the God of Abraham when they are ignorant of his mystery and faith, not choosing the works of the gospel but those of the law of works in new moons, circumcision and so on, as godless and irreverent troublemakers? These are works which do not know God.

## Titus 2

***1But as for you, teach what befits sound doctrine.***

What is called sound doctrine knows God, for his teaching saves us.

***2Bid the older men be temperate, serious, sensible, sound in faith, in love, and in steadfastness.***

Paul shows what sound doctrine consists of in order to point out that those who are less sober, less serious, unbelievers, loveless and impatient are followers of unsound teaching. Neither God nor his righteousness is known by such works.

***3Bid the older women likewise to be reverent in behavior, not to be slanderers or slaves to drink; they are to teach what is good, 4and so train the young women to love their husbands and children, 5to be sensible, chaste, domestic, kind, and submissive to their husbands, that the word of God may not be discredited.***

Paul advises the older women to set an example of good living to those who are younger so that if they have unbelieving husbands they may rejoice in them rather than blaspheme the name of God, when they see that because of the fear of God they are more ready to obey their own husbands.

***6Likewise urge the younger men to control themselves. 7Show yourself in all respects a***

[9]Jn 8:39.

***model of good deeds, and in your teaching show integrity, gravity, [8]and sound speech that cannot be censured, so that an opponent may be put to shame, having nothing evil to say of us.***

Since young men have a habit of going astray and are therefore more prone to fall away, Paul orders them to be subjected to remedial discipline, so that what is unbridled [by nature] may be governed by divine laws. In order that this should not prove too difficult or arduous a task, he advises the master to set an example and show how the things which he teaches can be put into practice, so that those who are godless and enemies of the faith may be ashamed when they see that what he teaches in words he shows to be true in his deeds.

***[9]Bid slaves to be submissive to their masters and to give satisfaction in every respect; they are not to be refractory, [10]nor to pilfer, but to show entire and true fidelity, so that in everything they may adorn the doctrine of God our Savior.***

Paul says that the Lord's teaching should be illustrated by good works and faith. It will be attractive and beautiful if the one who professes it does not make it repugnant by denying it in practice, but instead makes it lovable and true, for nothing which is true can be unattractive. When what is said is borne out by the deeds which accompany it, it is shown to be true, and for that reason it is also attractive. When that happens, masters will not only not be able to prevent their slaves from becoming believers, but they will rejoice when they see them mature in their faith. No one who keeps faith with God can be faithless toward other people.

***[11]For the grace of God has appeared for the salvation of all men, [12]training us to renounce irreligion and worldly passions, and to live sober, upright, and godly lives in this world,***

Paul says that the gift of God has shined on human beings through Christ, which means that the truth of the one God has been revealed in Christ, so that we may preach the Creator by a godly profession of faith in the unity of the Trinity. What previously was unknown to the human race the mercy of God has now brought to light, so that we can avoid the shadows of error, that is, we can flee the ignorance and ungodliness of worldly people, and turn to God, the parent of all things, confessing him in the truth which he gave as the gospel of his Son and do good works in order to receive a reward for this. Thus the person who preaches only the Father has no hope if he does not confess the Son as part of the same truth. His hope is also vain if he has only his confession of faith without good works.

***[13]awaiting our blessed hope, the appearing of the glory of our great God and Savior Jesus Christ, [14]who gave himself for us to redeem us from all iniquity and to purify for himself a people of his own who are zealous for good deeds.***

***[15]Declare these things; exhort and reprove with all authority. Let no one disregard you.***

Paul says that this is the blessed hope of believers, who are waiting for the coming of the glory of the great God. Then it will be revealed that Christ is the judge, in whom the power and glory of God the Father will naturally be seen, and they will receive the rewards of their faith. Christ has redeemed us for this, so that we might pursue a good life, filled with good works, so that we may be heirs of the kingdom of God.

## Titus 3

***[1]Remind them to be submissive to rulers and authorities, to be obedient, to be ready for any honest work,***

Paul reminds them what the hope of believers is in order to show that when they are criticized, they ought to realize what the good is that they are being prepared for, so that they will accept it without grumbling. They know that they are being disciplined for their own salvation and so that they will be slow to do evil and quick to do good, aware of what must be rendered to each one.

***[2]to speak evil of no one, to avoid quarreling, to be gentle, and to show perfect courtesy toward all men.***

Paul wants Christians to appear humble to everyone, for in that way unbelievers may be called to future hope.

***[3]For we ourselves were once foolish, disobedient, led astray, slaves to various passions and pleasures, passing our days in malice and envy, hated by men and hating one another;***

Paul recalls that these good things, which unbelievers do not have, are given to Christians so that they might be manifested as shining in all righteousness because they are worshipers of God. Once they were foolish, but now they appear to be well advised in all things and God is praised in them.

***[4]but when the goodness and loving kindness of God our Savior appeared, [5]he saved us, not because of deeds done by us in righteousness, but in virtue of his own mercy, by the washing of regeneration and renewal in the Holy Spirit, [6]which he poured out upon us richly through Jesus Christ our Savior, [7]so that we might be justified by his grace and become heirs in hope of eternal life.***

This good which is seen to flourish in Christians stems from the root of divine godliness. God in his mercy has saved us through Christ, by whose grace we have been born again and now receive the Holy Spirit in abundance, so that we may excel in good works. He will help us in everything, so that by these things we may inherit the kingdom of heaven. For this reason we must follow him with all devotion and obey his commands, because if there is anything beautiful in us, he has painted it with spiritual brushstrokes.

***[8]The saying is sure.***
***I desire you to insist on these things, so that those who have believed in God may be careful to apply themselves to good deeds; these are excellent and profitable to men.***

Nothing is more obvious than that mercy and humanity are good things in this life and useful for the future. The person who lives that way has praise now and will receive a crown on the day of judgment. Everyone who believes in God ought to practice mercy, because it is by mercy that he lives. The head of the congregation is therefore reminded to pay attention to this.

***[9]But avoid stupid controversies, genealogies, dissensions, and quarrels over the law, for they are unprofitable and futile.***

Paul calls these questions stupid, because they do nothing for our salvation, nor do they contribute any useful skill or knowledge. In these words Paul describes the dogmas of many heretics. Although everything which is not true may be called stupid, there is nevertheless a difference between the person who introduces mythical tales and the one who by the cleverness of his apostasy offers something full of poison, like Arius and Photinus. The law is not a myth, but heresy began with the Jews (and it was heresy even when it belonged only to the Jews), for some of them tried to claim special privileges on the basis of the origins of the patriarchs, which came out of their marriages, when there was no merit with God for anything like that, and some spent a lot of effort trying to wipe away the blood of a weasel by the ritual washing of pots and other vessels. [They also claimed] that the tomb of Moses was hidden so that he would not be disturbed by magicians (but if that were true, the tombs of the other saints would have to have been hidden as well), and [there is so much vanity in the tradition of the Manichaeans that it is better not to say anything about it.][10]

***10As for a man who is factious, after admonishing him once or twice, have nothing more to do with him, 11knowing that such a person is perverted and sinful; he is self-condemned.***

Heretics are those who attack the meaning of the law by using the words of the law to do it. They give their own meaning to the words of the law in order to promote the corruption of their own mind by the authority of the law. Ungodliness knows how important authority is, and so invents deception under cover of it, so that it will be commended by the good reputation of the name, since an evil thing will not be accepted on its own. It is therefore essential that such people should be disciplined once, so that they may be without excuse. If they are disciplined more often they will only become more expert in evil. Someone who disciplines them often will appear to be trying to force them to become more devious, to the destruction of many. Therefore they are to be sent away so that they may become more negligent and even perish—but on their own.

***12When I send Artemas or Tychicus to you, do your best to come to me at Nicopolis, for I have decided to spend the winter there.***

After sending the letter Paul wanted to see Titus personally because of his affection for him, and also in order to give him more detailed instructions concerning church discipline.

***13Do your best to speed Zenas the lawyer and Apollos on their way; see that they lack nothing. 14And let our people learn to apply themselves to good deeds, so as to help cases of urgent need, and not to be unfruitful.***

Each of these men is outstanding in wisdom and good works. Therefore Paul orders them to be provided with the money they need by those who have believed [in Christ]. That way they will refresh them, which is only right, because men who have shared spiritual things should not be wanting for material necessities. Although Paul calls Zenas a lawyer, it was Apollos who was skilled in the Scriptures, but Paul gives Zenas this title because that was what he had been in the synagogue.

***15All who are with me send greetings to you. Greet those who love us in the faith. Grace be with you all.***

Paul mentions only Titus in his greeting, but he is meant to represent everyone, whom Paul is greeting at the same time. He wants those who love him faithfully in the love of our Lord Christ to be regarded as worthy of being greeted.

*The grace of God be with you all.*[11] Here Paul greets the brethren and Titus's servants generally.

[10]An alternative version of this phrase reads: "that Solomon built the temple with the help of demons, in which work a large number of people were engaged—what could be more mythical?" [11]This is how Ambrosiaster read the last part of this verse.

# AMBROSIASTER
*Commentary on Philemon*

## Preface

Philemon was not ordained to any ecclesiastical office, but he was a worthy layman. Paul sends him a personal letter on behalf of his slave Onesimus, asking him not only to welcome Onesimus back but also to give thanks to God for him, because he would be receiving him not as a slave but as a most dear brother.

## Philemon

***1Paul, a prisoner for Christ Jesus, and Timothy our brother,***

***To Philemon our beloved fellow worker 2and Apphia our sister and Archippus our fellow soldier, and the church in your house:***

***3Grace to you and peace from God our Father and the Lord Jesus Christ.***

In order to indicate the importance of the letter being sent by him, Paul starts off by mentioning his own suffering. It is shameful to be imprisoned for wrongdoing, but to wear the chains of detention for the sake of Christ is the height of glory. Although Philemon was not a clergyman, he was nevertheless concerned with the needs of the church because of his devotion, which is why Paul says that he shared in his labors. There are many people who are worthy, but who apologize because they consider themselves inadequate for such a ministry, a characteristic which shows just how worthy of it they are.

***4I thank my God always when I remember you in my prayers, 5because I hear of your love and of the faith which you have toward the Lord Jesus and all the saints, 6and I pray that the sharing of your faith may promote the knowledge of all the good that is ours in Christ.***

Paul says that he rejoices and gives thanks to God in his prayers because Philemon was firm in his faith and persistent in doing good works. Whoever loves Christ must demonstrate this in the way he treats his slaves, knowing that the Lord will require of him whatever he expects from them. The apostle says that he is adding this to his prayers, that Philemon's works may be done with a recognition of their goodness, that is to say, that he may work in such a way as to expect a reward for it in the future.

***7For I have derived much joy and comfort from your love, my brother, because the hearts of the saints have been refreshed through you.***

It is clear that Paul says he is happy because Philemon was providing for the needs of the saints. For this reason he rejoices because he is certain that Philemon will obey his requests since it is clear that he is of higher rank than they are.

***8Accordingly, though I am bold enough in Christ to command you to do what is required, 9yet for love's sake I prefer to appeal to you— I, Paul, an ambassador and now a prisoner also for Christ Jesus—***

Within reason, the master was perfectly entitled on the basis of his apostolic authority to tell his disciple what to do, but because Philemon was a good man, Paul makes an appeal to him for compliance out of his love for him. Philemon was about the same age as Paul and also a "prisoner" of Jesus Christ, which means that he was obliged to do the Lord's business or even subject to imprisonment on account of the name of Christ, as the apostles themselves also were. Judas and Silas were similar, because although they were members of a congregation, the fact that they were leaders among the brethren obliged them to do things for God, and they struggled along with the apostles to promote the faith of God.[1] This was why Silas became one of the apostle's fellow laborers.

***10I appeal to you for my child, Onesimus, whose father I have become in my imprisonment. 11(Formerly he was useless to you, but now he is indeed useful to you and to me.) 12I am sending him back to you, sending my very heart. 13I would have been glad to keep him with me, in order that he might serve me on your behalf during my imprisonment for the gospel; 14but I preferred to do nothing without your consent in order that your goodness might not be by compulsion but of your own free will.***

It is no great thing for a humble man to give way, but for a prominent person to humble himself is praiseworthy. Thus the apostle asks Philemon, whom he had the right to order about, to be a model in all things for the growth of merit. During his imprisonment in Rome, the apostle had baptized Onesimus, a runaway who had fled to God for help, because he saw Onesimus's potential. He commends him by saying that with his own mind in him, Onesimus had been transformed from being useless to being useful in both secular and divine affairs.[2]

***15Perhaps this is why he was parted from you for a while, that you might have him back for ever, 16no longer as a slave but more than a slave, as a beloved brother, especially to me but how much more to you, both in the flesh and in the Lord.***

Having offended his own master, Onesimus took refuge with the apostle after having made a long journey. He wanted to show that he was not going back to his previous life as one who was bound in sin, but rather as one whose sins had been wiped out. He was going back as someone useful, because he was now not only his master's equal in merit, but also his teacher's brother. In order to stop Philemon from taking a haughty approach to Onesimus, as masters often do toward their slaves, Paul humbled him by saying that Onesimus was his brother both in the flesh and in the Lord, for once the issue of human subjection is removed, we are all of the same Adam and ought to recognize ourselves as brothers, particularly when faith, which takes all pride away, unites us.

***17So if you consider me your partner, receive him as you would receive me.***

Paul shows that his love for Onesimus is so great that he says that Philemon, whom he has already praised, will become his partner if he receives Onesimus as if he were the apostle. This is what Solomon said: *Free men will serve a wise slave.*[3] This was meant to frighten Philemon into at least taking him back, if he could not be persuaded to do so out of love.

***18If he has wronged you at all, or owes you anything, charge that to my account.***

Paul now removes any excuse for anger [on Philemon's part], just in case it turned out that he had been so hurt by Onesimus that he would find it impossible to forgive him. In that

[1]Cf. Acts 15:22. [2]The name Onesimus means "useful." [3]Sir 10:25.

case, Paul says it should be charged to him, through whom they were [both] future heirs of the kingdom of heaven, when previously they had been sinners.

**[19]*I, Paul, write this with my own hand, I will repay it—to say nothing of your owing me even your own self.***

If Onesimus has offended in any way, Paul testifies that the bond which he is putting up on his behalf ought to be good enough. To back up what he is saying, he stands up and says that he is asking for less from Philemon than he knows he ought to. Philemon has burdened himself with debt [to Paul], which he is obliged to pay off by [taking] his slave [back].

**[20]*Yes, brother, I want some benefit from you in the Lord. Refresh my heart in Christ.***

**[21]*Confident of your obedience, I write to you, knowing that you will do even more than I say.***

Paul treats Philemon gently in order that his obedience will be voluntary and reap some benefit. He urges him in such a way that Philemon will do more that he is asked to by the apostle. It is usually the case that if someone thinks he is well thought of he will perform better [than expected].

**[22]*At the same time, prepare a guest room for me, for I am hoping through your prayers to be granted to you.***

In order to make Philemon more concerned and willing to obey, Paul indicates that he will be coming to visit him, for those who are absent are usually ignored. Why should the apostle have refused to go there, when he was always suffering trials and afflictions, beatings, persecutions and imprisonment, and who had no rest other than in Christ? But Paul offered his flesh to suffering for the benefit of believers, in order to obtain immortal crowns for his soul and body. That way the enemies of Christ would be confounded and God's glory would be increased.

**[23]*Epaphras, my fellow prisoner in Christ Jesus, sends greetings to you, [24]and so do Mark, Aristarchus, Demas, and Luke, my fellow workers.***

Paul bears witness that all these share in his glory.

**[25]*The grace of the Lord Jesus Christ be with your spirit.***

This is the apostle's signature, confirming that the letter was sent by him.

## Scripture Index


**Genesis**
1:27, *95*
2:24, *59*
3:16, *96*
3:19, *90*
9:4, *9*
9:25, *98*
12:7, *17*
13:15, *17*
17:8, *17*
19:24, *145*
20:4, *22*
21:10, *26*
24:7, *17*
32:28, *83*

**Exodus**
3:2, *83*
3:2-6, *109*
20:3, *60*
20:4, *60*
20:7, *60*
20:8, *60*
20:12, *59, 60*
20:20, *1*
23:20, *19*
24:8, *25*
28:43, *49*
32:34, *19*

**Leviticus**
18:5, *16*
19:2, *56, 80, 128*
19:3, *1*
19:18, *29*
25:7, *1*

**Numbers**
16:5, *148*
16:26, *148*

**Deuteronomy**
5:16, *59*
10:16, *1*
18:15, *20, 85*
18:19, *85*
21:23, *16, 17*
25:4, *136*
27:26, *16*

**Joshua**
5:14, *109*

**2 Kings**
5:26, *87*

**1 Chronicles**
6:31-48, *129*
24:1-19, *129*

**Job**
1:21, *139*

**Psalms**
1:2, *55*
1:6, *44*
19:6, *48*
24:1, *44*
24:7-10, *44*
36:9, *141*
68:18, *48*
85:11, *38*
104:15, *124*
118:20, *44*

**Proverbs**
3:34, *70, 127*
10:23, *55, 75*
25:17, *118*
30:8, *110*

**Ecclesiastes**
7:16, *52*

**Isaiah**
1:4, *39*
10:22-23, *1*
29:13, *58*
54:1, *26*
59:20-21, *20*
65:1, *39*

**Jeremiah**
1:5, *6*
4:4, *1*

**Ezekiel**
3:19, *23*
3:21, *23*
20:25, *156*

**Daniel**
2:44, *45*
2:47, *87*

**Habakkuk**
2:4, *5, 16*

**Haggai**
2:8, *94*

**Zechariah**
13:7, *153*

**Malachi**
1:2-3, *26*
1:6, *37, 79*
3:1, *19*

**Sirach**
10:25, *162*

**Wisdom of Solomon**
1:4, *107*

**Matthew**
4:4, *49*
5:9, *47, 57*
5:16, *47*
6:5-6, *126*
6:20, *79*
6:24, *145*
7:2, *61*
9:16, *27*
11:27, *71*
12:8, *91*
12:24, *131*
12:36, *55*
14:33, *70*
16:18, *42*
16:25, *74*
18:23-35, *54*
21:43, *17*
22:37, *28*
22:39-40, *28*
23:10, *47*
23:15, *156*
24:23, *109*
25:12, *147*
26:53, *50*
26:56, *153*
26:64, *38*
27:52-53, *48*

**Mark**
2:21, *27*
8:38, *51, 137*
9:50, *57*
10:5, *156*
10:18, *123*
13:35, *109*

**Luke**
1:5, *129*
2:36-37, *134*
2:48, *7*
6:5, *3*
6:36, *54, 56*
6:45, *123*
7:4-5, *27*
7:42-43, *89*
11:42, *132*

12:47, *94*
13:16, *124*
14:11, *70, 127*
15:10, *53*
16:10, *97, 127*
16:11, *127*
16:16, *5, 27*
18:9-14, *31*
18:11-12, *70*

**John**
1:3-4, *67*
1:4, *26*
1:18, *83*
1:45, *7*
2:19, *2*
2:21, *2*
3:13, *48*
4:22, *66*
4:24, *28, 58*
5:14, *124*
5:18, *69*
5:21, *19*
5:21-22, *84*
5:26, *26, 84*
5:43, *115*
5:46, *85*
7:5, *7*
8:33, *28*
8:39, *157*
8:56, *1*
9:16, *29*
10:30, *69*
12:19, *17*
12:26, *36*
12:32, *48*
14:9-10, *83*
14:30, *33*
15:19, *149*
15:22, *130*
15:26, *45*
16:15, *39, 45*
16:24, *38, 71*
17:3, *124*
17:6, *65, 71*
17:12, *71*
17:24, *26, 38*
19:11, *55*
20:17, *37*

**Acts**
3:15, *40, 84, 93*
3:22, *20*
5:28, *105*
5:40-41, *33*
5:41, *102*
6:5, *49*
8:5, *49*
8:38, *49*
9:15, *39, 43*
10:48, *49*
14:19, *62*
15:1-29, *4*
15:10, *16, 41, 156*
15:22, *162*
16:1-3, *10, 120*
16:9-10, *64*
16:16-24, *103*
16:33, *49*
18:3, *154*
18:6, *57*
19:1-7, *15*
20:34, *104*
21:9-10, *49*
21:13, *33*
21:20, *44*
21:26, *10*
22:21, *42*
22:25, *42, 153*
22:28, *153*
25:10-11, *29*
26:27, *27*
28:16, *145*
28:30-31, *35*

**Romans**
1:8, *102*
6:6, *93*
7:14-25, *29*
8:16, *22*
8:29, *36*
8:32, *54*
9:5, *70*
9:24, *36*
9:28, *1*
11:26-27, *20*
11:32, *20*
12:18, *57*

**1 Corinthians**
2:9, *40*
3:15, *148*
4:15, *120*
5:12, *149, 150*
7:5, *129*
9:14, *146*
10:4, *1, 69*
10:9, *69*
11:7, *95*
12:25, *62*
12:28, *42*
15:12, *148*
15:32, *35, 62*
15:49, *94*
16:22, *29*

**Galatians**
2:14, *33*
3:11, *5*
5:6, *10*
6:3, *127*

**Ephesians**
2:4, *107*
2:14-15, *19*
2:17, *42*
6:12, *72*

**Philippians**
2:27, *108*
3:19, *156*

**Colossians**
1:15, *69*
2:3, *75*
2:19, *38, 116*

**1 Thessalonians**
4:13, *73*

**2 Thessalonians**
3:10, *104*

**1 Timothy**
1:9, *1, 30*
2:5, *19*
2:7, *11*
5:17, *110*
6:10, *94*

**2 Timothy**
1:16, *154*
2:24, *31, 57*

**Hebrews**
7:9-10, *143*

**James**
5:20, *28*

**1 Peter**
2:9, *50*
5:8, *154*

**2 Peter**
1:4, *65*
1:20, *125*

**1 John**
2:15, *92*
2:15-16, *30*
3:16, *54*
4:1, *111*
4:18, *96*
4:20, *29*

**Revelation**
7:9, *26*
11:7-13, *109*
12:7, *36, 108*
12:9, *116*